Captain Carey's Blunder

CAPTAIN CAREY'S BLUNDER

The Death of the Prince Imperial

by

Donald Featherstone

Leo Cooper Ltd, London

First published in Great Britain 1973
by Leo Cooper Ltd
196 Shaftesbury Avenue London WC2H 8JL

ISBN 0 85052 060 6

Printed in Great Britain by
Clarke, Doble & Brendon Ltd
Plymouth

ILLUSTRATIONS

INTRODUCTION

THE death of the Prince Imperial was the biggest story of the year 1879, arousing even more interest and sympathy than had the massacre of an entire British force at Isandhlwana a few months earlier, in which fourteen hundred men lost their lives. It is a story which poses the question—is it preferable to be a live coward or a dead hero?

It is not easy to pick up the threads of a man's life when that man is a relatively ordinary member of the public who has been dead for nearly one hundred years. It took eight years of plodding, patient research to compile this analysis of Captain Jaheel Brenton Carey, who, for reasons explained in this book, might so easily have been a hero. It is a colourful, tragic tale, set in Victorian England, France, Ashanti, British Honduras, Jamaica, South Africa and India.

A true story in every aspect, it is written with a minimum of surmise and conjecture. The words spoken by the characters are those which contemporary reports attribute to them.

In the past attempts were made to 'hush up' the matter : the original court-martial documents were destroyed, and an embargo of one hundred years was placed upon its findings and recommendations, in contrast with much shorter embargos of thirty to fifty years which have been placed upon seemingly far more important State and political documents.

One can only guess as to the effects upon European history of the Prince Imperial's death—a very different pattern might well have emerged had this young man, with his enthusiasm, character and love-of-country, ruled France at the end of the nineteenth century.

To savour the situation fully, one must try to visualise what

7

would occur if Prince Charles, heir to the throne of Britain, were permitted, at his own insistence, to go to Viet-nam, and was then killed in an ambush having apparently been abandoned by a young American officer.

PROLOGUE

At about ten o'clock on the morning of 22 August 1879, the Indian troopship *Jumna* arrived at Spithead. As it steamed into the harbour, its careful manœuvring was watched by a large crowd which had assembled at the railway jetty in the dockyard and at neighbouring piers and landing places. Many had come to meet the Portsmouth and Chatham Divisions of the Royal Marines, who had left the port in the first week of June for the Zulu War and who now returned with their strength undiminished, having seen no action. The ship tied up and the crew began to unload baggage. When they were told that the troops were not to disembark until later on in the day, the crowd resignedly settled down to waiting, craning to see the celebrity whom everyone knew was on board.

When the gangplank was lowered, the crowd surged forward to cluster round it in a tightly packed knot. A curtained carriage had been waiting unobtrusively at the back of the jetty; from it emerged a clergyman and two ladies, one middle-aged and one young. Clinging tightly to the parson's arms, they were shepherded before him as he forced his way through the crowd and up the narrow gangplank. They were followed by a group of newspaper reporters. Arriving on deck, the party halted momentarily, and two army officers came across the deck to meet them, one remaining a few paces in the rear. The leading officer flung his arms first around the younger woman, then the other, and then exchanged embraces with the clergyman. Finally, he introduced his companion, Captain Evans of the Royal Artillery.

The reporters crowded around the group :

'Captain Carey ! Will you make a statement ?'

The tall, well-built officer turned towards them, spreading out his hands in a gesture of appeal.

'Gentlemen ! Be so kind, so courteous as to grant me a few

precious minutes with my loved ones after which I will be delighted to place myself unreservedly at your service . . . to give you full and frank information and answer any questions you may see fit to put to me!'

Tilting his head to one side, he hunched his shoulders and gestured with his hands in a manner more French than English. Wearing a weather-stained patrol jacket, he presented a picture of the seasoned campaigner returning from the wars; keen eyes gazed from a bronzed, full-bearded face that mirrored robust health and apparent good spirits. Spreading his arms protectively around his father, mother and his wife, Captain Carey shepherded them to a quiet corner of the deck. His fellow officer who, so far, had not spoken a word, followed slowly in their wake, looking embarrassed.

Then Captain Carey strode back across the deck to the expectant reporters.

'Now gentlemen! What can I do for you? Where would you like me to begin? Yes, I am very pleased to be back in my beloved country and in the bosom of my family . . . everyone has been very kind and cordial. . . .'

Breaking off, he strode to the rail, the reporters still following.

'Excellent band . . . the Royal Marines I believe . . . I presume they are here to welcome their comrades?

Do you know, when we arrived at Plymouth, there was a band waiting to greet *me*. . . . I'm a Devon man you know . . . my countrymen came to meet me with a band!'

'Captain Carey! Is it true that the Mayor of Plymouth presented you with an address of welcome?'

'Well . . . yes . . . in a way . . . the rules of the service preclude the personal presentation of an address, therefore Mr Lewis, acting on behalf of the Committee, came on board and described the address to me . . . he told me that it was signed by between two and three thousand persons and it is to be sent to me later by post!'

'Captain Carey! We hear that the people of Portsmouth would have prepared a written expression of their confidence in your gallantry and soldierly qualities but for that of the inhabitants of Plymouth being refused presentation.'

Carey turned to face the speaker and he placed his hands over his heart :

'How good of them! It is so comforting to know that, by their spontaneous expressions of confidence, my countrymen show that

10

public opinion is pre-eminently in my favour. Gentlemen, I have a statement for publication in your illustrious journals . . . may I suggest we retire to a cabin where I can give it to you in comfort and at your leisure?'

1

IN the autumn of 1846, Adolphus Frederick Carey was appointed Assistant Curate at Burbage in the County of Leicester. He brought with him his young bride, Harriet Mary. On 6 August 1847 she painfully brought a son into the world, and Adolphus, who had been signing the Baptism Register since the beginning of the year, carefully and with great pride, now put his signature to the entry confirming the birth of Jaheel Brenton Carey.

Adolphus viewed these names with reservations; he was not convinced that a minister's son should be named after Sir Jaheel Brenton, a militant sailor of Nelson's days whose exploits on board the *Caesar* at Gibraltar in 1801 and in command of the frigate *Spartan* at Cerigo and Pesaro had won him a baronetcy. Not wishing to upset his young wife in her delicate state of health, and conscious that she wanted to name the child after the grandfather from whom her private income originated, the curate kept his objections to himself. He found consolation in the knowledge that Jaheel was the third son of Zebulon, that tribe of whom Deborah sang 'they were a people that jeoparded their lives into death in the high places of the field'.

A few months later, in the spring of 1848, Adolphus was appointed Curate at Higher Brixham in Devon, and the family moved to the quiet little fishing village. In 1849 Reginald Orme Brenton was born, to be followed, in the manner of the time, by a regular output of brothers and sisters. Because of Harriet's private income, they were able to live far more comfortably than did the families of most curates at that time.

Harriet found that the performance of her necessary parochial duties as a clergyman's wife became increasingly difficult as her family grew larger. In order to cope with the situation, she devised a strict régime which knew no deviation—rigid discipline for

13

each and every member of her family with swift punishment following any transgression.

Impulsive and self-willed, Jaheel soon fell foul of the new system. In some awe, Adolphus Carey and his children watched the clash of wills between the eldest son and his mother. Her battle-cry became : 'Where is Jaheel? Go and tell him to stop whatever he is doing at once!'; and the frequent thrashings he received taught the boy the meaning of fear at an early age.

Strong-minded and ambitious, Harriet felt that the small village school, which was attended by the unpolished sons and daughters of fishermen, was not a fitting environment for the Carey children; thus they were taught at home by a French governess. For some time, Harriet had been looking for a suitable scholastic establishment to which her eldest son could be sent, and, in the mid-1850's, she told her husband of her plans. Louise, the governess, had spoken frequently of her brother, who was the principal of a Lycée Impériale in Paris. Now Louise was returning home to marry her fiancé and Harriet had arranged that the boy should accompany her and live with the couple in their new home whilst attending her brother's school. Adolphus Carey could not understand why it was necessary to send an eight-year-old boy to school in a foreign country, but Harriet replied that he would have his outlook broadened, that he would be bi-lingual and that it was quite the thing now for the sons of the aristocracy to be educated in France. Adolphus Carey felt that there was nothing more he could say, and so the tearful boy was packed off to school in France.

When he had become accustomed to the strangeness of it all, Jaheel Brenton Carey discovered that he liked the noisy, demonstrative people amongst whom he had been pitched. Soon he was indistinguishable from his classmates, dressed in the same fashion, making the same gestures, waving his arms and using the same colloquialisms as though he had been born to them.

With the English Channel between him and his mother's wrath, Jaheel, aided by retrospect and maturity, found a respectful affection for her. Although his father had always given him understanding and comfort, it was his mother whom he most missed and to whom he wrote long, descriptive letters.

In March 1856 he wrote to his mother telling her of the exciting time they had had in Paris during the celebrations of the birth of the Prince Imperial : '. . . the boulevards were one line of light from the Madeleine to near the Bastille . . . private houses were lit up from top to bottom . . . and the coloured lights hung even in the alleys and back streets . . .' and told her of the full Royal salute of 101 guns fired by the cannon of the Invalides. On the day following the christening of the young Prince, Jaheel spent what was perhaps the most exciting day so far in his young life. Paris, its boulevards crowded, was *en fête*—the people were entertained by military bands, circuses and every conceivable kind of amusement, culminating in a grand firework display with the Emperor himself letting off the first rocket.

In his letters, Jaheel told his mother how Prince Louis had been enrolled at birth as a grenadier and how at eighteen months he had acquired a Lilliputian uniform and miniature busby. At the age of three, he was promoted to epaulettes and began to appear in uniform at official gatherings. Woodcuts in French newspapers showed him at reviews sitting stiffly before the Emperor, saluting with childish gravity and importance. The seventh anniversary of the Prince's birth, 16 March 1863, was celebrated by a splendid fête of the boy soldiers of the Army of Paris, in which the Prince shared. Jaheel wrote enviously of the three hundred children who went to the performance of *Marengo*, a great military play in which cannon were fired and regular battles put on the stage. The little Prince was in the Imperial box with his parents.

2

NAPOLEON III had lived in exile as a child, returning to France only when he was old enough to engage in intrigues with opponents of the Bourbon monarchy. The plots uncovered, he fled to America, a step ahead of the secret police, returning later when things had quietened down to resume the secret meetings and plots. This time, however, Napoleon did not escape when the plotters were discovered, and he spent six years in prison. On his release, he came to live in England and did not go back to Paris until after the Revolution of 1848, when he was 40. Before the year was out he had been elected President of the Republic, and in 1852 he was proclaimed Emperor. In the following year he married Eugenie de Montijo, the vivacious and attractive daughter of a penurious Spanish hidalgo. Because of their less than-regal backgrounds, they were not entirely accepted by continental royalty. However, Queen Victoria invited them to England as her guests, and her journal indicates that she found them charming.

The Emperor, who longed to be the forerunner of a dynasty, was overjoyed when the Empress Eugenie was safely delivered of their son, and the Prince Imperial was presented to the people with pomp and ceremony. The Pope consented to stand as godfather, and Napoleon offered himself in the same rôle to all legitimate French children born on that day. Before the Prince was six hours old, the Diplomatic Corps paraded through the throne room to see him draped with the ribbon of the Legion of Honour. A large crucifix rested on the small body.

The French nation felt that this child, who had found birth so difficult, would ensure the future of the dynasty and end the era of revolutions. Napoleon rode high—he had conquered anarchy and conquered Russia; Great Britain, the hereditary enemy of the French, had become an ally; he had invited Europe to an Exhibition demonstrating France's productive energy, her genius in art and industry. On the eve of the meeting in Paris of a Congress of Powers, called to ensure a lasting peace, fortune crowned his successes with the birth of a son.

Twelve years later the Abbé Deguerry told the Prince:

'Mon cher petit seigneur, do you know that I paid you my first visit with many grown-up gentlemen when you were still not quite forty-eight hours old? You had the red ribbon already. Now, what had you done at two days old to have deserved the grand cross of the Legion of Honour? You had been given the cross, not for the services you had rendered, but for those you will one day have to give. The cross is the symbol of sacrifice. The one that was placed in your cradle meant that you had been marked out from your birth to devote yourself to the people.'

3

I<small>N</small> December 1856, when he was nine months old, the Prince Imperial was entered on the roll of Commissioned Officers of the First Regiment of the Grenadiers of the Guard. His first formal dress was military attire—he could barely stand when he was arrayed in a minature grenadier's uniform. Before he was out of his cradle, long before he could walk, he was strapped to the saddle of a Shetland pony. Peering in bewilderment the child attended a military review with his father, his pony led by a mounted groom. At six years of age he was able to ride a full-sized horse. It was said of him :

'He was a horseman at heart . . . uniting agility with suppleness with that noble French horsemanship of which we were justly proud before the invasion of English methods.'[1]

Napoleon's critics, and he had many, derided the manner in which he directed his son's upbringing, calling it a military masquerade. In this they misinterpreted the Emperor's motives; he reasoned that the throne would be strengthened if the people felt they had a prince who might one day follow the same glorious path pursued by his illustrious uncle. To achieve this end, the Emperor sought a spectacular relationship between his son and the army and directed the general course of his education with that in mind.

A devoted and indulgent tutor, Auguste Filon, took charge of the rather delicate child; but he did not receive much in the way of a formal education. Later, when the Emperor established his son's military household he put at its head General Frossard, aide-de-camp to the Emperor, together with four aides-de-camp taken from the navy and from the different branches of the army.

The young Prince grew up with certain features which might have been envied by a girl—delicate skin, long eyelashes, slender

[1] Auguste Filon, *Memoirs of the Prince Imperial* (London, 1913).

18

wrists and ankles and grace of movement. These features became less obvious as he developed into manhood, but they were never completely effaced. Filon, his tutor, wrote fondly :

'. . . he was a regular boy . . . as I was soon to perceive through his rash feats, the very remembrance of which makes me shiver. . . .'[2]

Excitable and nervous, the young Prince had an incessant restlessness that he was sometimes unable to control and which made him almost uncontrollable. When other threats failed, he could usually be brought to heel by the threat that he must not 'disgrace the uniform'. When playing with other children, he seemed to lose every idea of what was real and what was possible—once started, he was likely to smash his way through a closed door or jump from a window. On Sundays, the Prince and his friends would play war games, attacking or defending a little fort constructed at the end of the terrace of the Tuileries, on the plateau commanding the Place de la Concorde. When it came to the inevitable hand-to-hand fighting, the Prince would be difficult to control. That there were no serious accidents was due solely to the sense of respect which his young friends felt for their royal comrade. Poor Filon hardly knew a day without worry due to the royal taste for dangerous games.

As he grew older, the Prince Imperial seemed to achieve his greatest pleasure from danger, courted willingly and in cold blood, and his feats became notorious.

During his travels in Scandinavia he terrified the Prince Royal of Sweden with his rash escapades, until finally the latter left him, feeling that his presence encouraged the Prince. This incurable passion asserted itself despite the Prince's awareness of his position.

In September 1867 a naval despatch boat, the *Chamois*, on which the Empress and the Prince Imperial were cruising, struck some rocks at the base of the jetty while trying to enter Saint Jean de Luz. The dark, a freshening wind and the confusion made it hard to estimate the danger. The Empress cried out :

'Louis, don't be afraid !'

The Prince answered :

'A Napoleon is never afraid.'

Surrounded by uniforms, flags and all the military trappings of the age, the Prince was borne along in a dream-world of glory and ostentation, encouraged by the eternal vision of the great

[2] Auguste Filon, *Memoirs of the Prince Imperial* (London, 1913).

Napoleon Bonaparte; the duller details of tactics, strategy and staff-work were ignored.

The Emperor was the boy's constant companion, and he succeeded in cultivating in his son the desired enthusiasm for military matters. Unfortunately, it all went too far—the taste turned into a consuming passion. A contemporary writer commented :

'The tunic they had put upon him as a mere child would be a shirt of Nessus to him. . . .'

In fact, the many tunics he was to wear tell the story of his short life—from the ludicrous minature grenadier's outfit to the undress uniform of an officer in the British Royal Artillery, slashed and bloodied by Zulu assegais.

4

IN mid-1863 when he was just sixteen Jaheel Brenton Carey left the Lycee in Paris and returned home to his family in Brixham. He had gone away a tearful boy of eight, he returned a mature, demonstrative young man of the world. His easy, almost glib manner of speaking pointed by un-English gesticulations modified slightly his mother's habitual sharpness, but not enough to prevent it from being irksome to him. Although he was pleased to be back with his family, lording it over his adoring brothers and sisters, he found Brixham a sad substitute for Paris, and it was not long before he was bored. He chafed to embark on something, he did not know what, only that he had to get away.

Harriet Carey reluctantly realised that it would be best for her eldest son to leave them again and to take the first steps towards a career. Adolphus had always hoped that Jaheel would go into the Church, but he could see that whilst the boy might become a Catholic priest, he was hardly the stuff of which English country clergymen are made. Jaheel himself seemed to have no ideas at all on what he wanted to be, except a vaguely-expressed interest in the Army. Recalling her illustrious naval ancestor, his mother tried to persuade him to go to sea. The attempted dominance hardened the boy's views until, in a short time, the conflict had driven Jaheel into an uncompromising desire to take the Queen's Commission. Knowing herself to be beaten, Mrs Carey sought out an influential family friend, and in February 1864 Jaheel Brenton Carey was admitted to the Royal Military College at Sandhurst.

The RMC was founded in 1799, and had been housed in the Old Building at Sandhurst since 1812. From 1858, it had trained 16- to 18-year-old boys who had received a Public School education. In 1864, the establishment was only just settling down after a cadet mutiny that had taken place eighteen months before, which had had to be settled by the personal intervention of the

21

Duke of Cambridge, Commander-in-Chief of the British Army. It had arisen in rebellion against the rules which were originally formulated for boys of 14 years of age. The cadets were spied upon constantly and could be searched at any hour of the day or night; the discovery of an 'improper article' such as a tobacco pipe would result in 48 hours' confinement in a cellar six-by-eight feet, without light, heat or bedding. They were restricted to £2 pocket-money every six months, they had to undress in the dark and were confined for exercise to a small playground. In 1862, tiring of these conditions, the cadets took food supplies and defended a prepared redoubt, bombarding the Commandant with loaves of bread when he approached to remonstrate. Although the ring-leaders were sent down, conditions subsequently improved; games and sports were organised and the officers were brought into more personal contact with the cadets.

In 1864, when Jaheel arrived, the college had about 300 cadets who lived and messed with the officers while they took the year's course of military subjects. The cadets entered straight from school, in the majority of cases with a healthy disinclination for concentrated study. Pleasure-seeking and irresponsible, their high spirits caused them to carry on the Public School tradition of fierce ragging, so often indistinguishable from bullying. Encouraged by the legends of the Mutiny, the cadets felt that they had to be a closely-knit group. Inevitably, this left no place for the non-conformist—all had to adapt themselves to the common pattern or be persecuted until they departed. A few hardy characters managed to withstand the physical and mental indignities put upon them by their fellows, but the majority conformed.

Cursed with a name like Jaheel, lacking a Public School background and conspicuously non-English with his involuntary Gallic gestures and demonstrativeness, it was inevitable that the boy should quickly become a prime target. Before February was out, Jaheel knew all the terrors and pains of the traditional Sandhurst ragging. He had been 'drawn'; 'ventilated'; 'bed-launched'; 'shovelled'; 'roasted'; 'aired' and 'adamised'.[1]

---

[1] 'Drawn'—teased and goaded.
'Ventilated'—tied to a ventilator and pricked with forks.
'Bed-launched'—to have the bed overturned with its occupant still in it.
'Shovelled'—laid on a table and whacked with shovels and racquets.
'Roasted'—held close to a built-up fire when wearing only a night-shirt.
'Aired'—held upside-down by the feet from a third-story window for a certain period.
'Adamised'—kidnapped after dark, stripped naked and lowered to the

The porter who carried his bag from the railway station on his arrival day told him that only tough fellows could live through Sandhurst. Jaheel, who did not consider himself tough, wondered how he would stick it; and unconsciously he drew about himself a protective cloak compounded of an almost hysterically light-hearted resilience and a buffoonish garrulity, tempered by an obvious and apparent willingness to conform. His tormentors, baffled by this sponge-like ability to absorb punishment, and deriving decreasing satisfaction from their efforts, began to turn their attentions to alternative victims.

Jaheel was now free to work at his studies and by sheer industry he finished his year's study at Sandhurst in the first twenty, thus qualifying for a commission without purchase.

The insidious practice of buying commissions in the British Army was abolished in 1871, but on 31 December 1864, when Jaheel Brenton Carey left Sandhurst, 'Queen's Regulations' set out the price of an Ensign's commission as £450. It was a great relief to Harriet Brenton Carey that she did not have to find such a large sum—her constantly-increasing brood had made great inroads into her small private income. Jaheel's Parisian schooling had taken his share, and she was unable even to give him an allowance once he was commissioned. Knowing that he would have to live on his pay, Jaheel realised that he could not serve in England where his monthly Mess bill would probably be far more than he earned. There was keen competition among those officers who did not have a private income for postings to the Indian Army, in which the higher pay enabled them to live without assistance from home. Unfortunately, Jaheel's free commission made an Indian posting impossible; thus, with a Home commission out of the question, he was forced to look for an overseas regiment in a disagreeable station.

Such a vacancy existed in a regiment serving in West Africa, and on 24 January 1865 Jaheel Brenton Carey was gazetted as Ensign in the 3rd West India Regiment. He was $17\frac{1}{2}$ years of age.

> parade-ground, from which the only means of re-entry into the college was through the guard-room.
> (From Major A. F. Mockler-Ferryman, *Annals of Sandhurst*, and E. S. Turner, *Gallant Gentlemen*, p. 215.)

5

ON 23 March 1865, two months after receiving his commission, Ensign Carey sailed from Liverpool for West Africa. As the ship made its way up the Mersey, he gazed at the patchwork of vari-coloured fields dotted with scattered homesteads and wondered if he would ever see England again. He soon retired to his hammock, to struggle up on deck two days later having served his apprenticeship to the sea. He was scarcely ever seasick again.

The early novelty gone, it was a dull voyage. With few books available, Carey occupied himself by keeping an elaborate journal and by drawing, for which he had considerable talent.

When land was sighted everyone lined the rails; the ship moved in slowly and dropped anchor about a mile from the shore, where she lay rolling and heaving monotonously. From the sea, Cape Coast Castle standing on a projecting point was quite a pleasant sight. On rising ground to the left of the massive old Dutch castle stood the white-washed buildings of the town.

Carey had been warned that landing here was a difficult business, and he was therefore prepared for the apparently hazardous procedure that necessitated his clinging desperately to a gyrating rope-ladder a few feet above the churning surf, until a surf-boat surged upwards underneath him and he could drop into it. The surf-boats were like strongly-built whale-boats, with six or eight Kroo boys with paddles sitting on the gunwale on either side and another in the stern who steered with an oar; they chanted a dirge as they paddled.

When the boat finally arrived at the shore Carey stepped onto the hard sand in an atmosphere that quivered with heat. Behind him the surf thundered and roared endlessly, and at the top of the beach was the entrance to the castle through which passed files of porters carrying casks and cases. He looked about him for someone who might be expecting the arrival of a freshly-joined Ensign.

The West India Regiment was made up of coloured soldiers officered by white men who wore a Zouave-type uniform that reminded Carey of a parade down the Champs-Elysée in 1859, when the French Zouaves returned from Solferino. The West India Regiment wore a red bolero trimmed with yellow over a white jacket, and very full pale-blue trousers bearing a broad yellow stripe and ending in white gaiters. On their heads they wore flat white turbans with white tassels—on active service peakless caps with white covers and neck flaps were sometimes worn. Dress Regulations laid down that the officers dressed 'as for infantry', with a forage cap bearing a badge composed of the letters 'W.I.' and the battalion number.

Under the command of Lieutenant-Colonel Conran the 4th Battalion of the West India Regiment, together with detachments of the 3rd and 4th Battalions, had gone to Ashanti in 1863. After moving up to Prasu to construct defences so many men had died of fever and dysentery that the force had come back to the coast late in 1864. In mid-1865 the tribes became troublesome again, and Ensign Carey's first operation was on a small punitive expedition sent to Prasu.

They moved on a well-trodden path running through what might be called a gigantic shrubbery some thirty to forty feet high, with huge cotton trees rising above the greenery. Apart from the inhabitants of the mud-hut villages through which they passed, they saw no one. At each halting place, bamboo huts were erected, well thatched to combat the heavy dew that soaked everything. Rations were plentiful and included fresh meat from cattle which were driven with them, but it was so tough that Carey could hardly get his teeth into it.

At last they reached Prasu, where the River Prah separated them from the country of the rebellious natives. The expedition crossed the river on a light bridge and marched to the Adausi Hills. From here, the country stretched out in a rolling carpet of the deepest green, with an occasional gigantic tree towering above the lush jungle. After struggling through this dense forest for days without encountering a single native, the force returned wearily to the coast. Carey finished the expedition in a rough litter carried by four soldiers; for two days he had felt sick, faint and giddy, and he finally collapsed.

Back at the coast, he lay delirious for days in a stuffy hut where the temperature reached 109°, in spite of which his teeth chattered and he was wretchedly cold. He was shakily back on his feet some weeks later when another, larger expedition set out to suppress the natives; but Carey was left behind, with a small garrison, in command of Fort James at Accra. It was an old, dilapidated building erected by the British in 1673 and practically indefensible. Still too weak to worry, Carey vaguely realised that neither he nor the fort were capable of putting up much resistance if attacked; he wished that he had been fit enough to go with the expedition.

The force advanced to the mouth of the Volta river to attack the camp of the Anlo tribe, who had been incited by a slave-trader, Geraldo de Lema, to attack the town of Kpong in the British protected area. After the camp had been shelled, the native tribes supporting the British refused to cross the river and, as the troops were too small in numbers to cross and fight successfully on their own, the next fourteen days were spent arguing and wrangling amongst themselves, until finally in disgust Captain Humphrey, the senior British officer, retired with his 4th West India Regiment. Seeing the troops go, the Anlo rebels attacked the remaining allied force of natives and were only defeated when they ran out of ammunition and were attacked in the rear. This ended the campaign and the expedition straggled back to Accra.

Late in 1866, the West India Regiment thankfully quitted West Africa and sailed to Jamaica.

6

SLOWLY the vessel approached the Palisadoes, the seven-mile-long sandpit that swings from east to west, forming the eastern side of the narrow entrance to Kingston Harbour. They moved past Port Royal, the town that had grown up on the protected semi-circular beach around the seventeenth-century Fort Charles, taking the same route as that of the buccaneers who claimed to have made Port Royal, 'The finest town in the West Indies . . . and the richest spot in the universe'.

Jamaica was only now beginning to settle down after the native insurrection of October 1865, which had been quelled by Governor Edward John Eyre with the British troops stationed on the island. The island was now considered to be adequately garrisoned by the ten companies of British troops and eight companies of the West India Regiment, so no sooner had the troops returning from West Africa set foot on land than they were ordered out again. Brigadier-General Harley was taking a force to British Honduras to recover British territory from Indian invaders led by Canûl, a rebellious chief.

Although his health had progressed steadily during the voyage, Carey was still weak and unable to endure hard exercise. Remembering his ignominious litter-borne conclusion to the Ashanti campaign, he wished fervently to justify himself to his fellow-officers by going on the expedition. Insisting that he was perfectly fit, his enthusiasm was enough to get him returned to duty. Nevertheless, the march over the pot-holed, unsurfaced road that led to Belize became a nightmare to Carey.

Honduras had been declared a British colony only five years before. When Carey arrived in January 1867, Belize was a lively, bustling place of 25,000 inhabitants, whose narrow streets at night echoed with the roistering of drunken seamen.

Since the beginning of the eighteenth century, the bloodthirsty

Maya tribes from the Yucatan had come raiding and killing in Honduras. These were a people obsessed with war, either with inter-tribal guerrilla raids for prisoners and loot, or formal battles that opened with deafening drums, whistles, shell-trumpets and war-cries. Their braves, the 'holcan', were foot soldiers who fought with spears, poisoned darts, bows and arrows and slings. Some of them wore cuirasses of quilted cotton. In 1848, a horde of 10,000 Mayas from Santa Cruz burst upon the town of Bacalar and burned it to the ground. A gunboat was sent from Belize to the River Hondo, where a town, Corozal, was founded to house the refugees. In 1857, the Chinchenha Mayas mounted a raid on Northern Yucatan, killing nearly 2,000 Spaniards at Tekax. Crossing the Hondo, they took Bacalar, roasting their captives alive in a 'sacrifice to an idol in the moonlight'. Over the years the raiding and murdering continued, and troops were sent repeatedly from Jamaica to prevent the tribes from penetrating further into the colony.

The column marched out on 30 January 1867; it consisted of 400 men of the 3rd and 4th West India Regiments, 30 men of the Royal Artillery and a contingent of 500 local Militia. The roads over which they marched were winding, pot-holed tracks, covered by a thick, white dust.

For many yards back from the road the bush was thickly coated with the dust. At other times, they marched through dank rain-forests where the huge trunks of the Sapodilla were covered with creepers and exotic orchids. For most of the time they plodded along under leaden skies that reminded Carey more of an English winter than of the Central American tropics.

Against such a large force, the Indians offered little resistance; San Pedro, their principal stronghold, was taken and the only casualties of the operation occurred when three men were wounded in an assault on a village called San Jose. General Harley divided his force into flying columns and sent them in different directions to dislodge the few stubborn pockets of resistance; he also established frontier posts to prevent further invasions.

With the resilience of youth, Carey soon regained his strength and went ahead of the column reconnoitring and drawing maps. Impressed by his industry and enthusiasm, General Harley mentioned Carey favourably in his despatches at the conclusion of operations.

Back at Belize, the campaign seemingly over, the troops settled down to make the most of the pleasures offered by the rowdy, turbulent town which, in spite of its remoteness, had a colourful history. For generations it had been a base for hard-living logwood-cutters and pirates. Time had brought sobriety, and in 1867 its elite included landowners, merchants and ship-owners, many with daughters of marrying age. They vied with each other in offering hospitality to the eligible officers of the West India Regiment. Carey was a favourite with both mothers and daughters, captivating them with the spontaneous French gestures that had never left him. The men were not so sure of him, wondering what, if anything, lay beneath the posturing and the gallantries.

Carey sometimes suffered from fits of depression; especially since his illness, he had become a prey to introspection; death and disease held a morbid fascination for him. Wandering one day through St John's Cathedral, he came across many inscriptions and memorials to early settlers who had died of yellow fever. In the Mess one evening a local doctor told him of the Essex brick-layer who had come out to build the cathedral, how he had seen all his family die one by one, had buried them in Yarborough Cemetery and had eventually followed them himself. The doctor reckoned that missionaries, doctors and soldiers were lucky if they survived five years. Carey recoiled in horror; the doctor patted his arm.

'Don't worry, lad! You won't die of yellow fever, you're too young and healthy! You'll live to be hacked to pieces by those murdering Indians from Yucatan!'

The next morning word came that the Indians had risen again and were ravaging the country above Corozal. The 4th West India Regiment were ordered out and Carey was attached to them in place of an officer down with fever; as he rode out of Belize, Carey's fears were replaced by visions of glory. They marched up the great Northern Highway, a fairly straight road running between banks of high bush. Later, it crossed the sandy pine ridges of the northern plain, which was dotted with ragged patches of vegetation and pock-marked by countless small ponds. Everything was parched and baked; the dusty, unmade road dissolved beneath their plodding feet into a mouth-clogging grit. The only source of drinking water was the stagnant ponds; the officers were ordered strictly to supervise the boiling of water before it was drunk.

No one knew the whereabouts of the Indians, except that they were somewhere beyond Orange Walk, the district capital. Major Mackay, the commanding officer, rode at the head of the column;

by his side, in civilian dress already white with dust, rode a Civil Official from Orange Walk, who was to parley with the Indians in their own language.

After marching for some hours, the column approached San Pedro, where the last expedition had seen a little action. They were moving slowly between clumps of botan, a bay-leaf palm used by the natives as thatching, when suddenly Major Mackay held up his hand. Carey stood in his stirrups and craned his neck to see what had happened. Through the settling dust he saw patches of bright colour and dark skin in the vegetation ahead; as he stared, the patches multiplied until they blended together in a mass that transformed the greenery into a backcloth. No one moved, there was nothing to be heard except the chirruping of insects. Major Mackay turned in his saddle and gazed back down the column. A shout broke the stillness.

'Carey! Ensign Carey! Come up here quickly!'

Carey spurred his horse forward and pulled up in front of the commanding officer, who returned his salute. Alongside Major Mackay, the Civil Official sat staring stolidly at the Indians, still quiescent two hundred yards away.

'Carey, I want you to go forward with Lieutenant Ferguson, as an escort, you will carry a white flag.'

Tightly clasping a rough branch to which was tied a white handkerchief, Carey led his horse forward some ten yards behind the Civil Official. By his side, Lieutenant Ferguson talked quietly, his eyes ceaselessly scanning the bush on either side of them.

'I hope this fellow knows what he's doing. We're in a sticky spot if the Indians take no notice. He's asked the Major not to order the men into defensive formation in case it alarms the Indians and they attack before he's had a chance to talk to them!'

Ferguson's voice took on a more urgent tone.

'You know, I think those Indians are making their way through the bush onto our flanks while we are watching this lot in front.'

Carey thought the whole business a waste of time. Why not let the Indians have the jungle? It was no good to anyone.

At length the Civil Official stopped. His gaze travelled along the massed ranks of Indians, as though to awe them by his indifference. Slowly, he raised his right hand. It was the traditional gesture of peace, but the most uncivilised war cry could not have caused the Indians to react more violently. Screaming and yelling, they flung themselves upon the Civil Official. Carey saw him dragged from the saddle, his dust-whitened face and clothes turning bright red as razor-sharp weapons hacked and pierced him. This was the moment in his life in which for him the glory went for ever out of war, to be replaced by fear, horror and disgust. Carey knew that he would be killed within a few seconds, but was unable to move a muscle. Dragging his horse round, Ferguson bumped into him :

'Come on! Get back!'

Life flowed back into Carey; galvanised into activity, he turned to flee, brushing aside a native who struck at him with a spear. In a cloud of dust the two officers galloped furiously back down the track towards the column.

Major Mackay and the other officers were frantically trying to get the men into a defensive formation, but since he was unable to deploy his men on the narrow track, the Major was in a bad position. Reluctantly, he ordered the column to retreat, and to a background of ragged musketry volleys, the column laboriously retraced their steps. The Indians pushed them hard and were held off only with difficulty. Showers of spears fell upon the unfortunate section who had originally been at the head of the column but who were now the unwilling rearguard. Men began to fall as unseen Indians infiltrated through the bush and threw spears at close range. The troops were fast getting out of hand and only the constant urging and shouting of the officers kept them in any semblance of an organised force. Notwithstanding the midday heat and their fatigue, the retreating column moved faster and faster until everyone was proceeding at a shambling trot. Without orders, the men discarded their packs and equipment, so that the track became littered like a fairground after the crowds have departed. Perched upon his horse, conspicuous above the foot soldiers, Carey was uncomfortably conscious that he presented an obvious target. Each spear and arrow that hissed through the air made his flesh cringe and contract as though already pierced. Twice he emptied his pistol at unseen foes in the bush.

In spite of the efforts of Major Mackay and his officers, the withdrawal degenerated into a panic-stricken stampede, and Carey was thankful that night covered their orderless return to Belize.

A few days later, Lieutenant Ferguson and Ensign Carey were ordered back to Jamaica to give evidence before a court of enquiry sitting to examine the conduct of Major Mackay at Orange Walk. *The Jamaica Gleaner* of 5 March 1867 recorded the affair :

'4th West India Regiment. We understand that Major Mackay,

31

late in command of a detachment of the 4th West India Regiment at Honduras, has been ordered to report himself at headquarters in this city, to undergo examination before a court of inquiry, touching his conduct when in command against the Indians at Orange River. Lieutenant Carey and Ferguson, who were with the detachment, have also been ordered to Jamaica to give evidence before the Court, which will consist of three officers, who will investigate the case, and report to their Major-General commanding. If the report warrants a trial by court-martial, then the general will summon a Court, to consist of thirteen officers, from the other available regiments than that with which Major Mackay is connected. It will be remembered that the major was in command of the detachment which went up the river Hondo to intercept the Indians and drive them back; and the detachment are reported to have met the Indians near San Pedro, and the major, apparently believing that he was being surrounded by overwhelming numbers, ordered a retreat, which speedily produced a panic, and in the night returned to Belize, according to the accounts that have been published. It is to establish the truth or falsity of the conduct attributed to the major that the inquiry, we understand, will be instituted; and we trust the result may be such as to vindicate the honour of the British service, and prove creditable to the military character of Major Mackay.'

7

CAREY rode out to Morant Bay one day, to see the place where two years earlier a bloody series of events had taken place. In August 1865 a deputation, led by one Paul Bogle, had walked 45 miles from their little village of Stony Gut to King's House in Spanish Town. They wished to explain their difficulties to Lieutenant-Governor Edward John Eyre but were refused an audience and were turned away roughly by police. Bogle then led the villagers to the town of Morant Bay, where they were fired upon by local militia. In the affray that followed, there were men killed and wounded on both sides, until the militia barricaded themselves in the courthouse. The building was then set on fire and the militia men were murdered as they were driven out by the flames. Bogle and his followers then walked back to Stony Gut.

Immediately declaring martial law, Governor Eyre marched at the head of his troops to the village, where hundreds were arrested and their homes destroyed. After a drum-head court-martial, Eyre personally presided over the hangings of 439 men and more than 600 floggings, many of the victims being women. Bogle and some of his followers were caught a few days later in the mountains and were hung from the yard-arm of a warship in Morant Bay. George William Gordon, the editor of a local newspaper, was accused of inciting rebellion and, with eighteen others, he was hanged from a boom in front of the gutted courthouse at Morant Bay.

Carey crossed the Johnson River, fast flowing from recent floods, then over three converging tracks on the outskirts of Morant Bay and pushed his way through bush and nettles to a ruined church, half enveloped by the wild growth. From here a narrow street wound up to the now deserted square where he stood in front of the gutted courthouse and pictured the terrible

B

scenes that had taken place there. He shivered, and rode back to Kingston along the road by the seashore.

Jamaica was going through a bad time in the early 1860's. Sugar, the island's main industry, could give only irregular, badly paid employment to about 30,000 people; severe droughts, the collapse of several estates and fierce world competition had further depressed the industry. The provision crop had failed and the prices of imported foodstuffs had been forced up by the American Civil War. All this barely affected Carey, who found life in Jamaica very pleasant. As a gay and eligible young officer he was invited to all the parties. At first, he had found difficulty in comprehending the distinctions made in colour and class, whereby a free-born coloured person would be socially superior to a freed slave, even though both might be equally light-skinned. Both were considered inferior to white people; the only exceptions to this rule were the younger women, who were more than acceptable in the male-dominated society. There was a shortage of white women on the island, so that many white men had coloured mistresses; such women were considered to have a status superior to that of a coloured woman married to a coloured man.[1]

At first, Carey was stationed in Kingston, where narrow streets were bordered with dilapidated houses which had backyard gates opening into lanes originally used by slaves, servants and tradesmen. As time went by, these lanes were filled with shouting hawkers; then coloured people began to build small houses on them. Life in the streets and life in the lanes presented an incongruous contrast. The streets were packed with people of every shade of black, brown, white and yellow. Carey had expected to see characteristics of the African, the Indian and the Chinese, instead he could detect all and none in an inseparable mixture. Carey admitted to himself that it sometimes produced an irresistible fairy-like beauty in a young woman.

The lanes were equally full, but with a ragged, indolent population. Aged persons abounded, and Carey thought that he had never seen so many babies—almost every woman had an infant

[1] The offspring of a white man and a black woman is a mulatto; the mulatto and black produce a sambo; from a mulatto and a white comes the quadroon; from the quadroon and white come the mustee; the child of a mustee by a white man is called a musteffino, while the children of a musteffino were free by law, and were considered as white persons to all intents and purposes.

34

in her arms, and the dusty, litter-strewn tracks were playgrounds for children of all ages.

He liked to get out to Spanish Town, which was somewhat less crowded, although it was a drab, dusty little place made up of twisting streets, all of which seemed to lead to the square. This was surrounded by the King's House, the old House of Assembly and the Courthouse. A few yards away was the Cathedral of St Catherine, which, like the other buildings, had been laid out by the Spaniards and had been very little altered through the years, and was the oldest church foundation in the British Colonial Empire.

Carey tried to picture the sort of place that Port Royal must have been before fire destroyed it in 1704. He had read somewhere that it was '. . . a gilded Hades with Mammon holding sovereign-sway over its people. . . .' Gambling and drinking was paid for with precious stones and heavy gold coins thrown about by men who knew that their piracy placed them permanently in the shadow of the gallows. Carey now stood before a stone slab set into the esplanade. It bore the words 'Morgan's Line'.

Born in Wales in 1635, Henry Morgan became the greatest of the buccaneering captains, and had his headquarters at Port Royal; he brought enormous wealth into the town, and all Jamaica benefited from it. By 1669, Morgan had acquired large land holdings and spent his time among his estates, the social life of Port Royal and the capital, Spanish Town. With 800 houses and a population of almost ten thousand Port Royal became one of the three largest towns in the Caribbean. The houses, often two-storeyed, were built of bricks imported from England and were jammed close against each other right up to the seafront. The warehouses of the English merchants crowded the dock area, their doors flush with the unpaved narrow streets.

By 1867, more a much-battered village than a town, Port Royal had a population of about one thousand, who were mainly employed in its Navy Yards.

Ensign Jaheel Brenton Carey was promoted to Lieutenant on 6 March 1868 and was sent to command a detachment at Falmouth, on the other side of the island. The West India Regiment, in addition to quelling insurrections in Africa and North America, was also partly responsible for keeping order in Jamaica, a rôle considered even more pressing since the rebellion of 1865. The French Revolution had inspired the black slaves of the French colony of Saint Dominique to revolt near the turn of the 18th century, and fears of a similar uprising in Jamaica led to urgent demands for more military protection. The demands of the Napoleonic Wars precluded white troops being sent, so, in the face of violent protests by Jamaica's white population, the British Government authorised the raising of two regiments of black soldiers. They were slaves bought especially for the purpose and were still legally 'subject to the same laws as they would have been subject to had they been the property of His Majesty and employed in agriculture or public works'. Surprisingly, the scheme proved so successful that further regiments were raised until, in 1799, there were twelve regiments of black soldiers commanded by white officers.

Carey was sorry to leave Kingston; he was well established there and life held few dull moments. The road to Falmouth twisted northwest across nearly three-quarters of the length of the island, and he rode up through the Liguanea Plain and Spanish Town, stopping to look back as he arrived on the heights above Kingston.

He loved the picturesque names of the Jamaican villages—Dam Ford, Bog Walk, Linstead in the district of St Thomas-in-the-Vale, Ewarton. The road now passed through the mountains with a stiff climb over Mount Diablo to Moneague and the village of Retirement. Passing through the counties of St Andrew, St Catherine, St Ann and Trelawny, the road was dominated by mile after sweeping mile of thick-stemmed cane rising to a height of six feet and more. Passing Friendship Hill on his left he came to Claremont and into the mountain pass, with Canaan Hill on his left, to Bamboo and then on to the 'Towns'—Browns Town, Jackson Town, Stewart Town and Clarks Town, and finally to Falmouth.

Because he was not there of his own choosing, Carey at first failed to appreciate the peace of mind offered by the pleasant little town of Falmouth. Its wide streets and fine Georgian stone buildings, fronted by delicate wrought-iron balconies, rested quietly under the sun. But Falmouth had had its days of glory when it was one of the principal sugar ports of the island: in the heyday of King Sugar and slavery, the town had been the social and commercial capital of the north coast plantocracy.

Social life in Falmouth was very different from the roistering in Kingston. When he became accustomed to the formal social customs Carey found to his surprise that the placid, self-contentment of these gentle people produced a sense of relaxation that he had not known in Kingston. The Vines, a leading family in the district, were particularly kind to the young officer; he frequently found himself acting as escort to Annie, one of their daughters. Back in the early days of the century, Falmouth had been the seat of organised Christian opposition to slavery, and the Vine family had been among the most fervent supporters of William Knibb's chapel in the town. At midnight on the day in 1834 when the slaves had been freed, the Vines had echoed Knibb's cry, 'The monster is dead! The Negro is free!'

Placid, devout and home-loving, Annie Vine was nevertheless strong-willed. She found Jaheel Brenton Carey very different from the few young men of local birth still in the district. He seemed to glow with a cosmopolitan vitality, a joie-de-vivre that evoked a hidden vivacity in the girl. When he left, as he surely must, she felt that her world would come to an end. Her fears were allayed by her confidence that God in His Goodness would indicate the right manner for them to come together, if it was to be. In the months that followed, Carey was surprised to discover increasing pleasure in her company; she had a talent for listening in rapt silence to his voluble and demonstrative chatter, and together they explored the pretty villages in the district—Unity, Refuge, Alps, Troy, Bounty Hall and Wait-a-Bit—laughing as they made up reasons for the names.

Being the son of a clergyman and having been brought up in a vicarage, Carey's religious beliefs were gradually resuscitated by Annie's devoutness. Confused by the awareness of his growing affection for Annie, by his disturbed beliefs and by a lingering nostalgia for his past life in Kingston, Carey sat pondering in his quarters one night. He felt that some test was needed, some means of finding out if the pleasures that had until so recently filled his life were pleasures still.

It was well after midnight and a clear, fine night, as he saddled his horse, leapt into the saddle and clattered off down the Kingston road. On the climb over Mount Diablo he ran into dense mountain fog, and the mountains assumed a great size in Carey's mind, became frighteningly over-powering and seemed about to crush him. Mindful of sheer drops and precipices along the road, he pulled his horse to a walk. Gradually, it dawned on him that he was lost, that he had somehow missed his way on a road that he knew like the back of his hand. For hours, horse and rider stumbled through the mist; chilled by the moisture that beaded his clothes, face and hair, frustrated to the point of fury, Carey

37

cursed and chafed at his helplessness. Suddenly, his discomfort left him and realisation flooded over him. Gazing skywards, he cried : 'Oh Lord, You have come to me. . . . You have given this sinner a sign by sending forth Your wonders to prevent me returning to my evil ways . . . I will never again forsake you, Lord.'

Glowing with a nobility and an emotion such as he had never before known, Carey dismounted, tethered his horse and lay down. He was asleep almost at once. It was bright daylight when he awoke, an early morning with no trace of fog or mist, the sky above a brilliant cloudless blue. Carey mounted his horse stiffly and walked down to the sea where, full to overflowing with a deep contentment, he stretched out on the white, soft sand and let the sun envelop him.

Lieutenant Jaheel Brenton Carey, 3rd West India Regiment, married Annie Isabella Vine at Falmouth, Jamaica, in 1869.

8

ON 15 July 1870, with Paris echoing with patriotic songs and cries of 'To the Rhine!' France declared war on Prussia. It was almost certainly the one action likely to bring down the Empire that Napoleon III had been nurturing for his son, the Prince Imperial. Blundering into needless conflict with the greatest power ever organised in Europe, France was trapped, without allies, by a disastrous mixture of incompetence, foolishness and misfortunes. The Minister of War, Leboeuf, asserted that the Army was ready for the war, but the Emperor Napoleon had a shrewd idea of the lack of preparedness behind the glittering military façade. Napoleon had inherited none of the military genius of the first of his line, and any romantic dreams of war that he may have had were purged from his system by the horrors and blood of Solferino. Although he suffered from a bladder condition that made horse riding a nightmare, the Emperor Napoleon departed for the front to take command of his armies. The Empress Eugenie was to remain in Paris to act as Regent.

Thus, on the morning of 25 July 1870 a special train was drawn up near the Orleans gate on a private line which left the park and joined the main line from Paris to Versailles. The Empress was seeing her husband and her son off to Metz. In a fever of excitement, radiant even in the drab uniform of an infantry sub-lieutenant, the fourteen-year-old boy had no conception that this little world was soon to tumble in ruins. As the train was pulling out, the Empress called out :

'I trust, Louis, that you will do your duty.'

His answer was lost in the crowd's roar of 'Long Live the Emperor!' It was perhaps the last time that the loyal cry was raised in France.

On 2 August the boy saw sixty thousand Frenchmen laboriously

39

dislodge one thousand Prussians from Saarbrücken in the opening action of the war. A passing soldier gave him a spent bullet picked up from the battlefield. This bullet was to be commented on repeatedly by Republican newspapers and was thrown in his face until the day he died. The same evening the Prince exercised his talent for drawing by making a sketch of the engagement. It was very neat and precise, depicting the marching troops, the bridge and the encounter with the enemy; he clearly indicated the spot where he had stood with the Emperor throughout the affair. Louis presented the sketch to a great friend, M. Tristan Lambert, who was serving as a volunteer in one of the Guard Regiments. In one corner of the drawing, Louis wrote :

'A mon ami Tristan Lambert. Le 2 Aout, après avoir vu le feu pour la premiere fois.

Louis Napoleon'.

This minor action at Saarbrücken was the only fragment of glory that the young Prince saw during the war; soon the débacle began.

The French Army, an undisciplined mob of unwilling and bewildered conscripts, mobilised in a chaotic manner, was no match for the highly trained, confident and experienced Prussians. A succession of shattering defeats followed rapidly; the French, in two separate armies, were unable to unite and quickly degenerated into formless masses of dispirited men. Back in Paris, the Empress was unable to believe or accept the demoralising reports coming from the front. She issued a wild stream of unrealistic edicts, and finally she dismissed her husband from command of the army and forbade him and his son to leave the front.

For days, made memorable to the Prince by the utter confusion and the sullen disrespect of the soldiers, the pain-racked Napoleon and his bewildered son rode amid their disintegrating armies. Eventually the Emperor sent his son, under the charge of Commander Duperre, to Mauberge near the Belgian frontier; and at half-past three on the afternoon of 4 September they received a telegram : 'Start at once for Belgium'.

Louis and his officers laid aside their uniforms with anguish and donned civilian clothes. Only a few minutes after receiving the telegram they got into an omnibus and passed through the Mons gate; soon over the frontier, the Prince left French soil, never to set foot on it again. His father, the Emperor, had been captured at Sedan, and was at Verriers in the charge of a German general.

The Prince and his party crossed from Ostende on the morning of 6 September, aboard the packet *Comte de Flandres* and landed at Dover in the early afternoon. His mother, the Empress Eugenie, had also just arrived in England after a hazardous journey, and they were reunited at Hastings.

The journalist Archibald Forbes, in his book *Souvenirs of Some Continents*, describes the Prince Imperial during this phase of his life.

'He was a buckram boy from his swaddling clothes, poor little toy and tool of sham Imperialism down to the 'baptism of fire' (Saarbrücken). No trace is discernible of him as a boy in the fashion of other boys; he is ever found a mere padded clothes-horse or rather clothes-pony. Now attired in cumbrous uniform of the Compiegne hunt, with the couteau-de-chasse and a huge hunting horn hung about the poor melancholy little chap; now bedight in military garb, with a puny bit of a sword hung about his shins and his gloved hand raised in the frequent form of salute. The boy of the Second Empire is perhaps the most melancholy figure in its story, because we are fain to expect some human nature of boyhood, and the boyhood of this unfortunate child was as unreal as was the fantasy of which he was a victim.'

9

EARLY in June 1870 Lieutenant Jaheel Brenton Carey took his wife to England—he was returning to attend a course of instruction at the School of Musketry at Hythe in Kent. But the reunion with his family was marred for Carey by a division of loyalties with respect to the war between France and Germany. At that time it was the fashion in military circles to admire the efficient Prussians whilst deprecating France, the old enemy; a number of Englishmen were serving as officers in Bismarck's army. Nevertheless, Carey felt a strong sympathy for the French cause and sought ways in which he could aid them. Although it was an era in which officers applied for sick-leave to go to fight in some distant colonial campaign, Carey, as a serving British officer, could not volunteer to fight for a foreign power.

Then, out of the blue, came the news that the 3rd West India Regiment were to disband and that Lieutenant Carey would be on half-pay from 29 August 1870.[1] He soon volunteered for the English Ambulance, a body which was to send doctors, nurses and helpers to work alongside the French and German medical services. He went across the Channel with the first party, which included both English Ambulance personnel and those of the British National Society, under Captain Brackenbury of the Royal Artillery.

Carey was shocked to see the demoralisation of the French army, but he soon discovered that there was little time for emotional reveries; his own problems threw him into an atmosphere of horror, pain and confusion. Many of his English helpers were useless; having undertaken the service in a moment of enthusiasm,

[1] Half-pay was said by a contemporary writer to be '. . . a miserable dole designed to enable the War Office to keep up a cheap pool of ҉ . . . officers'. It was abolished, after two centuries, by Minister of War, Leslie Hore-Belisha, in 1937.

they turned out to be completely unfitted for the realities. Neither side displayed much gratitude for the services they were offering. Since most of the ambulance drivers were French, the Germans viewed them with great suspicion, sometimes not without cause. A Prussian officer disdainfully informed Carey that '. . . the English Ambulance, sir, is an infernal nest of spies !'

In the early morning of 15 August, an ambulance *fourgon* bearing a Union Jack clattered along the dusty road towards a French camp pitched around the château of Longueville. In the front sat J. S. Young, the superintendent of the English Ambulance, and Carey; both men wore the Red Cross brassard on their arms. They were very tired, having covered twenty-five miles, half of it under heavy fire. Twice the men, horses and wagon were spattered with showers of earth from shells exploding in the fields they were skirting. As they approached the château, its peace was shattered by the explosions of shell after shell landing on the building—a Prussian horse-battery had galloped up to within five-hundred paces of the building and opened fire upon the un-suspecting French.

Passing a garden, Carey saw three half-dressed French officers rising in indignant surprise from the breakfast table they had placed on the lawn. Suddenly they vanished in a turmoil of smoke, earth and fragments as a shell crashed upon them. Carey and Mr Young ran to the garden; but there was nothing they could do. Straightening up, Carey gazed towards the château, to see a group of officers hurriedly emerge, mount their horses and trot towards them. The foremost rider, wearing the uniform of a Lieutenant-General and the star of the Legion of Honour, had a thin, drawn face and a small pointed beard. By his side rode a slight, young officer whose uniform was only partially buttoned as though he had dressed in haste. Carey heard him say :

'Are they dead, father?'

The older man looked across at the tableau and nodded. Realising that they were in the presence of the Emperor Napoleon of France and his son, the Prince Imperial, both Mr Young and Carey uncovered their heads in salute. The Emperor responded perfunctorily; the Prince straightened in his saddle and stiffly returned their salute.

The days passed for Carey in a kaleidoscope of exhaustion and horror. Before leaving England and on the boat coming over he had read the accounts of the war written by the war correspon-dent William Russell in *The Times* and thought he knew what

43

to expect, but nothing had prepared him for the miseries he encountered. Russell, writing after the battle of Spicheren on 6 August, told of finding '. . . the earth strewn thickly with the evidences of mortal strife and, what was even more shocking, crowds of countrywomen wandering about, chattering and laughing. A party was observed picnicking among the blood-stained uniforms, the shattered limbs, the empty helmets and one person had actually done its duty, without stint, as a table. These people who had not themselves suffered from the war looked upon an excursion to a battlefield as one of the pleasantest trips that could be made.' Going over the battlefield of Worth in the pouring rain, Russell wrote that he saw the ground covered with dead horses, swollen to an enormous size, with their legs sticking up in the air; with Prussians who had fallen dead in the act of charging; and with Zouaves and Turcos in attitudes of fantastic rigidity, the faces generally covered with little pieces of linen placed there by the country folk. The burial parties were at work, but they had more to do than they could accomplish at one time. There were pools of blood in hollows, and for two miles on each side of the road a foul, sour smell was perceptible.

On 19 August, Carey and his ambulance were at the field of Rezonville, where he saw heaps of bodies lying to a height of nearly six feet. In many places they found bodies clasped together, and in one ravine the corpses were so close that they stood erect, buttressed up by one another.

Being told that there were wounded men still lying in a clump of woods, Carey led his helpers through the thick undergrowth, passing heaps of French corpses lying putrefying, poisoning the air. The Prussians had conscripted the local peasants to dig graves; a column of these reluctant workers, with shovels on their shoulders, shuffled past Carey. They reminded him of the brigades of snow shovellers he had seen clearing the roads in winter during his boyhood. Emerging from the woods with three wounded men, Carey and his party were suddenly surrounded by a patrol of Prussian Uhlans. These were lancers who advanced many miles ahead of their army into villages and farms, demanding food and forage and information of enemy movement which were sent back to their commander. Carey's French driver cowered in terror, but the Uhlans, seeing that one of the wounded men they were carrying was a Prussian Jager, wished them good luck and went on their way.

With the French armies constantly in retreat, the work of the volunteer ambulance units took place principally in areas occupied by the Prussians. In spite of his French sympathies, Carey found himself admiring their dogged German efficiency, and realised that their organisation for the care of the sick and wounded was far superior to that of the French. There was a corps whose special duty was to carry the sick and wounded; care was given them by assistants called Krankentrager. Some of them were enlisted soldiers, or men from the Reserve, whilst others were students from hospitals and universities. The soldiers wore uniform and the students wore plain clothes, but all wore the Red Cross worked or stamped on a white cloth tied around the left arm. Sisters of Mercy accompanied the army, marching on foot, each group having with them a priest or pastor; Carey noticed that they were often on the battlefield before the firing had ceased. The Krankentrager also proceeded on foot, except when they rode in waggons in charge of stretchers and medical stores.

Carey and his party were again taken prisoner by the Prussians after the battle of Gravelotte, but they were released as soon as it was seen that they were treating Prussian and French wounded with equal care. Never before in his life could Carey recall being so exhausted or existing for so long without sleep. Unattended wounded were still lying on the field three days after the battle had ended, and corpses were still unburied after eight days, in spite of every exertion. Every barn, shed and deserted farmhouse was filled with wounded men lying packed together on straw. The floors were drenched with blood and excrement, there were no brooms, cloths, soap or water to clean them, nor indeed even to wash the sufferers. There were no candles and no matches, and when darkness fell, men died unattended in the dark. Snatching a brief moment, Carey wrote to his wife, his mind full of the horrors amidst which he was living.

'Taking advantage of a lull in the firing about three o'clock, I went forward over the open ground in front towards the wood, which I thought the French had left. In a little hollow over which the Bavarians had twice passed, by a willow tree (the only sign of vegetation around), I found some eight or ten wounded men— five French, the rest Germans. With my little stock of bandages and my flask I did what I could for the poor fellows, but before I could return the firing recommenced. The bullets and balls whistled and hummed over me and around me, and patted or thudded the ground close to my feet. I crept under the slender shelter of the willow stump, and sat down among my wounded friends. I thought that half-hour would never end. The wounded Frenchmen groaned dreadfully. The Germans, though equally badly wounded, were more quiet and less complaining. This I found, too, in the hospitals. I think the French are more tenderly made. It was heart-rending to see so much misery I could do so little to relieve. I laid this one on his back, with his knapsack for a pillow, turned that one on his side, covered another's head with a cloth to shelter it from the burning sun, put a bit of shirt on this man's wound, unbuttoned the throttling coat of the fifth, took off the boot from the wounded foot of another, gave all a little cognac, and then sat down and talked with them. How grateful they were! How polite, in the midst of all his sufferings, was one poor French soldier! and, most touching of all, how kindly helpful the poor fellows were to one another, French and German alike! "But, monsieur," asked one poor Frenchman, "are the Prussians Christians?" "Certainly," said I. I knew he was thinking of those heathen Turcos of his. "Then," said my poor friend, breathing heavily (he was badly wounded in the chest), "why do we kill one another?" I interpreted our conversation to his German neighbours, and, the fire having slackened, I left them to seek the bearers to carry them off. The one question each asked was, "Tell me, tell me, shall I die?" I am not a doctor, so I took refuge in a hope for each; but how some lived a minute I cannot tell. One poor fellow, a Bavarian, had been struck down by a bullet just between the eyes, leaving a clean hole as large as a fourpenny piece. He was lying on his back yet I saw him raise himself deliberately on his elbow, and heard him distinctly ask me for water. I gave it him. He drank it, said "Thank you, thank you," and lay down again. In the evening, when the firing had again ceased, I brought back bearers with stretchers, and carried off all my poor friends to the field hospital.'

By mid-September the French armies were mostly in captivity, and Paris itself was under siege for nearly four months; together with other English volunteers, Carey suffered the same perils and discomforts as did the Parisians. Under constant bombardment and living on ever-decreasing rations, with horseflesh as the only available meat, Carey found Paris miserably changed from what it had been in his carefree schooldays. The volunteer ambulance workers performed courageous services throughout the siege. *The*

Daily News correspondent, writing of their exertions, said :

'They dragged the maimed and shattered out of the ruined houses; they collected the corpses from the streets and the ruins, and buried them with some semblance of decency. They went round the town, urging on the people that the women and children should go forth from the doomed town, and retire into Paris. The women and children were huddled in the semi-security of the cellars. The shells were crashing into the streets, and avalanches of stone and brick were ever crashing upon the side walks. The women, peeping forth, shudderingly declared that they would rather die where they were than incur a more certain and fearful death by sallying forth into that iron tempest. So they turned into the dark caverns to hunger and cold, and, cuddling their children to their bosoms, utterly refused to budge. The Pasteur Saglier went to the Commandant, and begged that he would allow him to go out as a parlementaire to the Germans, to ask for two hours' cessation of the bombardment, to give the woman and children a chance to get away without being struck down as they went. The Admiral refused, and the ruthless devilry went on. Then the Pasteur sent an appeal to the Paris journals, begging all who possessed means of conveyance to send them into St Denis to remove the perishing women and children. The response was but weak, and there appeared not a solitary representative of those ambulances whose members took delight in flags, and gave themselves to the vanities of buttons and uniforms. About half a dozen private vehicles turned up, and with the help of these the sick and wounded were got out of the hospitals in the town, and located in two large factories on the plain between St Denis and Paris. Then children followed, and women great with child, such as cared to go, till the plain houses became like caravanserais. Meanwhile, the few vehicles belonging to the ambulance were toiling assiduously in conveying to the rear the wounded struck down at the guns; a few men, and a few only, so far as I can learn, toiling with a zeal and energy that merited better support. As for the bold National Guards, their location was the wine-shop. Therein they imbibed the courage that prevented them from creeping into the cellars; and when their cups had made them reckless, they sallied out into the streets, only to give the ambulance more trouble with their worthless carcases. Not a few were killed as they staggered about; others were brought

47

to the ambulance, wounded indeed, but as drunk as lords.'

Before Carey left Paris at the end of January 1871, the Société de Secours aux Blessés presented him with a diploma of thanks, as well as a cross and ribbon, in gratitude for his faithful services to the French wounded.

10

THE Empress Eugenie and the Prince Imperial were reunited at the Marine Hotel in Hastings. Curious onlookers gathered outside the small sea-front hotel and peered through the bow-windows. When the Royal party took the air, they were followed on foot and through telescopes. But their greater troubles left them insensible to such petty vexations; both the Prince and his mother walked in silence, deep in their respective thoughts. Naturally concerned for her husband who was a prisoner in the hands of the Prussians, the Empress was even more worried by the changes which had occurred in her son. From an irrepressible boy whose every thought was reflected in his mobile face, he was now pale and impassive like his father; he moved lifelessly, consumed with such fatigue that it seemed he would be unable to withstand the physical and mental trials he had so recently undergone.

During the latter part of September the Empress moved to a house called Camden Place, at Chislehurst in Kent. The spiritless boy entered the house that was to play so prominent a part in their lives; eight years later he left it '. . . a bold and spirited young man, radiant with intelligence, overflowing with energy, glad to be alive and eager for action'.[1]

Soon, several refugee families who had fled from France took up their residence in the vicinity of Camden Place, and a small colony formed around the Empress. Rather to their surprise, the Royal party found themselves greeted with considerable enthusiasm, and many English visitors came and went—Queen Victoria paying her first official visit in the spring of 1871. Some time before that, however, she had made a public demonstration

[1] Auguste Filon, *Le Prince Imperial, Souvenirs et Documents* (Paris, 1912).

of her sympathy and affection for the exiles by inviting the Prince to attend a military review in Bushey Park. English newspapers remarked on the '. . . somewhat melancholy grace of the young Prince' and noted the ease with which he handled his horse. France, however, was still in the throes first of war then of revolution, and the Prince Imperial was so involved in these events that he seemed hardly conscious of where he was living. Not until his country was in a state of comparative calm did he take any interest in what was going on around him in England.

On 20 March 1871, after a short period of captivity under the Prussians, the Emperor rejoined his family and they settled down to make the best of things until conditions were propitious for their return to France.

In the autumn of the same year, the Prince Imperial was sent to study at King's College in London. It was not a success; he felt out of place in his surroundings and he made little effort to learn. Subsequently, in 1872, a friend, Colonel Manby, suggested to the Emperor that the Prince Imperial should take a course at the Woolwich Royal Academy where the officers of the Engineers and the Artillery were trained. The prospect of entering a military school so stimulated the Prince that he suddenly began to apply himself diligently to his lessons. The War Office was approached, then arrangements were made with Major-General Sir Lintorn Simmons, the Governor of the Academy. After a private examination before the professors of the Academy in November 1872, the Prince went to take his place at Woolwich. He was accompanied by Louis Conneau, his best friend, the son of a doctor who had followed Napoleon into exile. Together with Filon the tutor and Uhlmann, Louis' valet since early childhood, the boys lived in a small house near the Academy. Each day, as 'snookers' of the lowest class, they took their places among the two hundred Gentlemen Cadets at 'The Shop'. No attempt was made to spare him the 'roshing' suffered by all snookers, and it is recorded that on at least one occasion he was tossed fully dressed into a cold bath by his seniors for some failure to conform. In spite of an un-English tendency towards exhibitionism, particularly so far as riding and fencing were concerned, he seemed to be accepted as an equal by his fellow cadets. Showing his characteristic disregard for danger, he took part in the reckless night-time climbs of the 'Alpine Club' whose speciality was to decorate the lofty towers and spires of Woolwich with chamber-pots and flags.

The health of the Emperor Napoleon III had deteriorated

steadily while he was in England, and, after a number of operations, the Emperor died in the early hours of the morning of 9 January 1873. Called from his class at ten o'clock that morning, the Prince rushed home and fell on his knees beside the body of his father. It was said by those close to him that when Louis knelt down he was still a boy, but that he arose a man. From then on he signed himself the Prince Louis-Napoleon, to indicate that he now considered himself the head of the family and the heir to its dynastic rights; but he believed that the title of Emperor could not be conferred upon him except by a formal manifestation of the will of the nation. So strongly did he feel on this point that it is said that he showed great disapproval when friends bent the knee before him and called him 'Sire', and when French workmen hailed him with the cry of 'Vive l'Empereur!'

Louis slipped quietly back to Woolwich and carried on with his studies, his classmates sympathetically respecting his new reserve. In the summer of 1873, he filled in a questionnaire in an autograph album which indicates his thoughts at this time:

'What is your favourite virtue?—Courage.
Your leading passion?—Patriotism.
Your idea of happiness?—To do good.
Your idea of unhappiness?—To live in exile.
Where would you like to live?—In France.
Your present state of mind?—Sad.'

On 16 March 1874, when he was eighteen, Louis was declared of age at a gathering organised at Chislehurst by the Imperialist Party. In a huge tent on the lawn, the Prince delivered a speech, written by himself, which created an excellent impression.

Louis graduated in 1875, 7th in a class of 34 cadets, being first in riding and first in fencing. He was chosen to give the words of command to the entire student body when they manœuvred as a battalion before the Duke of Cambridge on the great parade ground of the school—it is recorded that he acquitted himself admirably. The ten top-ranking cadets were permitted to opt for the Royal Engineers, the most coveted commissions in the British Army; the rest of the class were commissioned into the Royal Artillery. In spite of his placing, Louis, coming from a family of gunners, opted for the Royal Artillery.

In the spring of 1875 the Prince took up his duties with a permanent battery at Aldershot. He found life at Aldershot very pleasant and was happiest on manœuvres when he was able to live a real soldier's life. Among the friends he made during this period of his life were Frederick George Slade and his battery commander, Arthur Bigge.[2]

By 1878 the Prince had reached full maturity; his features had lost their childish delicacy and taken on a firmer character, his complexion had darkened and he affected a thin moustache. Of middle height, he had a well-proportioned body made supple by riding, fencing and other outdoor activities. It was said that '. . . his presence lit up and warmed the atmosphere around him . . . by a smile, a pressure of the hand, by every word and every gesture, he shed light, life and joy on those who approached him even for a moment.'[3]

Although he had now drawn closer to his mother, she was not an easy woman to live with, particularly now that her husband's death had dashed her hopes of an early recall. Eugenie never doubted that she and her son would return eventually, but the political stability which France had achieved since 1871 gave her no alternative but to wait. It was, in fact, far from certain that the Prince and his mother would be welcomed back in France. The French press carried on a continual campaign of ridicule against the Prince Imperial, casting aspersions on his military career and on his achievements at Woolwich, even claiming that he had been ostracised by his fellow cadets. As the Imperialist party had indeed been unhappy at the French Prince Imperial being placed on the same level as ordinary English cadets and then becoming an officer in the English Army, the propaganda had subtle implications. Less subtle were those French journalists who labelled the Prince, 'Napoleon $3\frac{1}{2}$' and 'The Imperial Baby' or the 'fruit sec' (idiot). Louis ignored it all, quietly submitting his name when his age group in France came up for conscription.[4] Needless to say, he was not called.

The English were interested by him, he was popular with all classes, and his melancholy background and good looks attracted women. But his thoughts were constantly of France, personified by the French Army. In a letter written to the Duc d'Elchingen, he said:

'What concerns the army, as indeed you know, interests me passionately. I love the French army not merely because I am a soldier and a Frenchman to my very marrow, but also because

[2] Later Lord Stamfordham, Secretary to King George V.
[3] Auguste Filon, *Le Prince Imperial, Souvenirs et Documents* (Paris, 1912).
[4] Frenchmen abroad who ignored the summons were outlawed.

I consider that in it alone dwells the force that can first save French society, and then restore its greatness.'

He followed the events of the Russo-Turkish War of 1877 with great interest, hoping that England would join in it so that he could see some action. On 28 March 1878 he wrote to one of his friends:

'The English army will go gallantly to this unequal combat . . I hope to seize the opportunity for showing that I'm good for something. The quiet state of French politics allows it. . . .'

To his friend Captain Bigge, Louis wrote:

'. . . I am thirsting to smell powder.'

In the same letter he analysed the general situation in Europe, writing that he believed Austria would soon find herself in opposition to Turkey. Should such a war occur, he longed to take part in it; and he persuaded his mother, the Empress, to request of the Emperor Franz Josef that he should be given permission to serve with the Austrian Army. He was as deeply disappointed at the inevitable refusal as his mother was relieved.

At the beginning of 1879 he was 22 years old and he faced it soberly, believing that it was filled with nothing more exciting than the possibility of a marriage to Princess Beatrice, the daughter of Queen Victoria.

11

ON 22 April 1871, after gaining a First Class Certificate from the School of Musketry at Hythe, Carey was posted to the 81st Foot.[1] On 17 June 1871, accompanied by his wife, he joined the regiment in Gibraltar, where he served until 31 July 1872. On 25 January of that year, Annie Brenton Carey gave birth to a child, who was christened Edith Isabella Oranstoun Brenton.[2]

Early in 1873, Carey transferred to the 98th Foot (later the North Staffordshire Regiment (the Prince of Wales)), who were, at that time, stationed in Barbados. He joined the regiment at Litchfield, and in mid-1873 sailed to the West Indies with his family. On 1 December of that year he was appointed Garrison Adjutant to Jamaica, a position he held until the end of 1875, when he rejoined the 98th Foot in Malta.

An ambitious man, Carey had the additional stimulus of having to maintain, with moderate means, a young and increasing family. He felt that the small letters p.s.c. (Passed Staff College) on his documents would greatly further his career and decided to apply to the Staff College at Camberley.

This establishment existed to '. . . obtain the best regimental officers procurable, train them practically, give them a reasonable assurance of the Staff employment for which they have been trained, and place them in the appointments for which they appear best fitted.' Founded earlier in the century by the Duke of Cambridge, the Staff College came into being on the bare heathland of the Sandhurst Estate along the London road. In the course of

---

[1] In 1881 the 81st Foot combined with the 47th Foot, the Loyal Regiment (North Lancashire), to form one unit.

[2] This child was almost certainly their first; it is known that there was a second, Pelham, and a third, but I have been unable to discover where or when they were born.

time, the institution acquired a population of wives, families and other supernumeraries so that a regular village gradually took shape along the road to the west of the entrance lodge. Initially called Cambridge Town, by the time Carey came there the name had changed to Camberley, a flourishing residential neighbourhood with its own railway station.

The Council of Military Education, with a view to excluding the undesirable, insisted on the following :

'I hereby certify that I have examined —— in the various subjects connected with his duty as a regimental officer, and more especially on the points which form the chief qualifications of a Staff Officer, with a view to his competency for admission to the Staff College, Sandhurst; and to the best of my belief and judgment I considered him, from his general knowledge of the Service, character, habits, and disposition, to be qualified in those respects for employment on the Staff. He is a (good, fair, or indifferent) rider, and is not short-sighted.'[3]

Before an officer-candidate could get the coveted signature on his admission certificate he had to struggle with a stern entrance examination. Most candidates were of mature age and had to prepare under great difficulties; few men put themselves forward unless they had reasonable hopes of success—it was not a good idea to be marked afterwards in your regiment as having failed. At the same time, no commanding officer was willing to send off his best officers, although they allowed officers they could well spare to leave for Camberley.

Carey had never before worked so hard as he did to pass his entrance examination. He had no illusions as to what he was undertaking, he had known of officers going to the College from an active regimental life, already suffering from the unaccustomed strain of cramming for entrance, who had become so ill with nervous exhaustion that they had had to send in their papers. Mostly, they had been like himself, men of moderate means who had undertaken the course in order to obtain the advancement upon which they were dependent. He could not afford the expense of a 'crammer', because residence at the College made greater demands on his income than did regimental soldiering. He would not be allowed a soldier servant, and the meagre allowance *in lieu* was quite inadequate. Carey had worked out that an extra £100 a year over and above his pay was required if he was to live in anything like the expected style. He was going to gamble,

[3] A. R. Godwin-Austen, *The Staff and the Staff College* (London, 1927).

in all, some £300 on securing a p.s.c., and he could not risk losing it through his own lack of effort.

The course consisted of a number of compulsory subjects and a lesser number of voluntary ones. Those that were obligatory were :

Fortification, field engineering, and road-making.
Artillery.
Military drawing, field sketching, and surveying.
Reconnaissance.
Military art (strategy), history, and geography.
Practical military signalling.
Military administration and law.
Either French, German or Hindustani.
Riding.

Voluntary subjects included a second language, geology and science; telegraphy and photography (as applied to copying maps and plans) had recently been made optional, so that it was no longer essential for a Staff Officer to know 'the part played by the collodion layer in a sensitised plate'.

Riding was a compulsory subject, though an officer was supposed to be able to ride before he was admitted. Many who arrived at the College were poor riders and found the riding-school at Sandhurst a sore trial; and the more studious resented the time spent twice a week in the school.

Carey came to Camberley on the first day of February 1877. He found the College a noble building on top of a slope, which fell gently to an ornamental lake bordered by beech, rowan, chestnut and alder trees. The entrance hall was designed on the lines of a Roman bath, with passages leading from it and running the whole length of the building. On the left was the main stairway made of Craigleith stone and leading to a gallery with an ornamental balustrade overlooking the hall; from this gallery corridors, with rooms for forty officers opening off them, ran round the whole of the first floor.

In front of him lay two years of lectures, interspersed with frequent tests and papers, all carrying marks affecting the final order of merit, and the yearly examinations. It might all have been less grim had there not existed the grinding effect of competition, which tended to develop the worst qualities in the poorer students and stifled the best in the others.

There was also a system of Confidential Reports, which

entered minutely into the character and abilities of every officer at the College and his qualifications for Staff employment. These were forwarded by the Commandant to the Commander-in-Chief at the end of every term. Any student reported as unlikely to make an efficient Staff Officer was required to leave the College.

Similar Reports were tendered at the end of the course, stating for which branch of the Staff each officer appeared to be best fitted. They included many probing questions :

'Is his conduct marked by steadiness and prudence, and is he temperate in his habits?

'Is he extravagant in his mode of living?

'Does he display zeal, activity, and intelligence, as well as discretion, in the performance of his duties, and does he appear to take an interest in his profession?

'Report any other characteristics of the officer which renders him suited or otherwise for the duties of a Staff Officer.

'Is his disposition such as would enable him to perform those duties with tact and discrimination, in a manner calculated to ensure their being cheerfully carried out by those to whom orders would be conveyed by him?

or,

'Are his manner and temper objectionable, and likely to cause him to disagree with those with whom he might be associated, or be brought in contact?

'Is he active and energetic in his habits?

'Is he a good (fair, or indifferent) rider, and is he short-sighted?'

One of the most enjoyable features of the indoor programme were the 'Kriegspiel' or wargames sessions, in which officers fought desperate table-top encounters against opponents with whom, in later years, they were to co-operate on the battlefield.

Social life was a safety-valve; Staff College balls were milestones in the quiet life of the country. 'We must not forget the dances. Talk to any of the fair of the 'seventies and 'eighties, and they love to recall Camberley gaieties. The romantic drive, perhaps from Guildford, across the eerie moor; the penetration of the mysteries of this military monastery—"All such clever men, my dear! You must be your brightest." '[4]

When Carey left the Staff College on 15 December 1878 for Christmas leave, he had heard rumours that there was likely to be a war in South Africa against the Zulus. Before his leave had ended the war had begun, and the world had been shocked by the

[4] A. R. Godwin-Austen, *The Staff and the Staff College* (London, 1927).

news of a British column annihilated at Isandhlwana. Carey volunteered for service at once '. . . in any capacity'. He sailed from Portsmouth on 1 March 1879 in the transport *Clyde* which was carrying replacements for the 24th Foot.

With him went a report from the Staff College : 'Passed. Passed a good examination in Photography as a voluntary subject'.

12

In December 1878, convinced that the powerful Zulu nation should be restrained, Sir Bartle Frere, the High Commissioner in South Africa, imposed almost impossible conditions upon the Zulu Chief Cetewayo, demanding a definite reply before the end of the month. As anticipated, no such reply was received, and at the beginning of 1879 Great Britain went to war with the Zulus.

In the Colony of Natal, war had long been a foregone conclusion, so that preparations had been under way for some time. Commanded by Lieutenant-General Lord Chelmsford, a force had been collected, consisting of seven regiments of English Regular infantry, a Naval Brigade, seventeen guns and a rocket-battery of the Royal Artillery, together with two companies of Royal Engineers. Lacking regular cavalry, the force included two squadrons of mounted infantry, nearly 800 Colonial volunteers and Police, with more than 300 Native Horse, and a hastily trained native infantry contingent about 9,000 strong. There was also a transport train of about 700 waggons with 800 conductors and drivers.

Divided into five columns, the force was to march into Zululand at different points, all moving on Ulundi, the Zulu capital, where they anticipated a victorious concentration. Lord Chelmsford and his staff went with the third and strongest column, which was under the immediate command of Colonel Glynn. It consisted of the 1st and 2nd Battalions of the 24th Regiment, 200 Natal Volunteers, 150 Natal Police, two battalions of the Native Contingent and some Native Pioneers with six Royal Artillery guns and a squadron of mounted infantry. Crossing the Buffalo River on 11 January, the column moved forward over broken country with some difficulty, constructing roads over swamps and heavy ground as they went.

A young lieutenant, destined to escape at Isandhlwana and to make his mark in World War I, wrote of this :

'28 days to do 65 miles . . . creditable performance . . . enormous difficulties . . . very little flat ground, no roads, deep valleys, precipitous hills—many covered with rocks and boulders—to climb, muddy river-beds . . . we had 600 to 1,000 waggons each drawn by 16 oxen. Occasionally, we did 10 miles a day but generally far less; once we were 36 hours doing 1 mile. Ideal country for sharpshooters and ambushes, very little really open, much of it covered with bush, waggons moved sometimes 20 abreast over rolling veldt covered with rich luxuriant grass. Skilful handling of 16-oxen teams made great impression . . . Afrikander driver wielding a long whip . . . oxen were named and, when a pull became very heavy, were urged forward by name and pistol-like whip cracks. Called "Dootchmann . . . Germann and Englischmann".'[5]

By 20 January they were encamped at the foot of the Isandhlwana Hill. But although the tents of the infantry and the lines of picqueted horses were regularly spaced, the waggons which should have been ranged end-to-end around the camp in a laager were drawn up uselessly in line at the rear.

When his scouts reported the enemy in large numbers on a range of hills about twelve miles from the camp, Chelmsford determined on an attack in strength, believing it to be his chance of striking an early paralysing blow. Placing himself at the head of the second battalion of the 24th Regiment, the Mounted Infantry and four guns, he marched out with the first grey light of the morning of 22 January. He left six companies of the 24th Regiment, two Royal Artillery guns, about 80 mounted men and four companies of the Native Contingent, all under the command of Lieutenant-Colonel Pulleine of the 24th Regiment, to defend the camp. By ten o'clock they were strengthened by the arrival of Colonel Durnford with some of the second column and the rocket-battery.

Reports began to come in that large numbers of enemy were approaching from all directions. With two troops of Natal Native Horse and the rocket-battery, escorted by a company of the Native Contingent, Colonel Durnford moved to the front of the position, while two other troops of Native Horse went into the hills on the

[5] General Sir Horace Smith-Dorrien, *Memories of Forty-eight Years Service* (1925).

60

left. About five miles from the camp, the force was suddenly confronted by a huge force of Zulus advancing upon them with disconcerting rapidity. The rocket-battery, deserted by its escort of the Native Contingent, was overrun and all the crew slain. Durnford extended his small force and opened a steady fire, slowly retreating in the face of the overwhelming numbers of the enemy. In spite of the fact that they were sorely pressed, Durnford's men disputed every inch of ground, until they were almost back at the camp where, reinforced by thirty or forty Natal Volunteers, they made a last desperate stand in a dried-up river bed.

The Zulus were taking the camp in a half-circle, with another Zulu regiment pushing round the English left to gain possession of the waggon road and the line of retreat upon Rorke's Drift. The two guns and the 24th Regiment were in line with the Native Contingent on the right of the 24th, and then came Durnford's shattered and weary band. The 24th, one of the smartest battalions in the service, was firing withering volleys, and the enemy fell in hundreds as the guns, which had been firing shell, now poured in case-shot. Even Zulu courage could not maintain an advance against such fire; they began to waver and seek shelter, covering the valley in detached groups to a depth of about three-quarters of a mile.

By now, the horns of the Zulu army had worked their way round the flanks and were beginning to show themselves in the rear of the English position. Suddenly, the Native Contingent broke and fled, laying open the 24th's right and rear. The intensity of firing began to slacken because there were no tools to open the reserve boxes of ammunition. Seizing their opportunity, the Zulus poured through the gap in the line and the English soldiers were lost in a fierce hand-to-hand struggle. Horse and foot, English and Zulu, in dire confusion, were pushed slowly through the camp towards the road to Rorke's Drift. The 24th stood their ground and fought to the last man. The road of retreat already barred by the enemy, fugitives tried to escape over the broken, boulder-strewn ground to the Buffalo River. The guns were hopelessly impeded and the drivers were in their saddles. The long ravine, the path to the river, was a scene of continuous slaughter as the Zulus chased and caught the fleeing mounted men. Then, less than half of those who managed to arrive on the river bank succeeded in crossing; the fierce current and the sharp rocks caused many to drown while others were assegaied.

Many acts of heroism took place : Captains Melville and Coghill of the 24th saved their regiment's Queen's Colour after they had fought to the last in its ranks. On their way to the river, Coghill, in trying to rescue Melville who had lost his horse, had his own mount shot under him. Exhausted and wounded, both officers succeeded in reaching the Natal shore, but there they were overtaken and killed; the Queen's Colour was later recovered from the river. It is worthy of note that Melville, who passed entry exams for the Staff College in 1877, was in 1878 denied his place because there was no available vacancy; thus he would normally have entered in 1879 had he not sailed for Zululand. And on almost the very day that he should have joined at Camberley he lay dead, among the rocks of the Buffalo River at Fugitives' Drift.

Nearly 900 Europeans and more than 500 Natal Kaffirs perished at Isandhlwana. Because of their belief that if a fallen enemy was not disembowelled their own stomachs would swell up when that of the dead enemy did, the Zulus slashed open the bellies of all the dead. This ritual led Europeans to believe that the Zulus were a savage people who killed the wounded and mutilated the dead. They were in fact a very noble race, with high standards of morality.

On board the troopship *Clyde*, Carey was finding the voyage as boring and uncomfortable as always, the small 2,000-ton boat being very crowded. When they were within two days' steam of Cape Town, they encountered an appalling south-easterly gale, and for the six days which it took them to get to Cape Town, the ship was battened down, with everyone imprisoned below in a foul atmosphere of lamp oil and bilge-water.

Because of this unforeseen delay, at Cape Town extra efforts were made to get the *Clyde* quickly on its way to Durban. Coaling was carried on throughout the night, with all the troops pressed into service. Carey spent a weary night urging, bullying, cajoling and even physically aiding his men in their unpleasant task. On the following morning, he was gratified to receive the personal thanks of Colonel Davis of the Grenadier Guards, commanding troops on board the *Clyde*.

The *Clyde* left the docks at Cape Town on 2 April and almost at once became enveloped in thick fog. They groped their way along for more than twelve hours until, just after six on the morning of 3 April, the watch suddenly saw that they were within a few lengths of some rocks. The engines were reversed instantly, but too late to be of any avail, and the ship struck Gaza Rock, between Dyers' Island and the mainland. Although it was still foggy, the sea was calm, and it was easy to maintain discipline on board. By half-past eleven all the troops and horses were ashore, and the vessel was abandoned.

Bivouacs were set up on the shore and the camp was established; provisions were conveyed from the beach to the camp in a waggon borrowed from a nearby farmhouse. A crew of strong men was selected, and a boat set off to row to Simon's Bay, seventy miles westward; it arrived there in fourteen hours.

During the night the *Clyde* sank, taking with her one-and-a-half million rounds of Martini-Henry ammunition, four gatling guns and many stores. The *Tamar* was sent to pick up the stranded soldiers; and HMS *Encounter* brought divers to the wreck which was sunk in seven fathoms of water inside the north-west corner of the island.

The *Tamar* arrived at Durban on Friday morning, 11 April. On board there were fifteen officers, three staff sergeants, two officers' servants and 528 privates, making a total of 549, one of whom was Lieutenant Jaheel Brenton Carey of the 98th Regiment.

Later Press reports stated that :

'. . . when the ship was wrecked, he (Carey) was again commended for his zeal and ability; while on the march up country to Dundee it was he who preceded the drafts of the 24th Regiment, surveying the road and marking out camping-grounds; and he, again, who, for his cool-headedness and skill, was placed on Lord Chelmsford's staff, and was appointed to survey and map the road of advance to Ulundi.'

13

To the Prince Imperial, the Zulu war came as a gift from heaven. The Zulus represented a perfect enemy, a savage, martial nation against whom he could fight without causing the inevitable political repercussions which would occur if he fought for England in a Continental war.

Thus, one evening after dinner at Camden Place, early in 1879, the Prince moved restlessly about shifting chairs, playing military tunes on the piano. At last his mother said:

'What is the matter with you tonight?'

'If I told you, you would not sleep all night!'

'You imagine I shall sleep after what you have said to me? I shall conjure up terrible things, for instance, that you have been asked to serve in Africa against the Zulus!'

Louis confessed immediately that he had that very day sent a request to the Duke of Cambridge for permission to serve in Africa. Before his alarmed mother could discuss the matter, the Prince added:

'Wait until tomorrow, I beg you; I shall tell you my reasons and will hear yours, which will have all the more weight because you will have reflected longer.'

Next morning the Empress entreated her son to abandon his project; in his turn he told her that all the officers belonging to his battery had volunteered to go, among them Bigge and Slade, both of whom had already received their marching orders. 'While even one of the officers in my battery stayed in England I might have honourably remained here myself. When Wodehouse came in his turn to say good-bye to me, my mind was made up. How could I show myself at Aldershot when they will all be out there?'

The Empress continued to plead with him:

'If anything happens to you, your adherents will not weep for you . . . they will have a grudge against you!'

'Listen, mother, I will fully explain my position and then you can judge for yourself. Owing to the accident of my birth I am not my own master. God has willed it so, and I cannot, even if I would, escape from the destiny which He has appointed for me. Whether I like it or not, I happen to be the nominal, and eventually the effective head of a great party which believes itself to be—and which we believe to be—truly representative of France. Now what have I done hitherto to justify the hopes that people place in me? I have been an exile from my childhood, and I have grown up under the trees of Camden Place. I have worked with the teachers you have given me to acquire for myself a sound education, and to grow up into a man. But of all I have done, of all I have learnt, of all the things of worth that may be in me, nothing, so to speak, has gone outside the walls of my study. Apart from a small number of my personal friends, nobody knows me, and I can say that in France, although my name may be an emblem, my personality and my moral value, such as they are, are unknown. They still see me as I was when I left the country. In the eyes of my party I have never grown up, and at the age of twenty-three I am still a child to them, and the majority of them treat me as one. This is so true, that whenever on any important occasion I have attempted to direct the Imperialist party, and to impress upon them a uniform policy in conformity with my opinion and my personal wishes, I have not been listened to, and, as often as not, the party has acted in direct opposition to my advice. . . . It is imperative, therefore, that I should take some step to assert myself, and to obtain the influence which is indispensable to my future. There is one thing a man can always do—that is, to show that he does not value his own life too highly, and is prepared to risk it without counting the cost.

'I am continually having it thrown at my head that the Orleans Princes have seen fighting, and that I have not seen any. My enemies have even gone so far as to call me a coward, simply because I have never had the opportunity of proving the contrary. During the war between Russia and Turkey, Russian and English interests were in direct opposition, and the two Powers were watching one another with their hands, figuratively speaking, on the hilts of their swords. To take sides with either would have been to show myself ungrateful to one or to the other. England gave shelter in the past to my father; she has sheltered us also in our exile, and now shows us all manner of kindnesses. On the other hand, when the Emperor of Russia visited London he evinced, as is well known, the greatest interest in my welfare, and displayed the most affectionate feelings towards me. He was, so he told me, my sincere well-wisher, and I should always find a warm friend in him. It was therefore impossible for me to take any part against either country. In the Afghan war the situation was identically the same. At the present time, on the other hand, the war is one against savages, no European interests are involved, and no one can take offence at my participation in hostilities. In Africa I shall be able to show that I am no coward, and when I have proved that I am willing to risk my life for a country which is not my own, but to which I owe a debt of gratitude, I shall *a fortiori* have proved that I am equally ready to risk it in the service of my own country when she has need of me.

'You must, therefore, see that the moment has arrived when I must do something, and that my decision is a reasonable one.'

Discussing this conversation in later years, the Empress said:

'Notwithstanding all the fears of which my heart was full, and the agony which I seemed to foresee, I could not fail to realise the justice of many of my son's remarks, and this will explain why, although I still argued with him, I resigned myself at last to the inevitable.'

Her decision may have been influenced by the realisation that Louis was trying to reply to that hostile section of the French press who never ceased to attack him, although, as she said later:

'We thought him indifferent to these attacks.'

In later years, she revealed that after the Prince's death, among his effects, was found a scrap of a French newspaper rolled up like a cigarette, in which a marked paragraph stated that the indisposition that had kept him from taking part in the war as soon as he arrived in Africa could be attributed to the 'hereditary disease of the Bonapartes'.

Although he was fully aware of the possible dangers, the Duke of Cambridge was inclined to let the Prince go; he felt that if Louis went out there in a private capacity, as 'a spectator', it was his own business if he subsequently appeared in uniform. The Prime Minister, Disraeli, however, conscious that the inevitable uproar from across the Channel would fall upon him, '. . . had never heard of anything more injudicious. . . .'

On receiving the refusal, the Prince immediately wrote a letter to the Duke of Cambridge:

'21 February 1879.

'Monseigneur,

'I have just received the letter you wrote me. Before telling you how much it distressed me, I must thank Your Royal Highness for the flattering approval it gives to the motives that led me to this step. I should have been glad to share the fatigues and dangers of my comrades, who all have the happiness of being on active service. Though I am not so conceited as to think that my services can be useful to the cause I wished to serve, I nevertheless looked upon this war as an opportunity of showing my gratitude towards the Queen and the nation in a way that would be very much to my mind. When at Woolwich and, later, at Aldershot, I had the honour of wearing the English uniform, I hoped that it would be in the ranks of our allies, that I should first take up arms. Losing this hope, I lose one of the consolations of my exile. I remain none the less deeply devoted to the Queen and deeply grateful to Your Royal Highness for the interest you have always displayed in me. I beg you to believe in the feelings of sincere attachment of your very affectionate,

'Napoleon.'

The Empress now reviewed the situation, taking into consideration any possible political advantages of allowing him to go. Except from the climate and the rough camp life, she could not conceive that there was any risk involved, and, anyway, Lord Chelmsford and his soldiers would keep between the Prince Imperial and the savage Zulus. She visited the Duke of Cambridge and then the Queen, who was delighted to hear that the young Prince wished to go and fight in her Army. The triumvirate concocted a scheme which allowed the Prince Imperial to go to the war in the semi-official rôle of an observer, but not as an officer. The Duke of Cambridge wrote a letter to the Governor of the Cape indicating that the Prince would leave for Zululand '. . . in the capacity of a spectator.

'He was anxious to serve in our Army, having been a cadet at Woolwich, but the Government did not think that this could be sanctioned. But no objection is made to him going out on his own account, and I am permitted to introduce him to you and to Lord Chelmsford, in the hope, and with my personal request, that you will give him every help in your power to enable him to see what he can . . . he is a charming young man, full of spirit and energy and the more you see of him the more you will like him.'

He also wrote a letter to the Commander-in-Chief, Lord Chelmsford, which he gave to the Prince Imperial as a letter of introduction.

Although it was not quite what he had in mind, any permission was better than none—as long as he could get out there he could then trust to luck. He wrote to his friend, d'Espeuilles:

'I've had all the trouble in the world to get leave from the English Government. Today I've got it at last, but with all kinds of restrictions. I'm supposed to be sailing for the Cape as a traveller, and only when there am I to put on a uniform and attach myself to the general in command of artillery. So we must be careful to warn our journals not to say I start with my battery —it will be all right for them to say that I am hastening out to share the toils and perils of my comrades. They are too definite about my rank in the English Army, for it is quite unofficial.'

To Louis, it seemed pointless to be there at all if he were not going to fight—indeed, there was no other way in which he would be said to share the lot of his comrades. The letter can justifiably be said to contain the inference that he intended to throw off all restrictions on arriving at the Cape and to plunge into the war.

Dazed and incredulous, the entire French nation rose in arms at the news. His own party pleaded frantically with him not to go; and the Republicans, although they regarded him as a political threat and ridiculed him as a person, took the view that since he was a Frenchman they had a proprietary interest in him. Everyone in France assumed that he would be risking his life and completely ignored the statement that he was going out 'as a spectator'. Both political parties were aghast that he should give them only two days' notice before deserting them to risk his valuable neck for the disliked English in an obscure Colonial war.

In a letter written from Africa on 20 April the Prince outlined all the reasons that induced him to go to Zululand.

'Although my departure is already ancient history, I should like to go back with you to the causes that determined it. I asked no one's advice, and made up my mind in forty-eight hours; if my resolve was swift, it was because I had reflected at length on such a contingency and made my plans.

'Neither my mother's fears, nor the despair of the people about me, nor the exhortations of M. Rouher and my party, caused me to hesitate a minute or to lose a second of time; this will seem only natural to those who know me, but how many are they?

'The reasons that caused me to go are all political, and outside these, nothing influenced my decision.

'1°. I might have hoped, before the events that followed May 16th, that if my party increased its strength, the restoration of the Empire might take place without an upheaval, either through Parliament or through the Army.

'This restoration in the Spanish manner would have made me, like Alfonso XII, the slave of certain men and of a whole party. I would never have accommodated myself to such a position, and I dreaded rather than desired it.

'2°. Since October 14th, the scene is changed; the Imperial party has grown weaker, and can effect nothing by its own strength. All hopes are centred in my person; if that becomes great, the strength of the Imperial party becomes tenfold. I have had proof that no one will be followed but a man of known energy, and my care has been to find a way of making myself known.

'3°. Writing letters of condolence, harbouring politicians, patting journalists on the back, hob-nobbing with them, and working with them to stir up social problems, that is what the headstrong call "making myself conspicuous".

'Others want me to travel throughout Europe with a great retinue, going like the fairy-tale princes, to view all the princesses and boast of my political elixir that will heal all social evils.

'This comedy, think the authors, must end like every good play, with a marriage.

'I have turned a deaf ear; I have not cared to let my wings be clipped by marriage, and my dignity refused to stoop to the part of princely commercial traveller.

'4°. I have come to the conclusion that that was not my part.

'When one belongs to a race of soldiers, it is only sword in hand that one gains recognition, and he who wants to learn by travel, must go far.

'I had, then, long ago promised myself, first, to make a long voyage. Secondly, to lose no opportunity of seeing a campaign. The disaster of Isandhlwana gave me the opportunity I wanted.

'In France there was no crisis immediately to be feared to hold me back, as before the senatorial elections. The African war became suddenly popular in England, and was developing on a great scale without involving any European complications.

'The scene of the war in itself was worth the trouble of an uprooting, for the interest it offered a traveller.

'Everything, therefore, urged me to go, and I went. . . .'

Before he left England, the French press apparently realised that they could not change his mind and they now began to portray the Prince as the whole war. They hinted that the command of the English army would be handed over to the Prince, who would rout the foe. Asserting that his return from Africa would resemble that of the great Napoleon from Egypt, French newspapers talked of his '. . . leading Cetewayo in chains'. On the other hand there were those who believed that his sole motive in going was to get away from the Empress, being unable to stand any longer her parsimony and the humiliations she inflicted upon him.

The Prince decided to take with him as his sole companion his valet and body servant, Uhlmann, a big man, very serious and reliable and extremely devoted to his master. Louis intended leaving him at the base camp. Many other young Frenchmen wished to accompany Louis, begging leave to share in the campaign, but he refused to hear of it, saying :

'. . . I could not take a bodyguard into an English camp.'

14

Oᴺ 27 February 1879 the Empress Eugenie, with the Comte Laurent de la Bedoyere and all the members of her household, accompanied the Prince Imperial to Southampton. In the evening they attended a farewell banquet arranged by some officers of the British Army, and toasts were proposed in honour of the Empress and of her son. He sailed on the following day in the *Danube*, which was carrying drafts for the 3rd/60th Rifles.

For some time before the actual moment of parting, the Empress wept intermittently; although she was trying to be brave, she was in a state of wretched confusion. Conscious that she had aided in his going, she would now have given anything for him not to have gone. She wanted him to achieve the object of his going, to come back a hero, yet the very thought of the risks that this would involve tormented her to distraction. At their final parting, she implored him to do nothing rash, to be cautious and, above all, she made him promise not to serve with Irregulars. The Prince, in a state of elation, readily gave his word to everything she asked.

From the hotel window overlooking Southampton Water the Empress watched the ship sail away; then, when it had finally gone from her sight, she sank to the floor in a faint. She returned to Chislehurst on the verge of hysteria. So that she could obtain news of the army as quickly as possible, Eugenie kept in close touch with her English friends. She made all preparations to leave for the Cape at a moment's notice if Louis were wounded or ill. In a letter to her mother she said :

'If God preserves him and gives him the opportunity to distinguish himself, the days we are now passing through, which are so dark and sad, will be the most brilliant of my life.'

From Plymouth, where the *Danube* touched before starting off, the Prince Imperial wrote to his mother :

'For the seven hours I have been on board, I have nothing particular to tell you, except that I find myself very comfortably settled in my cabin, and that the sea is as calm as Lake Constance. However, there is a thick fog that only allows us to get along very slowly.

'I can say to you in writing what I did not wish to tell you *viva voce*; how much the grief of leaving you is mingled in my heart with the delight of being on active service. To tell you all I felt while bidding you good-bye would have been to agitate you to no purpose for you must know me well enough to read my heart. . . .'

At first he was exultantly happy, he chased around the ship meeting everyone and being liked by them all. When the sea roughened, he chafed at the time they were losing. Later, the heat made him feel ill, and the journey became a long, drawn-out bore. In a letter written at the Cape he gave Eugenie a full account of the voyage.

'Government House, 26 March, 1879.
'Cape Town.

'My dear Mother,
'My first care on setting foot on *terra firma* is to acquit myself of a duty dear to my heart. I mean to spend the few hours of leisure that are left to me in talking with you of everything that has happened since my departure, for I have been deprived for a very long time, not only of the happiness of receiving news of you, but also of the delight of writing to you.

'Since my last letter, I have seen Madeira, I have seen Tenerife, and after that sky and sea for twenty days.

'From Madeira down to the Line we had fine weather.

'The heat under the tropics was overwhelming, and nothing but the flying fishes, whose portrait you see (he attached a drawing) could distract us from our compulsory idleness.

'From the Equator, the sea was extremely rough, and though the old ceremony of crossing the Line has fallen into disuse on board steamers, the Atlantic himself saw to it that we were baptised.

'The days are long between sky and sea : and so every means of diversion is sought after.

'Among the passengers are a great number of officers on leave or retired, militia captains, or simple adventurers who like myself are going to the Cape to make war or to seek their fortune. They call themselves "volunteers" and each of them flourishes his sword a little. We thought it would be amusing to break the monotony of the voyage by having a grand parade on board to which each man should come in full dress and equipment.

'Chosen Commander-in-Chief, I gave the order for a great review, and it was thoroughly diverting to see that line of Fradiavolesque uniforms rise and fall with the roll of the ship. (Another sketch.) This farce had a serious side, that of allowing us to improve our equipment and our uniforms by comparison.'

He described his arrival at Cape Town in another letter written at the time :

'I have just arrived in Cape Town, as my paper has already told you. The moment the *Danube* came into the roadstead, a naval officer in Lady Frere's suite came to meet me and invite me to accept the hospitality of Government House.

'I went in a carriage, acclaimed by a many-coloured population who had draped the windows with flags of as many hues.

'Lady Frere has just taken me to Constantia, where I have eaten some of the famous grapes. I must declare that they surpass those of Arenenberg, and I was delighted with the varied landscape that presented itself to my eyes, tired of a watery horizon.

'To-night Lady Frere is giving a grand dinner in my honour, and a reception afterwards.

'To-morrow I leave for Durban, where I am eager to arrive, for a battle is expected.'

He took to the sea again and arrived at Durban on 31 March. Here he was bitterly disappointed to find that Lord Chelmsford was not among the many officers who came to meet him; on all sides there was talk of a battle and it was only Chelmsford who could decide whether or not he would be in it. In a letter to Sir Lintorn Simmons, he said :

'However hard it is for a soldier to remain inactive when the others are fighting, I had to resign myself to my fate and wait here until the General comes back.

'I am anxious to deserve as soon as possible the praise that people give me too early, for I am ashamed to be made such a fuss about before having done anything when so many who have nobly done their duty seem completely unknown.'

Major Butler, the assistant Adjutant-General, attached him to an artillery battery to mess; and he awaited Chelmsford's return impatiently. In a letter to his mother he gave his first impressions of Natal:

'Durban, 2 April, 1879.

'Since my last letter, that is to say since I left Cape Town, I have lived in a state of anxiety and impatience, comparable to that of an old troop horse yoked to a plough when he hears the trumpet sound the charge. . . .

'My regret is not to be with those who are fighting; you know me well enough to judge how bitter it is. But all is not over and I shall have my revenge upon my ill-luck.

'I was received on my arrival in Natal like a crowned head, though I wore a lieutenant's uniform. The ships were dressed with flags and the military authorities came to meet me.

'The country, which I have hardly had time to see, seems to me superb. Picture to yourself green hills undulating as far as the eye can see, and covered here and there with groups of trees of every kind. The trees are not lofty, but they keep their beautiful foliage always; the loveliest plants and the rarest flowers of our climates spring by the wayside.

'When one takes in the whole landscape, one cannot help comparing it with what England must have been (the country of the green hills) when the Saxons landed upon it.

'Remember me to all those who are about you, and tell them not to imagine that I forget them.'

One of the two horses belonging to the Prince Imperial had been killed in an accident while landing, and the other was taken ill, so one of his first occupations was to buy a replacement horse. In his book *The Washing of the Spears*, Morris relates the event:

'Whilst in the lobby of the Royal Hotel, Louis glanced out of the window and saw a civilian trotting by on a magnificent grey which, to Louis' practised eye, looked everything that he wanted in the shape of a horse. Quickly he sent Uhlmann out to buy the animal on the spot. It was ridden by Meyrick Bennett, the Managing Director of Randles, Brothers and Hudson. Every suitable horse in Natal had been commandeered for the campaign and even broken-down crocks were going for sky-high prices; Mr Bennett did not wish to sell the grey, named "Percy". Identifying his master, Uhlmann appealed to the owner's feelings and, after some hesitation, Mr Bennett reluctantly sold his horse; he remarked that it was apt to be skittish.'

There is a difference of opinion as to the name of this horse; other sources say that it was a tall grey called 'Fate', an animal with a good character but a habit of plunging and resisting when mounted. It is also reported that this was a characteristic which did not displease Louis, as he rather liked to be seen vaulting onto the horse's back without the aid of stirrups.

During his seemingly interminable period of waiting for the return of Lord Chelmsford, Louis went down with Cape fever. When the General finally came to see him, he was convalescent and suffering from an almost intolerable chafing. As soon as the formal preliminaries were over, the Prince Imperial eagerly presented his letters of introduction. The first was from the Duke of Cambridge :

'25 February, 1879.

'My Dear Lord Chelmsford,

'This letter will be presented to you by the Prince Imperial, who goes to Africa on his own account, to see as far as possible the coming campaign against the Zulus. The Prince is very eager to go to Africa.

'He expressed the wish to be enrolled in our army, but the Government thought it impossible to grant this.

'However, the Government authorises me to write to you and to Sir Bartle Frere, to ask you to show him every kindness and to help him so that he may be able to follow operations as far as possible, with the columns of the expedition.

'I hope you will do this. He is an excellent young man, full of intelligence and of courage, and has many old friends among the young artillery officers. He will certainly have no trouble in making his way. If you can in any other way help him will you kindly do so?

'My one fear is that he may be too courageous.

'I remain, my dear Chelmsford,

Yours most sincerely,
George.'

The Prince Imperial also had a letter from the Governor of the Military Academy at Woolwich, Sir Lintorn Simmons, in which he introduced '. . . his former pupil, the Prince Imperial. . .'

'He is very intelligent, thoroughly amenable to discipline; very zealous and active, a quick and accurate observer and a good rider; can sketch ground tolerably and gives every promise of being a good officer. Having been attached to batteries during two series of manœuvres, he has a fair knowledge of the movement of troops. His only fault is that which is common to youth, viz : that he is rather impulsive, but of this I have little doubt he will soon get the better.

'I have thought you would excuse me for writing this concerning him, as it may be of use in disposing of him. He will be only too thankful if you can find some employment for him, and if there is no other way of accomplishing his object, he would, I believe, gladly accept a local commission. The Empress would not, however, like him to be attached to a native corps.'

This fresh burden was one which the harassed Commander-in-Chief could well have done without. Busy with the reorganisation of his force for the second invasion of Zululand, he had little time to spare for his Royal visitor. This young man was trained to serve as a lieutenant in an artillery battery, but Lord Chelmsford realised that in that capacity he would be only too likely to see the active service he wanted but which officialdom and commonsense must deny him. The General noted the vague wording '. . . see the operations' and tried to think in what capacity this could be done. He studied the young man, poised before him like 'a greyhound in the slips'. He was not handsome, but had an oval face striking for its liveliness and mobility. He looked somewhat Spanish, with his black hair and olive pallor.[1] He had short legs so that he was not quite of middle height; however, he was an extrovert, he had never been shy—once someone asked him if he was frightened of Queen Victoria, and he had said :

'Not in the least, the Queen is very fond of me.'

Lord Chelmsford sought a solution that would satisfy this military-minded Prince Imperial, so that he would not get himself into some scrape for which he, as Commander-in-Chief, would be blamed. The Prince was wearing uniform, although the Duke of Cambridge's letter had vaguely hinted that he was not a Regular officer; on the other hand, Sir Lintorn Simmons asked that he should be employed and the Empress Eugenie appeared to agree. It was unfortunate that she would not allow her son to serve in the Irregulars—the ideal place to farm off civilians. The Prince seemed intelligent, he could ride and was apparently a reasonable

[1] His tutor Auguste Filon said of him :
'. . . he had few French characteristics . . . he was a veritabe hidalgo with all the pride, the melancholy, the self-restraint yet ardour to shine, the courage trenching on ostentatious recklessness and . . . childishness in trifles. . . .'

hand at map making—but Chelmsford realised that he was dealing with a very impulsive young man. Thus, Chelmsford asked the Prince if he would serve on his personal staff as an extra ADC, and he wrote to Sir Lintorn Simmons:

'The Prince Imperial has consented to accompany me into the field, and without putting him in orders, I have arranged with him that he shall be considered as one of my personal staff.

'I have already begged the Duke of Cambridge to assure the Empress that I will take every care of the Prince. He will have to rough it with us all, but the climate is a healthy one and the out-of-door life we lead is one which seems to agree well with us all.'

In a letter home, the General wrote:

'I shall treat the Prince exactly the same as any other officer; I know that is what he wants.'

Of course, this was exactly what the Prince wanted; in fact, later, he took this for granted on all possible occasions, until restraint became very difficult. He wrote to a friend:

'. . . I am at present filling the post of a staff officer with the Commander-in-Chief; this is the best way of seeing, of learning, and of making war for me.

'I had courage enough to refuse the command of a squadron of volunteers! Tempting as the offer was, I thought that the position I now hold would allow me to obtain more experience and to render more service.'

Louis joined Lord Chelmsford's staff in Pietermaritzburg, where he spent three days waiting for the General, and so caught up with his correspondence. Writing to a friend on 20 April, he said:

'Pietri has communicated to me extracts from papers and private letters which prove to me that our party have reconsidered their first impulse.

'Public feeling in France has then been, as I suppose, favourable to my decision: but it is not enough to go, I must come back with honour! And for that I rely on God.

'The news I have from France shows me also that I was not wrong in denying the possibility of a speedy crisis. Without being a great doctor, it is easy to see that the country is dying of a lingering illness, and not of an acute disease.'

Impatient and bored, Louis succumbed to a display exhibitionism trying to ride a mettlesome horse that had already defied other riders. He was thrown onto a pile of stones, and suffered a mild concussion, but this was not enough to prevent him travelling with the staff when they caught up with Lord Chelmsford at Dundee towards the end of April.

15

WRITING at the beginning of May, the Prince Imperial told his mother :

'. . . I am beginning to be uncomfortable and want for everything. For the last two days we've been sleeping in our clothes ready to turn out at the first alarm. Since we crossed the Buffalo River, we have been in enemy country, and yesterday I thought we should meet some bands of Zulus, for we were riding by the Blood River with only a small escort.'

On the second day of the month, mounted on 'Fate', he accompanied Lord Chelmsford and his Staff when they went by way of Landman's Drift, Koppie Allein and Conference Hill to visit the camp of Evelyn Wood at Kambula. Here, Louis met the heroes of the campaign—General Sir Evelyn Wood, VC, Colonel Redvers Buller, VC, and Lord William Beresford, Buller's right-hand man, soon to be similarly decorated. The camp was the headquarters of Buller's Regiment of Horse, an irregular body of about 1000 down-on-their-luck gentlemen and fugitives from justice from every European country; there were solid Afrikanders, Boers driven from their farms by the war, and the sweepings of every town in South Africa, plus a number of runaway sailors. All were volunteers and dressed as they liked; the only uniform piece of equipment was a cartridge bandolier slung over their shoulders. Recruited solely for the campaign, they received 5s. a day and were armed with a Martini-Henry rifle. Bill Beresford was Buller's only Staff officer, but the force was considered a brigade, since it was formed of a number of sub-commands such as Baker's Horse, D'Arcy's Horse, Bettington's Horse and Ferreira's Horse.

Evelyn Wood was 'a loquacious, charming man' (although in later years his commander in Egypt, Lord Wolseley, said that he '. . . hid behind barriers of vanity and deafness . . .'). Redvers

Buller was a 'silent, saturnine, bloodthirsty man' with a very red face ('. . . as red as a Red Indian . . .' Wolseley said; he also wrote, in 1885, '. . . his . . . fierce manner is against him, but as a fighting soldier and as an organising officer he is A1 . . .'). He ruled his oddly-assorted command with a rod of iron; and he and Wood were ideal foils for each other. On his cob, 'Punch', an ugly tough little horse, Buller had explored the frontier from end to end; he was probably the most experienced soldier in the camp.

Overjoyed to meet his friends Bigge and Slade, Louis listened enviously as they related how they had served their guns in the open during a Zulu attack on the camp. Bigge, however, lectured him on foolhardiness, pointing out that it was his duty to his country and to his mother not to take any risks, that his life was too precious to be exposed rashly in some harebrained venture. None of it was new to the Prince—he had heard it all before, and he assured Bigge that he would be very careful.

Also in the camp was Archibald Forbes, the journalist who had written so cruelly of him in 1871; bearing no malice, Louis now captivated the famous war correspondent, who wrote:

'. . . the boy of the Empire when the shackles of the Empire had fallen from his limbs . . . was no longer a buckram creature but a lively natural lad. . . .'[1]

Seeking to imitate the 'professionals' who surrounded him, Louis refused to avail himself of the few amenities offered by the camp, roughing it, frozen at nights, in an open-ended canvas bivouac as used by the Irregulars instead of in one of the small tents issued to the regular soldiers. He was inevitably turned down for every expedition for which he volunteered, but despite the disappointments he told one officer that he felt happier than at any other time in his life. His enthusiasm impressed and captivated everyone; Sir Evelyn Wood said '. . . he has soldier-like ideas and habits and unwearied endeavour to acquire knowledge and military experience. . . .'

On 5 May, Chelmsford left Kambula and made his headquarters at Utrecht; Wood's column also broke camp and moved south. On 8 May Chelmsford appointed as his Acting Quartermaster-General Colonel Richard Harrison, RE, a stolid, experienced officer who had served in the Indian Mutiny and in China. He was responsible for supplies and transport; and being in command of all patrol work, he also had the task of reconnoitr-

[1] Archibald Forbes, *Souvenirs of Some Continents*.

ing a route into Zululand for the 2nd Division. As assistants, Harrison had Major Grenfell, 60th Rifles,[2] and Lieutenant J. Brenton Carey, 98th Regiment, one of the special service officers who were not attached to regiments but were available for odd posts.[3] The Acting Quartermaster-General found Carey's staff-work very useful and frequently used him for patrols and for forward map-making. Contemporary sources mention of Carey that '. . . he was an officer of outstanding promise and a glutton for duty . . . no more zealous or useful officer in South Africa . . . he had . . . got together an impressive amount of invaluable infor-mation and he toiled night and day. . . .'[4]

By now Louis had become probably the best-known figure in the small encampment at Utrecht. He nosed around asking innumerable questions and diligently scribbling down the answers in his field note-book; and almost at once he discovered an officer who stood out in sharp contrast to his stolid fellow-officers, as much through his Gallic gestures and lively manner as by his extravagant style of speech. Delighted to encounter someone who spoke French as well as he did himself, Louis was attracted to Lieutenant Carey, who so volubly admired France and everything French. Within minutes of their first meeting, Carey had pro-duced from a breast-pocket photographs of his lovely wife and children. Being a sentimental, Louis understood and did not share in the general amusement which was aroused by Carey who fre-quently kissed the photographs, oblivious to all who saw him. He talked freely of his private and family affairs, of his aims and ambitions. Although he was not a Catholic, Carey's deep religious feelings impressed Louis, who became aware of an affinity in their mutual conviction that the prayers of their loved ones would protect them from every peril.

The Prince Imperial also met another man to whom he was drawn, but in a different way—towards him Louis felt an instinct to protect. Deléage was a young French journalist who had per-suaded his paper, *Le Figaro*, to send him out to Natal to keep

[2] Later Field Marshal Lord Grenfell.
[3] In his book, *The Washing of the Spears* (London, 1966), Donald R. Morris relates that those officers who came out in time for the first invasion were known as aasvogels or vultures, because they had eaten up all the good assignments, and those who had only arrived in the April reinforcements were known as boomvogels, because they were up a tree and were generally assigned to transport duties.
[4] E. E. P. Tisdall, *The Prince Imperial* (1959).

the French people informed of the Prince's activities. More a Republican than a Bonapartist, Deléage almost against his will detected something heroic in the Prince's action, although he feared that his exile in England might have transformed the Prince Imperial into a 'dull-witted, Anglicised pretender'.[5] As soon as they met, Deléage found that his fears were groundless— he found as he wrote in his paper : 'not a young man, but a prince, with the simplicity and charm of an *esprit supérieur et distingué* . . . a Frenchman with all the qualities of his race.'

The Prince's pleasure at meeting a fellow countryman was further enhanced by his admiration for a man not much older than himself who, with no knowledge of the English language and without experience of Army life, had the courage to follow the campaign—virtually on his behalf.

Louis utilised every spare moment in activities which he considered would prepare him for the battles that lay ahead. He carried out interminable sword exercises, using the weapon carried by his Great-Uncle Napoleon at Austerlitz; he cut in two as they fell potatoes thrown into the air, sometimes performing the feat on a moving horse. The otherwise bored soldiers co-operated wholeheartedly by throwing at him sticks cut like assegais, which he would dodge.

Back in England, the Empress Eugenie, consumed by anxiety, had become obsessed with the idea of following her son to Africa. Hearing of this, Queen Victoria conferred with the Duke of Cambridge, '. . . and Lord Wolseley, who was on the point of leaving England to replace Lord Chelmsford at the head of the troops in Zululand, was entrusted, it was said, with the orders for the Prince's return.'[6]

[5] Morris, *The Washing of the Spears*, p. 519.
[6] Auguste Filon, *Recollections of the Empress Eugenie*, 1920, p. 292.

16

Towards the middle of May, Sir Evelyn Wood ordered Buller to find for the Flying Columns a way south from Wolf's Hill into Zululand. Colonel Harrison, who wanted to find a route eastwards from Koppie Allein for the 2nd Division, decided to go along with Buller. As soon as the news reached him, the Prince Imperial rushed to Harrison's tent, begging permission to go; hastily, Harrison referred him to Lord Chelmsford. The Commander-in-Chief weighed the matter . . . the Prince's wild enthusiasm might be partially satisfied by this safe expedition, with Buller and 200 men of the Frontier Light Horse and the Edendale contingent to protect him. He gave permission, and, on 13 May, Harrison rode out accompanied by the Prince Imperial and William Drummond, the Staff Interpreter. The night was spent at Conference Hill, where entrenchments were being built; Louis was delighted to be asked to christen them Fort Napoleon.

Feeling fitter than ever before, with the comforting pressure of his sword and his pistol against his legs, and mounted on a spirited horse, Louis joyfully greeted Colonel Buller and other acquaintances among the patrol. They crossed the Blood River into Zululand, passing through a country of jagged hills, plains deeply scored with dried-up water-courses and deep white-ant holes concealed by tall kaffir-grass.

That night the party bivouacked, formed in a tight ring without fires; it was bitterly cold. Throughout the long dark hours, his blood at fever-pitch, Louis marched up and down singing French military songs, to the ill-concealed irritation of the patrol.

Next morning, in the valley of the Ityotyozi, they encountered Lieutenant Carey with an escort of 80 Dragoons; such a large escort of Regulars aroused unrestrained laughter from the Irregulars. At midday, when Louis was beginning to think that the

Zulus did not exist, a small party of the enemy suddenly appeared on a hill, melting away as the patrol advanced. The few Irregulars who set off after them were sharply recalled by Buller. But Louis dashed up the hill, far in advance of the patrol, seeking a straggler whom he could engage with his sword. Alas, there was only a solitary black figure to be seen on a knoll beyond the hill; he set off on a solo chase.

Experienced and eminently practical, Redvers Buller did not intend to allow his patrol to degenerate into a Zulu hunt. If Louis got himself into danger, Buller knew he would probably lose valuable men in extricating him; redder than ever and in a furious temper, he sent a party racing after the Prince and told Harrison that this was the last time he would take out the young excitable hot-head. Having his own men under an iron control born of mutual respect, Buller found himself in a vastly different position with this Prince of the Blood.

Back at Wolf's Hill Camp on 16 May, Buller complained of the Prince's recklessness to Lord Chelmsford, saying that he could not be saddled with such a burden. He flatly declined to take further responsibility for the Prince Imperial, growling that it would be better for everyone if he were employed within the camp on Staff duties. Lord Chelmsford wrote an order to Colonel Harrison stating that under no circumstances was the Prince to be allowed out 'into the blue' without his express permission, and that he must always have an officer and an escort when doing survey work near the camp. He assigned the Prince to Harrison's staff and told Louis that he was never to leave camp without permission.

The Prince wrote to his mother :

'I have just returned from reconnaissance; we were away six days. A few shots were exchanged but nothing happened to speak of. We were in the saddle for twenty hours out of twenty-four.'

Deléage had talked with Lord Chelmsford at Newcastle, and, although he found some of the conversation rather worrying, he emerged with the idea that the Commander-in-Chief had some sort of 'gentleman's agreement' with the Prince. Lord Chelmsford told the French journalist that his initial inclination had been to forbid the Prince to move without an appointed bodyguard, but that he realised that under such circumstances '. . . the young man would quite rightly leave the Army in a rage'. He said that he was of the opinion that unless Louis' mother or his party had agreed to a certain risk, would he have come out entirely alone? He asked how he could 'show more solicitude for that precious life than those who had ventured it in the first place?'

Convinced that the British were, after all, concerned for the Prince Imperial's safety, Deléage was horrified to hear that the Prince had ridden deep into Zululand with a scouting party.

Colonel Harrison, who still needed to find a route for the 2nd Division, decided to go out again with a small party of six mounted volunteers and twenty men from the Edendale contingent. Inevitably, Louis volunteered and, inevitably, he was refused; then Harrison softened and agreed to allow him to go if Lord Chelmsford gave permission. Louis set out at top speed for Utrecht; on the way he fell in with General Sir Evelyn Wood whom he persuaded to intercede for him. Thus, he gained the permission he sought. When the patrol set out from Wolf's Hill, Colonel Harrison had both the Prince Imperial and Lieutenant Carey by his side.

As they were penetrating deep into unknown country, the patrol's main chance of safety lay in concealment; to ensure this, they were led by Major Bettington, commander of 3 Troop, Natal Horse, although Harrison was the senior officer. Bettington was a veteran of vast experience, and capable of using his mounted Irregulars to their best advantage. These Irregulars never failed to amaze Louis, their disregard for formal discipline and appearance were contrary to all his ideas of military training. They never paraded, mounting when they were ready; when their leader noted a reasonable gathering of men he set off with them following in a straggling file. Latecomers cantered after the detachment until they caught up. Irregulars depended more upon their horses than their weapons for safety, and they tended to get out of hand in a forward gallop unless they were restrained. Dismounted, Irregulars could maintain a hot fire with their Martini-Henry carbines; when they were mounted, the weapon was fired from one hand like a heavy, awkward pistol. It had no safety-catch and so was always carried unloaded although loading was a very difficult business when on the move.

It was intended to ride along the northern edge of the Nqutu Range, inspecting the valley south of the Ityotyozi and scouting to the east. They had a rendezvous at Sihayo's kraal on the upper Bashee with a larger force under Buller's command. They crossed the Blood River at Koppie Allein and then rode south of Napoleon Koppie completing forty miles on the first day. Buller decided to scout east between the Ityotyozi and the Tombokala and turned east at Incenzi Hill ten miles to the north; thus the two patrols did not link up. Bettington, believing them to be observed, waited until darkness and then led the party in complete silence for more than a mile until he reached a donga. Here, Basuto sentinels were posted; the horses were haltered in a circle, ready saddled and bridled, with their riders lying by their side. It was a chilly night with no fires, and no man permitted to speak above a whisper. The Prince was stretched on the ground with the others, sharing blankets with Lomas, his orderly. At one point Carey thought that he heard earth and stones rattle down the steep side of the donga; he alarmed the patrol in muted urgency—but nothing happened, and, grumbling, the party again settled down.

The next day, halting at intervals whilst the Prince Imperial and Carey sketched the ground, the patrol moved east along the ridge, passing north of the ravine where the Zulu impi had hidden before Isandhlwana. Suddenly, a hail of badly-directed bullets spattered and ricocheted off the boulders around them. Bettington ordered the troopers to charge up the steep path that led to a small kraal on the rocky kop from where the shots had come. It was a narrow gully made treacherous by loose rocks; climbing in single file, the horses stumbled and skittered, their riders crouched low over their necks under a ragged fire. Waving his sword excitedly, Louis charged behind Major Bettington, keeping his pistol in its holster. After a few more shots, a small group of Zulus scrambled over the rocks and got away.

After they had searched the huts and found a few stores which had been looted from Isandhlwana, the patrol burned them to the ground. While they were eating breakfast, Bettington advised the Prince not to bother with a sword, but Louis quickly replied:

'I should always have mine, not so much to charge but to defend myself if I was surrounded. I would die fighting and then death would have nothing painful.'

The site was ceremoniously marked on their maps as Napoleon Kraal; the patrol then rode until sundown, when they halted at a deserted kraal and cooked a meal. Sensing that groups of Zulus were collecting near them, Bettington left the fires alight and moved off as soon as darkness fell. He drove the patrol through the night, working north by stars and compass; they crossed the Blood River and reached Conference Hill before dawn. Coming up to the camp during the first-light stand-to, they identified themselves cautiously and rode in to a welcome breakfast.

Back at Utrecht, Louis wrote out a lengthy and detailed report of the patrol which had, in fact, found a practical route for the 2nd Division. Trusting Buller's judgment more, Lord Chelmsford decided to move by the route that he had discovered, ten miles to the north. Next day, in a letter to his wife, the Commander-in-Chief said :

'The Prince Imperial went out on a reconnaissance a few days ago and nearly came to grief. I shall not let him out of my sight again if I can help it.'

17

As he was riding into camp, the Prince Imperial was hailed by Sir Evelyn Wood:

'Well, Sir, you've not been assegaied yet?'

The Prince laughed: 'Not yet!' Then, more gravely: 'But while I've no desire to be killed, if I have to fall I should prefer an assegai to a bullet . . . it would show we'd been to close quarters.'

He met Deléage and told him of his adventures: 'I enjoy these little outings, they suit me perfectly—but if I had to be killed, I should be in despair at the thought of falling in one. In a great battle, very well, it's for Providence to decide; but an obscure skirmish—ah, no, that would never do!'

Recounting the meeting in later days, the French journalist confessed that at that moment he had wished with all his heart that he had been an old friend whose maturity gave him the authority and wisdom to advise this foolhardy young man. He yearned to remind the Prince of his heritage and of his duty to his people, to beg him not to allow his insatiable quest for excitement to blind him to the fact that he was out here only to gain general military experience.

Recalling that same day, the Frenchman wrote about an English officer named Carey who came running *avec force gestes*, begging him, in excellent French, to stop a little. He wished to talk of the Prince and of his part in the recent patrol, and since Deléage was sure that His Highness had probably minimised his rôle, he was delighted to listen. Carey told him of their night in the donga, of how they had been fired on from a hill-top at the close of day and of how it had been so cold during the night that the Prince had snuggled against him for warmth. Carey is reported as saying: 'I can't understand their making us pass the night in such a place, especially as His Highness was with us!'

Describing the charge up the rocky gully to the kraal, Carey is said to have become lyrical in his praise of the Prince's courage, intelligence, amiability and '. . . all the virtues of mind and heart'.

During their long conversation, Carey told of his schooldays in Paris and his ambulance work in France during the war with Prussia. Deléage took an instant liking to this officer of 'frankly cordial visage' who was so completely un-English. A day or two later, at Koppie Allein, when the Frenchman's baggage failed to come up, Carey offered to share his tent with him. They became fast friends, almost intimates—'it was a common thing for the journalist, awakened in the small hours by piercing cold, to lift his head and see his tent companion still working. Deléage was profoundly moved by that quiet figure, bent over a map and carefully enriching it with the fruits of a long day in the saddle. He only wished the credit might be given where it was due, but more likely, Carey's superiors would get all the thanks for the obscure devotion of their subordinate.

'The Lieutenant often spoke of his family. On the table, always before him as he worked, there stood a photograph of his mother and his three children; in his pocket-book there was a yet dearer pledge, which he used now and then to take out and salute with passionate kisses. For he was not merely *un homme sensible*, but highly emotional and perfervid. Those five dear ones, he exclaimed again and again, were all the world to him; they were the guiding stars of his life.'[1]

In the days that followed, the Prince Imperial appeared downcast—'his face bore a look of strain and fatigue . . . his manner was decidedly overwrought. . . .' In the sweltering QMG tent he toiled listlessly at his maps, wondering for how long he must '. . . sit still and apply himself' whilst everyone else was '. . . out there'. He had been caught by Colonel Harrison as he was about to ride out with a patrol; the Commander-in-Chief's written order had been invoked and he had been sent back to his map-making.

Major Grenfell could not help feeling that trouble lay ahead; on 24 May he wrote in a letter home :

'. . . he is a plucky little chap and will, I think, get himself shot before the campaign is over.'[2]

The days passed in preparation for the final advance into Zululand, to Ulundi, Cetewayo's capital. On 31 May Louis was dis-

---

[1] E. E. P. Tisdall, *The Prince Imperial* (1959).
[2] Field Marshal Francis Wallace Grenfell, *Memoirs* (London, 1925).

interestedly sketching a map of the ground which the column was
to traverse to reach tomorrow night's camp-site by the river below
Itelezei. Suddenly, he had an idea : he knew that the site for the
camp of 2 June had yet to be chosen. He rushed to see Colonel
Harrison—could he go out tomorrow with an escort past the next
day's camp site and on to the ground the column wo[...] re[...]
the 2 June in order to extend his sketch to cove[...] [...]?

Harrison considered the request; a short releas[...]
work would do the Prince good, he reasoned; an[...]
from a few hours free of the care of the he[...]
column on the march, Lord Ch[...]
ance, and the ground the [...] [...] been
declared free of Zulus . . . [...] [...] re[...]
had been sc[...]uting, w[...] [...] s large
escort, ar[...] e ha[...] [...] army close
at hand [...] wit[...] of the 2nd
Division a[...] the F[...] [...] us escort could
hardly com[...] to any [...] ie ground between
the Blood [...] er a[...] [...] mounted patrols of the
marching column, and t[...] ing would extend beyond the
new camp-site. This would not be a dangerous mission Harrison
decided—not with Major Bettington in charge of the escort. He
laid down that the escort must consist of at least half a dozen
of Bettington's troopers with six native scouts from the Edendale
contingent, the natives were notoriously quicker to spot distant
movements than were Europeans.

However, Major Bettington had been ordered to carry out
another task, so Harrison had to think of someone else to command the escort. At that point Lieutenant Carey entered the tent,
he had heard of the expedition and asked if he could accompany
the Prince, as he was anxious to verify some points on his map
of the route to the Ityotyozi Valley. Harrison considered for a
moment : 'I am glad you are a volunteer, for you can now look
after the Prince.'

He wrote out a warrant for an escort of six white troopers and
six Basutos and handed it to Carey. Herbert Stewart, the cavalry
Brigade-Major, who co-ordinated requests for mounted men, was
chatting with the journalist Archibald Forbes when Carey brought
in the warrant. The document did not state, nor did Carey think
it necessary to mention, that the escort was for the Prince Imperial.
Stewart ordered out six men of Bettington's Horse and gave
Carey an order to Captain Shepstone for the Basuto detail, re-

marking that it would save time if Carey took it over himself and gave the natives their instructions personally. Carey agreed, saluted and went on his way.

When he got back to the QMG tent, Carey found the Prince Imperial gazing ruefully at the map on which he was working. He confessed that he had made a frightful botch of it and Carey offered to re-do the sketch for him. Louis thanked Carey profusely and made a relieved exit. Carey sat up most of the night working on the map by the light of a lantern.

Out in the camp, the Prince Imperial gossiped with Archibald Forbes who talked to him of the Franco-Prussian war which had wrought both the Prince's ruin and his emancipation. The volatile Prince was in a noticeably happier frame of mind than he had been for some days and returned with zest to his former habit of bombarding his companions with questions. Lieutenant Horace Smith-Dorrien wrote of that night :

'The Prince Imperial, wearing the undress uniform of the Royal Artillery . . . endeared himself to all . . . he was especially friendly to myself. He took a deep interest in the organisation of every branch of our force . . . he was in my tent up to 11 p.m. on the night before going out on his last patrol . . . extracting from me a promise to write him a treatise on bullock transport.'[3]

At eight o'clock next morning, Sunday, 1 June 1879, Carey rode over to the cavalry lines and returned with six men of Bettington's Horse. On the previous night he had instructed the Basuto scouts to join them outside the QMG tent before nine o'clock. The men had been selected personally by Major Betting-ton : they were Sergeant Robert Willis, Corporal Grubb and Troopers Le Tocq, Abel, Cochrane and Rogers. Grubb spoke fluent Zulu and had been on the Langalabalele expedition; he was a veteran of sixteen years in the Royal Artillery and a decade's farming in Natal. Le Tocq was a French-speaking Channel Islander. With them was a Zulu guide who knew the area—learning that this man would have to lope alongside the mounted men, Louis ordered out his second horse, Fate, for the native. While they waited for the Basutos of the Edendale contingent, the Prince squatted on the ground and, using a saddle as a desk, scribbled a pencilled note to his mother :

'I write to you in haste on a leaf of my notebook. In a few

[3] General Sir H. Smith-Dorrien, *Memories of Forty-eight Years Service.* (1925).

minutes I am leaving to choose a camping-ground for the 2nd Division on the left bank of the Blood River. The enemy is concentrating in force and there will certainly be an engagement within a week.

'I don't know when you will hear from me, for the postal arrangements are not all that could be desired. I didn't want to lose this opportunity of embracing you with all my heart.

'Your devoted and respectful son,

Napoleon.

'PS—I've just heard of *la belle election de M Godelle*. Please let him know that I am delighted at the good news.'

This letter was carried to Landman's Drift by Archibald Forbes.

It was now past nine o'clock and the Basuto scouts had still not shown up; in fact, they had reported to the cavalry Brigade-Major who, in the confusion of the breaking up of the camp, assumed that the Prince's party had already left. He ordered the Basutos to ride after them and they trotted off into oblivion. Characteristically eager to be off, the Prince said :

'Let's start . . . leave orders for the Basutos to follow'.

Carey made no objection and he moved off, with the Irregulars following. They crossed the river and came up with Colonel Harrison and Major Grenfell on the far bank. Harrison noticed that the Basutos were not with the party and suggested they wait for them to come up. The Prince shrugged impatiently :

'Oh, there are quite enough of us !'

Distracted by his duties and possibly weary of cautioning the Prince, Harrison allowed it to pass. In his memoirs, Lord Grenfell distinctly states that the Prince refused to wait for the Basutos. The Official History records that the Prince :

'. . . having afterwards become separated from Lieutenant-Colonel Harrison, moved on with his eight companions to carry out the reconnaissance on which he was engaged.'

The Prince began impatiently to move off. As Carey opened his mouth to call him back, Colonel Harrison motioned him to follow, saying :

'Do not interfere with the Prince'.

From this moment, there seems little doubt that the Prince regarded himself as in command of the party, a fact tacitly acknowledged by Carey. On the other hand, there are grounds for believing that the Prince assumed, at the time of departure from the camp, that Carey was in command—but if this was so, he

92

did not later act in accordance with such an assumption. Afterwards, when the point arose, Carey denied that he had ever been
given such a command, maintaining that it would have been
impossible for him to command the escort and to perform his
own specific technical duties at the same time.

A further complication arose when Major Grenfell, finding
himself at a loose end for a couple of hours, decided to accompany the party for a portion of their journey. Not seeing the
Basutos, Grenfell '. . . concluded tha . . . were far ahead covering
the . . . as of c . . . they . . . l have been. . . .'[4] Not only
had Colonel Harrison . . . Carey . . . interfere with the Prince,
. . . Major . . . immedia . senior on the staff, had
. . . agreed . . . . in . . . . the Basutos—
. . . for Carey to clear.

Grenfell, Carey and the troopers rode after the Prince, with
none of the officers or the escort knowing who was really in command. Indeed, Major Grenfell, the senior officer present, later
asserted that he was unaware that the scouting party, as opposed
to the fighting portion of the escort, was not on the ground at all.

At about this time, back in the old camp, Lord Chelmsford and
his staff were mounting their horses to move off to Itelezei. The
Commander looked around and asked :

'Where is the Prince Imperial?'

An officer replied :

'Sir, he is with Colonel Harrison, who started for Itelezei at
dawn.'

Satisfied, the preoccupied Army Commander mounted his
horse.

The party rode over open grass country for seven or eight miles,
and then along a ridge running out into the Ityotyozi Valley. Even
with a small escort, the journey on the open ridge was reasonably
safe since the Zulus had no horses. The Prince and Grenfell rode
in front, with Carey behind them; the elegant Staff Officers,
neatly clipped and elegantly brushed under gleaming white
helmets and with highly polished boots, spurs and scabbards,
presented an incongruous contrast to the bearded Irregulars,
puffing at blackened clay pipes, in their patched assortment of
'uniform'. Before they reached the crest of the hill overlooking
the valley, Grenfell left them and turned back to attend to his
duties in the new camp at Itelezi Hill. He said goodbye to the
two officers, calling out over his shoulder as he moved away :

[4] F. W. Grenfell, *Memoirs*.

93

'Take care of yourself . . . and don't get shot!'

The Prince pointed to Carey:

'Oh no! Carey will take very good care that nothing happens to me!'

Colonel Harrison was far too busy at the new camp to give any thought to the Prince, nor did he mention to Lord Chelmsford when he was showing him around the new site that the Prince was out on patrol. Chelmsford had no time to play nurse to young officers, whoever they might be, and, in his wildest dreams, he would never have guessed that a young lieutenant fresh from the 'Shop' had been entrusted with choosing his camp-site for the next night. The recent disaster at Isandhlwana had made him incapable of taking any such chances—only an experienced Staff Officer could assess the defensive suitability of a camp-site, besides its nearness to water and fire-wood. As did Deléage, Lord Chelmsford assumed the Prince Imperial to be occupied unseen in some far corner of the camp.

18

SEVEN miles beyond Itelezi Hill the patrol reached the end of the ridge and, at 12.30, halted on a flat-topped hill above the river. Below them, perhaps a mile or so away, a small kraal nestled in a sea of tall yellow kaffir-corn; a stream meandered close by. The two officers searched the landscape of hills and valleys through their glasses, but could see nothing that moved. The Prince proudly pointed out Napoleon Koppie, to the south-west across the Ityotyozi river. They settled down, Carey completed his map and the Prince made a quick sketch of the surrounding country. When the party had rested for nearly an hour, the Prince Imperial called out to the men to off-saddle, but he changed the order almost at once to loosen girths, saying:

'It is hardly worthwhile to off-saddle for a quarter of an hour . . . we shall go down to the huts by the river where the men can get wood and water and cook something.'

Carey shook his head:

'I don't think we should go down there, Your Highness . . . it is rather enclosed . . . no, I don't like it. . . .'

The Prince laughed, jumped lightly to his feet and waved his hand in a flippant gesture as though chiding his companion for being unduly cautious. Carey shrugged his shoulders and moving over to his horse began to tighten its girth. At the Prince's order, the men mounted and started down from the end of the ridge into a valley of dry dongas; the deeper channel of the Ityotyozi curved away to the south.[1]

---

[1] The hill on which the party rested was a spur of the mountain range in which Sirayho and his small band of Zulus had hidden during Buller's last reconnaissance (in which the Prince participated). The kraal which the patrol was approaching was a Zulu outpost. As the party made their way down the hill they were under constant observation by the Zulus, who were gathering together in readiness for an attack.

The kraal was small, formed of five huts around a circular stone cattle-pen; kaffir-corn and tambookie grass grew to a height of six feet close up to the east, south and west sides of the huts. To the north, the ground was bare for 200 yards, before dropping away into a dry donga six or eight feet deep; in the rainy season the storm waters coursed through it on their way to the Ityotyozi river. Perched on the side of a hill with a covered approach on three sides, the kraal was easily accessible to the fast-moving Zulus; nevertheless, there is no record of any objections being voiced by the experienced Irregulars of the patrol.

The party halted at a spot near the huts where the grass had been beaten down, and the Prince gave orders to off-saddle and to knee-halter the horses so that they could graze. A fire was lit and coffee was brewed with water brought from the river by the guide. The men wandered off to search the huts, returning to report that they had been occupied recently since they had found freshly-chewed sugar-cane by the entrance to one of them and a mound of warm-ashes. A trooper called the attention of Sergeant Willis and Corporal Grubb to three native dogs slinking around the huts, commenting that where there were dogs there were men. The two NCO's looked across at their officers stretched out full-length on the ground; no orders had been given to post a sentry or to load carbines; they shrugged their shoulders and continued to drink coffee and puffing at their pipes.

This flatteringly close contact with the young Prince seems to have hypnotised Carey and banished all his commonsense, experience and military training. Both officers were immersed in their maps and sketches; afterwards they discussed animatedly, in French, Napoleon's 'Immortal Campaign of 1796. . . .'

Carey looked around to see if the men had finished their coffee, then glanced at his watch; it was half-past three.

'I think we should saddle-up now, Your Highness.'

Lazily, the Prince Imperial stretched his arms above his head :

'I am so comfortable . . . let us take another ten minutes.'

Suddenly the native guide appeared talking agitatedly. Uneasy, Carey waved a restraining hand at him and called for Corporal Grubb to interpret.

'Sir, he says he saw a Zulu come over the hill.'

The native nodded vigorously and pointed. Both men rose stiffly to their feet, and the Prince called to the five troopers lying stretched out on the sun-baked ground :

'Everyone! On your feet and collect your horses!'

96

1 & 2. Two early photographs of
the Prince Imperial

3. Captain Carey

4. A photograph of the Prince Imperial
taken shortly after the death of his
father in 1873

5. The Empress Eugenie in 1880

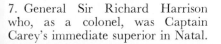

6. The Duke of Cambridge

7. General Sir Richard Harrison who, as a colonel, was Captain Carey's immediate superior in Natal.

8. General Lord Chelmsford

It took ten minutes to collect the scattered horses and saddle-up, but at last everyone was standing at their horse's head. Trooper Rogers, whose horse had strayed further than the others, was still fumbling with a girth. Carey was ready first and he mounted independently, to sit facing the long grass in the direction where the Zulu had been reported. In a clear, unhurried voice, the Prince called out :

'Prepare to mount.'

Gathering the reins and putting his left foot in the near stirrup, each man grasped his saddle and waited for the Prince's next command. If the word 'Mount' was ever uttered, it was drowned by the crash of rifles.[2] From the long grass a few yards away burst thirty or forty Zulus, screaming 'Usuthu!' as they flung themselves on the startled patrol. Frightened by the noise, the horses reared and stampeded; their riders, who were not yet in their saddles, clung desperately to their bolting horses. Rogers' horse plunged away leaving the trooper staring helplessly after it; then he collected himself and dodged into the shelter of the huts, loading his carbine as he ran. But a Zulu was close upon him, and Rogers missed him with the only shot fired by the patrol during the whole affair, and an assegai drove deep into his body.

When the first startling vision of the Zulus burst upon Carey's shocked eyes, he saw again the screaming Maya Indians of Honduras twelve years before and the Civil Official dragged from his saddle to be transformed into a bloody bundle as he was hacked and pierced through and through. Jolted back into focus by urgent reality, Carey controlled his frightened horse, and, pulling it round, he galloped off on a path that put the huts between him and the Prince Imperial. Clear of the kraal, Carey drove fast towards the donga with others of the patrol pounding beside him. Just before they reached the ravine, he called to his companions to bear to the left, as he could see that it would be easier to cross the donga away from the river and to rally on the far side.

Corporal Grubb was up but far from firm in his saddle; Trooper Le Tocq managed to mount his rearing horse but dropped his carbine. Slipping off, he grabbed it from the ground and, with his left foot in the stirrup, he threw himself face downwards across the saddle as the horse bounded away. The native guide dis-

---

[2] No one was hit by the shots, the Zulus were notoriously bad at handling the rifles they had taken at Isandhlwana and, as Donald Morris says, 'Zulus with rifles were merely Zulus without assegais'.

appeared on foot among the huts and was never seen again. All the time, the Zulus kept up a wild fire; a bullet smacked into Trooper Abel's back just below the bandolier, he threw up his arms and slid sideways off his horse. Now in the saddle, Le Tocq overtook Corporal Grubb, calling out as he went past:

'Stick firm to your horse, boy, and put in the spurs! The Prince is down!'

The sudden uproar of rifle-shots and screaming had caused Percy, the Prince Imperial's grey, to shy violently and gallop off. About to mount, the Prince was unable to curb the horse, nor could he get his raised foot into the wildly dangling stirrup; he

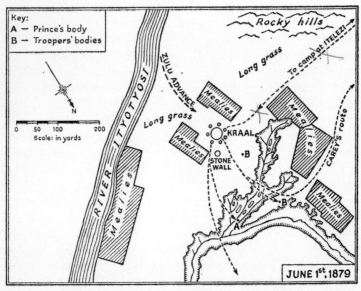

Ground plan of the area around the kraal where the patrol were surprised.

was only saved from falling by grasping with his left hand the leather of his holster. While he was struggling to hold on the grey plunged a hundred yards or so. Le Tocq galloped by calling out:

'Dépêchez-vous, Votre Altesse, s'ilvous plait!'

The Prince gathered himself to vault into the saddle, to save his life by performing the showy trick he had so often demonstrated—it was not going to be easy at this speed. He tightened his right hand on the pommel and flung himself upwards towards the saddle, but the strain was more than the holster strap could stand and it gave way. Rolled in the dust by Percy's trampling hooves, the Prince Imperial lay dazed for a few moments, a sharp pain in his right wrist. Head swimming, he sat up; Percy was fifty yards away, moving fast, beyond catching.

The Prince staggered to his feet and stared at the oncoming Zulus; there were seven of them. He reached for the sword with which he had said he would die fighting, the weapon of Napoleon Bonaparte. His fingers failed to find its hilt and he glanced wildly down to the empty scabbard from which the blade had slipped as he fell. He drew his revolver with his left hand and ran a weaving course down the slope that led into the bed of an arm of the donga, where he turned at bay by a little mound.

The young Frenchman's eyes flickered rapidly over the half-circle of Zulus, poised for the kill. They were big men, made taller by feathered headdresses and clay-stiffened hair fashioned into bizarre shapes; well-moulded muscles rippled under smooth, dark skin. Short kilts of monkey-skin and cow-brush garters were half hidden behind black-and-white cowhide shields held forward in the left hand; each right hand hefted a short stabbing assegai with a stout blade eighteen inches long. Four of them wore short, scrubby beards.

The momentary stillness exploded into action : a Zulu named Langalabalele drew back his arm and flung an assegai. Startled by the movement, the Prince fired a shot in that direction, but missed; the assegai caught him in the thigh, but before the projecting shaft had time to droop to the ground, the Prince tore the spear out. Holding it clumsily in his injured right hand, he rushed at the man, firing and missing again; the native dodged behind another, Zabanga, who halted the Prince in his tracks by transfixing his left shoulder with a thrown assegai. Then all seven closed in, hacking and stabbing; for seconds only the Prince fought with them, using his left hand with the revolver in it to ward off blows, so that he was unable to fire again. The Prince Imperial was beaten down to a sitting position; and the Zulus crowded over him, arms rising and falling in a flurry of reddening assegais.[3]

[3] The following extract is from a letter written by Sir W. Wyndham to Mrs V. G. M. Robinson (daughter of the late Sir Charles Saunders) and is taken from *The Last Zulu King* by C. T. Binns (1963). 'I went to Zululand with the British Resident, then Mr Melmoth Osborn, in January 1882. On his arrival at Rorke's Drift the local chief of the district (I think it was Tashingway), deputed his son Sityityili to act as a bodyguard to the Resident. We visited the site of the Prince's death and Sityityili personally related to us exactly what occurred. . . . In the excitement the Prince's horse

The fleeing riders came to the donga; Corporal Grubb was flung forward on to his horse's neck as it plunged into the ravine so that he dropped his carbine. Troopers Le Tocq and Cochrane crossed the donga with Lieutenant Carey on the left, and Sergeant Willis and Corporal Grubb lower down.

On the far side of the donga, Carey pulled up, and the two troopers halted with him. Hearing shouts, they looked across to where Willis and Grubb had crossed the ravine. Just beyond them, Carey was horrified to see the Prince Imperial's grey galloping along, riderless. Turning to the troopers, he asked if they had seen the Prince. Cochrane said simply :

'I fear he is dead.'

Trooper Le Tocq nodded his head in agreement.

Willis and Grubb turned in their direction, the grey, Percy, following them. As they reined-in, Carey asked if they had seen the Prince. Corporal Grubb answered :

'I looked back and saw the Prince clinging to the stirrup-leather and saddle underneath his horse for a few lengths . . . then he fell . . . I think his horse trampled on him.'

Carey's mind raced over the situation. The Prince had been seen to fall from his horse . . . he was a brilliant rider who could hardly have failed to mount . . . therefore he must have been hit by a bullet and unhorsed . . . in that case he had either been killed outright or despatched by pursuing Zulus. As the seconds ticked by without any sign of the Prince, the awful certainty that he was dead became plain to all. Glancing across at Percy, now grazing quietly a hundred yards away, Carey said absently :

'Someone must catch the Prince's horse.'

Corporal Grubb dismounted :

'My horse is fagged . . . I'll catch it and ride it into camp.'

He ran over and clambered into the saddle of the grey.

Carey realised that he must make up his mind quickly as to his next course of action—on his left he could see Zulus moving in the high grass, while others had already crossed the donga further down. Their line of retreat was almost cut off . . . if they went

reared as he tried to mount and while he made a second attempt Sityityili rushed in and stabbed him to death.

'I may say that Sityityili was one of the finest Zulus that I ever met. He succeeded his father as Chief and met his death in action during the Bambata Rebellion when loyally fighting for the Government. I have no hesitation in believing that his account is a strictly true version of the tragedy and he told me that when he realised later that he had killed a member of our Royal House he always deeply regretted the incident.'

now, they would have to take a long detour to the left over the Tombokala River and a hard ride along its far side before they came up with scouting parties from Wood's column which he knew to be moving down in a south-easterly direction. Only two alternatives were open to him : either return to the donga to look for the Prince and the other two missing members of the patrol, or to make a get-away while there was still time. If they went back, the small party would have to use mounted shock-action or dismounted fire-action. As only Carey had a sword, the first course was out of the question; anyway, with only three single-shot carbines among the four troopers, he would have only three armed men at his back to face an unknown number of Zulus on broken ground where their fleet-footedness made them the equal of horsemen. To dismount would be worse—Grubb was unarmed, and one armed man would have to remain with the six horses; thus he would have only two men with him. It was more than likely that the Irregulars would refuse to go back even if they were ordered.

Even if they did go back to actually see the Prince's body, Carey realised that his responsibility did not end there—he owed the same duty to Troopers Rogers and Abel and, indeed, to the native guide. So, if they fought their way back to the donga, they would also have to fight their way back to the kraal. No, it was not possible; Lieutenant Carey felt convinced that his duty lay in rescuing the living rather than adding to the dead in an abortive attempt to discover the fate of the missing.

A hail of bullets passed over their heads from the ill-aimed Martini-Henry rifles of the Zulus, then a party of the natives began to move quickly towards them. Lieutenant Carey called out :

'Let's make haste and go quickly . . . we'll try to find a drift over the Tombokala River then we'll meet up with General Wood's column!'

The riders turned their horses' heads and rode away from the place of ambush, Corporal Grubb rode Percy, leading his own horse.

19

L IEUTENANT CAREY reviewed over and over the events of those few irrevocable minutes, calling himself every sort of a fool for allowing the Prince to lead them to such an obviously dangerous place without scouting the area or posting a sentry. When the Zulus burst upon them, how was he to know that any member of the patrol was in a more dangerous position than himself? It was a matter of *sauve qui peut*—the fact that he had shouted to the others to guide them to a rallying point showed that he had not been thinking only of himself. He had reined-in as soon as the donga was crossed . . . but there was nothing that could be done by then. He realised that he was going to be blamed for the Prince's death. It was a grotesque injustice—he had done everything possible, there was no time for more, any concerted action had been out of the question.

About five miles from the camp, they saw a small mounted party to their right, and they turned their tired horses in that direction.

Early on 1 June No 3 Column shifted from Mundhla Hill. It was a bright, clear day, the sky was cloudless after the heavy rain that had fallen overnight to swell the water-courses. The force pushed on for seven miles, crossing two drifts made by engineers and native sappers, to the Ityotyozi River. A mile in advance of the column General Sir Evelyn Wood rode with Colonel Redvers Buller. Troopers of Buller's Frontier Light Horse scouted the ground in front and on either flank. At about four o'clock in the afternoon the advance group came to the deep river. Buller, going on ahead, had left a trooper to mark the ford that had been discovered. The vedettes on the higher ground were signalling the approach of mounted men, who, on seeing the column, changed their direction and came towards them at full gallop. It was later said that one of the riders was waving to them as though telling them to go back. The rest of the story must come under the heading of conjecture.

Without taking his eyes from the onrushing riders, Buller spoke from the corner of his mouth to the man riding alongside him:

'Why! They are riding as though they think the Zulus are after them!'

The fugitives pulled up and Buller addressed their leader sharply:

'Whatever is the matter with you?'

'The Prince . . . the Prince Imperial is killed!'

Buller's fierce red face hardened:

'Where? Where is his body?'

The officer pointed to a hill some three miles off, and Buller searched the area with his glasses to make out a party of Zulus leading three horses.

'Where are your men, sir? How many did you lose?'

They are behind me. . . . I don't know.'

Buller fixed him with steely eyes and from a mouth that had become a slit, rapped out savagely:

'You deserve to be shot, and I hope will be. I could shoot you myself!'

Buller pulled his horse round sharply. General Wood came up with them.

'Where is the Prince, Lieutenant Carey? Speak, Sir, what has happened?'

'The Prince, I fear, is killed, Sir.'

The General stared at Carey:

'Is that the case, Lieutenant Carey? Tell me instantly, Sir.'

'I fear 'tis so, General.'

The General's eyes narrowed, his lips set in a thin line:

'Then, Sir, what are you doing here?'

Of all the men in South Africa, Carey had at this moment the ill-fortune to meet Evelyn Wood and Redvers Buller—both holders of the Victoria Cross. Other versions of the story have William Beresford with the party. Archibald Forbes, the journalist, added to the detail by having Carey cry dramatically:

'Fly! Fly! The Zulus are after me!'

It is a dramatic incident that requires careful consideration. There is no doubt whatever that Lieutenant Carey and his troopers, during their flight from the kraal, came up with No 3 Column and that a conversation took place among General Sir Evelyn Wood, Colonel Redvers Buller and Carey. The incident appears, much as related above, in Colonel Melville's *Life of Sir Redvers Buller*. But it is not based on anything written by Buller himself, appearing in the form of a communication from Sir George Pomeroy Colley. Colley was not present on this occasion, and, in fact, he was not even in South Africa. Sir Evelyn Wood was a compulsive narrator, but he does not mention the incident in his autobiography *From Midshipman to Field Marshal*. His silence would certainly seem to indicate that he did not wish to lend the authority of his name to current legend. Neither Buller nor Wood ever referred to the exchanges of these few minutes, but the much-publicised reports of this meeting told heavily against Carey. They should be accepted with considerable reserve as no one now knows what was actually said.

The fugitives were brusquely ordered to carry on to the camp, and No 3 Column went on their way. Not even Redvers Buller, 'brave to the point of madness', saw any sense in going to the fatal donga in the failing light.

20

IT was almost dark when the party wearily rode into the new
camp at Itelezi. They separated, the Irregulars going to their
own lines; Carey handed over his horse to be rubbed down and
picketed, then walked slowly and stiffly to the Headquarters Mess
tent. Inside, Major Grenfell was sitting alone; he looked up.

'Why, Carey! You are very late for dinner . . . we thought
you'd been shot!'

Carey stared at the ground, then raised his head to look Grenfell
in the face:

'I am all right, but the Prince is killed!'

Grenfell leapt to his feet:

'Lieutenant Carey, is this true? Are you sure?'

Carey nodded. Indicating to him to follow, Major Grenfell
pushed aside the tent-flap and led the way to Lord Chelmsford's
tent. It took a few seconds for the Commander-in-Chief to absorb
the information; he sank down into his chair stunned by this
terrible news which arrived on the very first day of his campaign
that was to wipe out the stain of Isandhlwana.

Archibald Forbes and a group of officers were having dinner
in the tent of General Marshall, the cavalry brigade commander.
Suddenly, Colonel Harrison's head thrust through the open door;
his voice was choked:

'Good God! The Prince Imperial is killed!'

Although normally a stolid man, Harrison had a habit of jesting,
usually on macabre subjects. Lord Downe, Marshall's aide-de-
camp, threw a crust of bread at him, and Herbert Stewart, the
Brigade-Major, laughed aloud. Sitting by the door nearest to
Harrison, Archibald Forbes saw his face quite clearly, so that he
cried out:

'It can't be!'

Harrison made a despairing gesture; having questioned the

patrol he had no doubt of the facts; even so he found it difficult to believe or understand what had happened.

The news was spreading rapidly through the camp. The four Irregulars—Willis, Grubb, Cochrane and Le Tocq, were talking freely to large audiences. They were not ashamed . . . they had followed the officer . . . by frontier reckoning a man on patrol looked after No 1 and, if it came to making a run for it, it was every man for himself.

Archibald Forbes reported to *The Daily News* that, immediately on hearing the terrible news, he questioned each of the four Irregulars. Suspecting that they were in collusion to keep something back, Forbes claimed that all were bad witnesses. He wrote that it was generally agreed that Lieutenant Carey had headed the panic-flight. On the following day, Forbes inspected the band of leather crossing the pommel from holster to holster on the Prince's saddle; he discovered that the band had torn under the strain and that it was not leather at all, but paper-faced. The Prince's fate could be attributed to shoddy saddlery, he wrote.

Deléage had looked about for the Prince during the column's advance and, not seeing him, had made enquiries when he reached the new camp. An officer told him that he had seen the Prince with the cavalry; Deléage got on with settling his belongings into the tent he was sharing with Lieutenant Carey. That evening after dinner, he was walking back to the tent when an artillery officer stopped him :

'Have you heard? They are saying the Prince Imperial is killed !'

Deléage stared uncomprehendingly at the man :

'Repeat that please . . . can you say it in French?'

Then he rushed across to see the Commander-in-Chief. Lord Chelmsford was pacing slowly outside his tent, staring at the ground. As the young Frenchman approached Chelmsford showed no surprise at his violent and unceremonious approach; but answered Deléage's questions in a low voice :

'Yes . . . the Prince was missing . . . it was probable that he was killed . . . his horse had come back alone . . . Lieutenant Carey was in that tent over there. . . .'

Deléage burst into the tent where Colonel Harrison was sitting watching Carey eat a belated meal. Both men looked up defensively at the newcomer; they had just shaken off the persistent questioning of Archibald Forbes and the other journalists and resented this added torrent of interrogation in French and halting

English. Uncertain and shocked, Colonel Harrison masked his feelings by adopting a gruff, official manner. Carey, tired and overwrought, eating jerkily and quickly, used the meal as a defence.

'He could say nothing . . . there would be an official report . . . he had done all he could. . . .'

Frenzied at being treated by Carey, his former friend, as an inquisitive reporter pestering a tired man for news, Deléage pressed his questions. Wearily, Carey ceased eating and answered :

'There is little I can tell . . . the Zulus burst upon us . . . we had to run for it . . . only just got away myself . . . crossing the donga I looked back and saw the Prince's grey climbing out further down . . . I did not see the Prince at all . . . I lost two Irregulars and the native guide . . . I've no idea what became of any of them. . . .'

Deléage drew himself up, turned on his heel and left the tent without saying another word. Anxious to accompany the search party he assumed would go out at once, Deléage roamed the camp demanding from everyone where was it forming? He was shocked to discover that there was to be no search that night; senior officers told him that it was too late and too dark . . . nothing would be gained . . . better to wait until morning when a large expedition was under orders . . . they told him to report mounted in the cavalry lines at 5 am.

Aghast, Deléage pleaded and protested—there was light enough . . . there was a moon . . . the Prince might still be alive a few miles away . . . he might be wounded . . . waiting for help . . . if he was dead then his body was lying out there at the mercy of the Zulus and animals of prey . . . how could they leave him there all night . . . His Highness might have escaped !

To his arguments, the Englishmen replied that it would not be possible to find the Prince in such a black country even if the moon was brilliant . . . too many horses would break their legs in the ant-holes, anyway. Frantic at this exhibition of reticence, baffled and despairing, Deléage cursed them and followed them, shouting that they were cold-blooded and inhuman. They suffered his accusations, and in the mess tent they offered him brandy and soda.[1]

[1] The accounts of this night written by Deléage in *Le Figaro* helped to foster wild French rumours that the English had plotted the Prince's death. In reality, it is probable that the officers were thunderstruck and hoped against hope that the 'PI' would come bouncing along singing one of his

Deléage had moved his kit from the tent, so that Carey was left to sit alone into the small hours of the morning, going over the dreadful events of the day. For much of the time he wrote feverishly, unburdening himself to his wife.

'My Own One,—You know the dreadful news, ere you receive this, by telegram.

'I am a ruined man I fear, though from my letter which will be in the papers you will see I could not do anything else.

'Still, the loss of a Prince is a fearful thing. To me, the whole thing is a dream. It is but eight hours ago since it happened.

'Our camp was bad, but then, I have been so laughed at for taking a squadron with me that I had grown reckless and would have gone with two men.

'To-morrow we go with the 17th Lancers to find his body, poor fellow! But it might have been my fate. The bullets tore around us and with only my revolver what could I do?

'The men all bolted and I now fear the Prince was shot on the spot as his saddle is torn as if he tried to get up. No doubt they will say I should have remained by him, but I had no idea he was wounded and thought he was after me. My horse was nearly done, but carried me beautifully.

'My own darling, I prayed as I rode away that I should not be hit and my prayer was heard. Annie, what will you think of me! I was such a fool to stop in that camp; I feel it now, though at the time I did not see it.

'As regards leaving the Prince, I am innocent, as I did not know he was wounded, and thought our best plan was to make an offing.

'Everyone is very kind about it all here, but I feel a broken-down man. Never can I forget this night's adventure! My own, own sweet darling, my own little darling child, my own little Edie and Pelham! Mama darling, do write and cheer me up! What will the Empress say? Only a few minutes before our surprise he was discussing politics with me and the campaigns of 1800 and 1796, criticising Napoleon's strategy, and then he talked of republics and monarchies!

'Poor boy! I liked him so very much. He was always so warm-hearted and good-natured. Still I have been surprised; but not

French songs. Everyone was deeply disturbed and it was said that the men lingered in groups, talking in hushed voices, far into the night and that few slept soundly.

that I am not careful, but only because they laughed at all my care and foresight.

'I should have done very differently a week ago, but now have ceased to care.

'Oh, Annie! How near I have been to death. I have looked it in the face, and have been spared!

'I have been a very, very wicked man, and may God forgive me! I frequently have to go out without saying my prayers and have had to be out on duty every Sunday.

'Oh! for some Christian sympathy! I do feel so miserable and dejected! I know not what to do!

'Of course, all sorts of yarns will get into the papers, and without hearing my tale, I shall be blamed, but honestly, between you and me, I can only be blamed for the camp. I tried to rally the men in the retreat and had no idea the poor Prince was behind. Even now I don't know it, but fear so from the evidence of the men. The fire on us was very hot, perfect volleys. I believe thirty men or more were on us. Both my poor despised horses have now been under fire. The one I rode to-day could scarcely carry me, but did very well coming back.

'Oh! I do feel so ill and tired! I long for rest of any kind. . . .

'If the body is found at any distance from the kraal to-morrow, my statement will appear correct. If he is in the kraal, why then he must have been shot dead, as I heard no cry. *Enfin, nous verrons*. Time alone will solve the mystery.

'Poor Lord Chelmsford is awfully cut up about it as he will be blamed for letting him go with so small an escort.

'*The Times* and *Standard* correspondents have been at me for news, also the *Figaro*. . . .

'My own treasure, I cannot write more. Good-night, my own one; I will try and let you know a few words to-morrow. I will now try to sleep, till reveille at 5 am; and it is now nearly one and so very cold!'

It has been asserted that this letter was the damning confession of a panic-stricken man who, feeling betrayed, was trying to convince himself that he had rallied the patrol and that he had not abandoned the Prince Imperial. Critics claimed that Carey had omitted unpalatable truths from his effusion of misery; on the other hand in this letter Carey undoubtedly blames himself for not having asserted his authority. It would be fairer to say that it was a letter written when Carey was labouring under conditions of extreme weariness and shock which induced him to take the blame upon himself. Some of his statements could be twisted into an admission of responsibility, although there is nothing of real evidence as to the actual command. The letter was not produced at the court-martial; indeed, the circumstances under which it was written would have made it dubious evidence, particularly when it is considered in the subsequent light of Carey's reasoned statement and his cross-examination of witnesses at the court-martial.

21

NEXT morning the men were roused at 4 am; it was said that everyone longed to be on the road '. . . for the suspense and anxiety since Lieutenant Carey's arrival last night could hardly have been exceeded had he brought news of a second Isandhl-wana. . . .' The search party, if belated, was very large; under the personal command of General Marshall, it consisted of more than one thousand men—a squadron of Lancers and another of Dragoons, the Irregulars of the Flying Column, the Natal Native Contingent and a troop of mounted Basutos, with an ambulance unit. Fuming at the delays caused by the size of the expedition, and overlooking the fact that it was intended as a mark of respect, Deléage reflected bitterly that yesterday, when His Highness was alive, they had let him go out with only six men.

It was not until seven o'clock that the force set out, getting in each other's way as they manœuvred and positioned under the eyes of Lord Chelmsford who was perched on a hill-top '. . . like a commander exercising his troops. . . .' Impatiently, Deléage went forward with the advance party of Native Horse, avoiding Lieutenant Carey who was acting as guide. With them went an ADC, Captain W. C. F. Molyneux, 22nd Regiment, Lomas, the Prince's servant, and Dr Scott, who had attended the Prince in Durban. They proceeded about three miles north-east, then changed direction to east-south-east and moved on a further five miles. Raaf's and Baker's Horse pushed ahead in flanking parties to the highest ridges on either side of the line of march. From the summit of a nearby hill, the Helinstadt signal apparatus flashed and twinkled in the bright sunlight as it kept in touch with Wood's column.

Nearing the donga, the force split into parties, Irregulars, Native Horse and, further over, the fluttering pennons of the lances carried by the 17th Lancers. Slowly descending the slopes of the ravine, the eyes of every rider sought what they feared to find. Then the body of Trooper Rogers was discovered lying in the long grass, propped against a bank. His chest was lacerated with assegai stabs; a huge gash had been made in his abdomen, but only through the flesh, none of his intestines being injured. At first glance he appeared to be naked, his cord jacket and woollen shirt were drawn so high up round his neck. After killing the man, the Zulus had dragged him along the ground by his jacket and shirt. He had a number of wounds in the upper part of his chest and one through his right hand, showing that he had fought for his life at close quarters. A hundred yards from the kraal, just off the main donga, they found another mangled body with the belly ripped open; the face, horribly disfigured, was wrapped in a piece of flannel. It was not he for whom they were looking— this tall man had been Trooper Abel.

Then, searching lower down the main donga, Captain Dundonald Cochrane, 32nd Light Infantry, of the Edendale contingent, shouted. Naked save for a sock, the dead Prince lay stiff on his back, head bent to the right so that his cheek touched the ground.[1] A few feet away lay a light blue sock with an embroidered 'N', and a spur twisted out of shape. Round his neck, the Zulus had left the little gold chain on which was strung a locket set with a miniature of his mother, and a reliquary containing a fragment of the true Cross which had been given by Pope Leo III to Charlemagne when he was crowned Emperor of the West; it was a talisman which had since been worn by dynasty after dynasty of French monarchs.

The group around the body grew larger as more men came up.[2] Dr Scott and Deléage gently turned the body on its face to inspect

[1] Archibald Forbes wrote: '. . . his face, the features of which were in no ways distorted but wore a faint smile that slightly parted the lips was marred by the destruction of the right eye from an assegai-stab.'

[2] Deléage reports: 'We hastened forward, and all doubt was at an end; it was the Prince that lay before us. We could recognise, even from a distance, the small white and well-knit body, in which the grace of form did not interfere with strength and activity. The Prince was lying on his back; his arms, stiffened by death, crossed a little above the chest; the features showed no sign of pain, or any contraction whatever; the left eye was half closed; the right eye had been destroyed by an assegai stab. Judging from the position of the body and the expression of the features, the Prince must have been killed by the first blow, and Dr Scott, as well as Dr Robinson, of the 17th Lancers, who had then come up, estimated that the fatal blow that destroyed the eye and tore through the brain, was inflicted by an assegai thrown from a distance, and that death must have been instantaneous. Dr Scott and I ascertained that there were no wounds inflicted in the back.'

9. The Last Bivouac

10. The kraal where the Prince Imperial and his party dismounted and were fired on

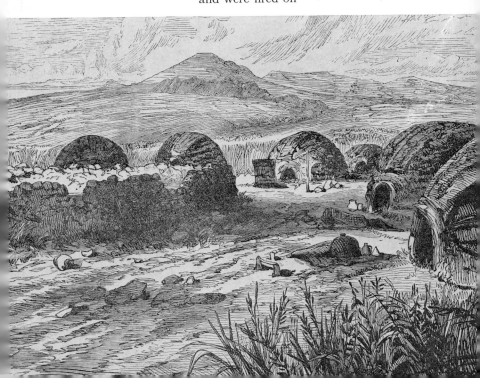

11 & 12. Two artists' impressions of the death of the Prince Imperial

the back; it was unblemished. The Prince Imperial had died facing his foes—there were seventeen separate wounds in the front of the thin body. At least two of them could have killed him—one that had pierced his right eye to the brain and the thrust over the heart.[3] In his right hand was some hair torn from a Zulu head; his left arm was hacked and lacerated. The Prince's abdomen had not been slashed open, only grazed.

Straightening up, Deléage turned and pushed his way through the group, followed by Lomas, the Prince's servant. The young Frenchman raised clenched fists towards the sky and dropped onto his knees in a frenzy of grief; Lomas burst into tears. It was reported that Lieutenant Carey, although obviously disturbed, was in better command of himself. One of the Prince's friends, either Arthur Bigge or Frederick Slade, detached the chain from the Prince's neck and placed it in an envelope together with some locks of the short dark hair. These were later sent to the Empress Eugenie.

As though fearing to trespass upon the quiet of the donga, everyone spoke in whispers and the men of the 17th Lancers were quietly called forward to remove the body. The body was wrapped in a cotton sheet and the Prince was laid reverently on a litter made of a blanket and four lances. Slowly '. . . the body was carried from the donga up the hill homewards by officers Major-General Marshall, Captain Stewart, Brigade Major; Colonel Drury Lowe, and three officers 17th Lancers; Surgeon-Major Scott, Brigadier-General's Staff; Lieutenant Bartle Frere, Rifle Brigade, ADC, and myself. Monsieur Deléage, correspondent of *Le Figaro*, specially requested to be allowed to assist, which was at once conceded to. At 11 am the ambulance waggon arrived, the body was placed in it, and officers' parties of the King's Dragoon Guards and 17th Lancers escorted it back to camp, which we reached at 2.15 pm.'[4]

[3] A letter written from Zululand by an army officer says:
'. . . I have seen a man with seven wounds from one Zulu . . . they stab away like maniacs. In this sad instance the agony was short, the wound in the eye reaching the brain, that in the neck cutting the great vessel; and the chest wound; any would have sufficed for nearly instant death. There is not a pretence for saying there was any spearing than "from above". He was fairly run down and finding that he could not get away, he turned at bay to face his enemy and met his death like a young hero, with his front to the foe. . . .'

[4] Extract from report of 2 June 1879 written by Captain W. C. F. Molyneux to Lord Chelmsford. *Accounts and Papers 1879*, p. 127.

Later that day Lord Chelmsford wrote to Sir Bartle Frere:

'The body has been recovered . . . I shall bury it here with such military honours as are possible. I have always felt that it was somewhat unfair to saddle me with the responsibility which naturally would be attached to such a charge, but I had to accept it with all the rest.'

Respectfully but firmly, Chelmsford's staff officers pointed out that to bury the Prince in South Africa was out of the question; it was imperative that his remains should be returned to England. Deléage backed their pleas.

In the late afternoon, the entire force paraded in hollow-square while Father Bellard, the Catholic Chaplain, conducted a funeral service over the Prince Imperial's body which was wrapped in a Union Jack and strapped to a gun-barrel. Behind the gun, leaning on his cane, stood Lord Chelmsford, the chief mourner, his face drawn and his shoulders bowed. Then, escorted by a squadron of Lancers, the body was taken to Koppie Allein where, throughout the night, army surgeons struggled over the unaccustomed task of embalming the body. It was packed in a rough deal casket, straw and sand being used to keep it in place during the long journey by ambulance to Durban.

As soon as the service had ended in the camp at Itelezi Hill, Major Bettington called the survivors of the ambush, one by one, to his tent. From each man he took a statement; Lieutenant Carey was the first to be questioned.

Lieutenant Carey's Statement

'Having learnt that his Imperial Highness would proceed on June 1 to reconnoitre the country in advance of the column and choose a site for the camp of the following day, I suggested that, as I had already ridden over the same ground, I should accompany him. My request was granted; but at the same time, Colonel Harrison, Acting Quartermaster-General, stated that I was not in any way to interfere with the Prince, as he wished him to have the entire credit of choosing the camp. Shortly before starting, I found that no escort was prepared, and applied to the Brigade-Major of Cavalry. I received the necessary orders, and at 9.15 six men of Bettington's Horse paraded before head-quarters. With

114

these and a friendly Zulu, provided by the Hon Mr Drummond, we started. Six Basutos of Captain Shepstone's Corps were also under orders to proceed with us, and before crossing the Blood River I sent on to him to ask for them. The messenger returned to say that they would meet us on the ridge between the Incenzi and Itelezi Hills. I again sent the man with orders to bring the escort back with him. On our right and left flanks I saw large bodies of Basutos scouting. Arrived upon the ridge, we dismounted, wishing to fix the position of some hills with our compasses. Colonel Harrison then rode up and told us that General Marshall's cavalry was coming up. When he had left I suggested to the Prince to wait for the remainder of the escort. "Oh no, we are quite strong enough." At a mile and a half we ascended a commanding and rocky range of hills beyond Ityotyozi River. I proposed that we should here off-saddle, but the Prince said that he preferred to off-saddle near the river. We remained for half an hour sketching and surveying the country with our telescopes. Seeing no one, we descended to a kraal in a valley below and off-saddled. No precautions were taken, as no Zulus were expected to be in the neighbourhood. The Prince was tired, and lay down beside a hut. The men made coffee, and I reconnoitred with my telescope. At 3.35 I suggested saddling up. His Imperial Highness said, "Wait another ten minutes"; but in five minutes gave me the necessary order. I repeated it, and then went to fetch my horse from the mealie-fields. I had saddled and mounted on the home side of the kraal when I heard his Imperial Highness give the order, "Prepare to mount." I looked round and saw his foot in the stirrup. At the same time I said, "Mount" and as the men vaulted into the saddles I saw the black faces of Zulus about twenty yards off, rushing towards us through the mealie-fields. They shouted and fired upon us as we rode off. I thought that all were mounted, and, knowing that the men's carbines were unloaded, I judged it better to clear the long grass before making a stand. Knowing from experience the bad shooting of the Zulus, I did not expect that anyone was injured. I therefore shouted as we neared the donga, "We must form up on the other side. See to the retreat of everyone." On looking back I saw one party following us, while another on our left was attempting to cut off our retreat across the ridge. Meanwhile we were under a heavy fire, and after we had crossed the donga a man said to me, "I fear the Prince is killed, Sir." I paused, looked back, and, seeing the Prince's horse galloping on the other side of the donga, asked if it was any use returning. The Zulus had already passed over the ground where he must have fallen, and he pointed out the men creeping round our left. I paused for our men to come up, and then galloped on to find a drift over the Tombocto River.'

Corporal Grubb's Statement

'We went, as near as I can guess, twenty miles from Blood River to a kraal. Before we got there the Prince told us to loosen girths, and went sketching with Lieutenant Carey to the brow of a hill. When he came back we mounted, and we went down to another kraal. The Prince came up, saying, "You can water your horses at the river and cook your coffee." We off-saddled there for an hour. The kraal had five huts, with a stone cattle-enclosure; two or three dogs were about, and there were traces of Zulus having gone away only shortly before we arrived. Tambookie grass six feet high, with kaffir corn and mealies growing amongst it, was standing all round it except in front of the way by which we escaped. Here there was twenty yards of open ground. We had our coffee while the native looked after the horses. The Prince said, "It is ten minutes to four; we will saddle at four." The kaffir came up saying something which no one understood till I interpreted. It was that he had seen a Zulu at the river on the other side. We lost no time in saddling, fetching our own horses. The Prince gave the order, "Prepare to mount". I took the time from him. He took hold of his horse, and said, "Mount". The Prince mounted; but before we had time to get our right feet into the stirrups a volley was fired from the mealies. We were all seated except Rogers, who was trying to catch his led horse. The volley was fired from about twenty yards. The Zulus shouted "Usutu" and "Here are the English cowards". I turned round, saw the Zulus, and put spurs to my horse. As I went I saw Rogers behind a hut, to the shelter of which he had run, and I shouted out, "Come along". I saw him level his rifle at a Zulu. I rode on with Abel full gallop.'

'Who was leading them?'—'Lieutenant Carey and Cochrane. When we had got a few yards from the kraals a bullet struck Abel full in the back about an inch below his bandolier. He was half a length in front of me. I saw they were firing high, and so lay along my horse. Le Tocq passed me saying, "Put spurs to your horse, boy; the Prince is down." I looked back, and saw the

116

Prince was clinging to the stirrup-leather and saddle underneath his horse for a few lengths, and he then fell. His horse, as far as I could make out, trampled on him. I unslung my carbine to have a shot at the Zulus, but the horse just then plunged into the donga, and I fell forward on his neck and lost my loaded carbine. When I recovered my seat I found the Prince's horse close beside me. I could not catch it, so I got behind it and drove it along till I caught up to Lieutenant Carey. He then said, "Someone must catch the Prince's horse" and I replied, "As my horse is fagged, I will catch it and ride it into camp." I dismounted and caught the horse and rode it into camp. The Zulus made one rush at us, but we were too quick, and they continued independent firing till we were out of range. We rode on till we fell in with General Wood, Colonel Buller, and two mounted infantry. We made our report, and they, looking through their glasses, saw six Zulus leading away our horses. I saw no more of the Prince.

'What was the last order given?' 'The Prince said, "Mount". I heard no order after that, but at the sound of the volley I watched Lieutenant Carey. We all of us put spurs to our horses and galloped.'

'How many Zulus were there?' 'I should say forty or fifty.'

'What were the Zulus firing with?' 'From the whizz of the bullet that struck Abel, I know they had Martini-Henrys.'

'Before you mounted, how were you standing?' 'We were in line, the Prince being in front of us. Our backs were to the kraal.'

Sergeant Willis's Statement

'We descended a hill to a kraal about a hundred yards from the Imbanani River. The kraal contained four or five huts. There was clear ground in front, but high grass and standing crops all round the other sides. We were ordered by the Prince to off-saddle, and, after knee-haltering, turned our horses into the grass. We lay down outside the huts and took some cooked coffee, while the Kaffir looked after the watering of the horses. At ten minutes to four the Prince gave the time, saying, "Let the horses have ten minutes more." The Kaffir drove up our horses, and at four we were ordered to saddle. The Kaffir said he had seen a Zulu across the river, going up the hill opposite. We saddled as quickly as we could. The Prince then gave the order to mount, and all of us did so, except Trooper Rogers, who was trying to catch his led horse. A sudden volley was at that instant fired, and we all

117

made our way out at once, except Rogers, and I saw him lying against the hut.'

'Did you see the Prince?' 'I cannot say. I saw two men fall from their horses, but cannot say who they were, because I was galloping hard. About fifty yards in front was a deep donga, and when we caught up to Lieutenant Carey I was told the order was to make for Colonel Wood's camp. The Zulus continued firing after us as we galloped for 200 yards, and yelling. We got back to camp about seven o'clock, all together.'

'How far do you think you went to the kraal?' 'About twelve or fifteen miles from the Blood River.'

'How many Zulus do you think there were?' 'From the shots, I should say fifty. Corporal Grubb caught the Prince's horse and rode him in, leading his own. I never saw the Prince again.'

Trooper Le Tocq's Statement

'The kraal we came to last was about fifty yards above the river. Here the Prince told us to off-saddle, and then the Kaffir was sent into the hut to see if anyone was there. He went down afterwards to the river for some water, and we had coffee. After an hour the Prince ordered us to saddle-up. When we had all saddled up he asked, "Are you all ready?" and we said "Yes." He then said, "Mount," and, just as we were springing to our saddles, the volley was fired from the mealies at fifteen or seventeen yards. We had gone to that very place to catch our horses. When we were saddling up the Kaffir, who had been to the river to water the horses, said he had seen a Zulu going up the river away from where the volley was fired. I dropped my carbine and had to dismount for it. In remounting I was unable to get my feet into the stirrups; my horse was galloping so hard from fright. I lay across the saddle. I passed the Prince, but was unable to stop for him, having no power over the reins. As I got clear away from the kraal I passed the Prince. He then had hold of the stirrup-leather and the cantle of the saddle, and was trying to get his foot into the stirrup, but his horse was going too fast. I said to him, *"Dépêchez-vous, s'il vous plaît, Monsieur, et montez votre cheval."* He made no reply. He had not caught hold of the bridle; he could not keep up with the horse, and I saw it tread on him, and the Prince fell down. The Zulus were firing all the time, but I could not see them. I saw no more of the Prince. I followed Lieutenant Carey. He was leading at first, but some of us

118

passed him. We galloped two or three miles, the Zulus trying to surround us. I saw Grubb and Willis could not catch up to us, and asked Lieutenant Carey to wait for them. He said, "We will cross the spruit and wait for them on the rise on the other side." Grubb and Willis were 300 yards behind us, for their horses were knocked up.'

'Were any orders given to stop or rally, or try to save the Prince?' 'No.'

'Did any of you mention the Prince, or did Lieutenant Carey say anything about him?' 'No; all that I heard Lieutenant Carey say all the time was, "Let us make haste, and go quickly."'

Trooper Cochrane's Statement

'We rode, I think, twenty miles from the river, meeting General Wood's column coming down the hill about ten o'clock. We then went to a kraal between the hill and the river. The Prince there ordered us to off-saddle. We stopped an hour, when the Prince ordered us to saddle up again. When we had done so Lieutenant Carey said it was half-past three, and the Prince gave the word "Prepare to mount," and afterwards, "Mount". I was next to him. We mounted, but I did not see him do so. He was, I think, doing something to his bit. All of a sudden a volley was fired at us, the Zulus giving a tremendous shout. The horses were frightened, and we could hardly hold them. Some broke away, and the rest bolted with us. When I got across the donga, or about fifty yards from the kraal, I saw the Prince on foot, closely pursued by Zulus. His horse was then galloping off in another direction. I saw no more of the Prince. I followed Lieutenant Carey. He gave no orders. About a quarter of an hour afterwards Grubb and Willis caught us up and told us that Abel, Rogers, and the Kaffir were killed.'

'In what direction was the Prince running?' 'He was running after us'.

'How many Zulus were pursuing him?' 'I think about a dozen.'

'How far off were they?' 'About three yards from him. They all had guns and assegais.'

'Was any effort made to rally or halt, or any attempt made to save the Prince?' 'No; we had only three rifles with us.'

'How far did you gallop?' 'About two miles without stopping.'

'Did anyone ask about the Prince?' 'No; we were separated.'

119

22

Extract from *Accounts and Papers 1879*.
Memorandum for the information of His Excellency the High
Commissioner, Cape Town.

'Pietermaritzburg, Sunday night 8th June, 8 pm.

'Great pressure of work prevents my sending your Excellency
such report on the sad end of the late Prince Imperial Louis
Napoleon as I could wish. The papers I send you will, I trust, give
you an idea of our endeavours to show our respect and heart-felt
sorrow for the sad end of the poor young Prince. His body arrived
here at 2 pm, and with the Lieut-Governor and all the military
and civil inhabitants of Pietermaritzburg, we received him at the
entrance of the town, and escorted him to the Catholic school
room, where in the presence of properly constituted legal authorities, M Uhlmann, the Prince's confidential servant, M Deléage,
correspondent of *Le Figaro*, Colonel Mitchell, Colonial Secretary,
and myself, we verified his identity and placed our signatures to the
necessary legal documents, one copy of which I placed in his
coffin, one I sent home for the Secretary of State for War, and
one to him also for the Prince's mother. I took the responsibility
of the transfer of the body to better coffins (wood and lead) on
myself, and am thankful I did so. Nothing could be better than
the medical arrangements made. The body is now resting in the
little Roman Catholic chapel here, and we are doing all we can
to show our deep sorrow and sympathy in this great national
calamity. After service to-morrow at 8.30, the body will be moved
under escort to Durban, where all will again be done that circumstances will admit of to show our sorrow and respect. I hope to
get to Durban on Tuesday; though I am very anxious at leaving
my post here at such a moment, still I think showing respect of
our late charge is now my first duty.

'(Signed) H. H. Clifford,
Major-General'

120

Uhlmann, the Prince's valet and life-long companion, had collapsed on hearing of his master's death; he was so grief-stricken that, although he travelled to Pietermaritzburg, he was unable to accompany the cortège to Durban, proceeding there by another route. On 12 June, at Port Natal, the coffin was conveyed across the bar on the tug *Adonis* and taken aboard HMS *Boadicea*; the cabin of the Commodore of the Naval Squadron served as a chapel.

The Times reported the arrival of the body at Simon's Bay:

'By the latest news from the Cape, which is to the 17th ult, we have accounts of the reception there afforded to the body of the Prince Imperial, which was sent from Natal on board HMS *Boadicea*, and arrived in Simon's Bay on Sunday, the 15th. The coffin was at once transferred to her Majesty's ship *Orontes*, being conveyed upon a pinnace towed by the steam-launch of the *Boadicea* through a line of men-of-war boats, the crews of which stood with their oars peaked and their heads uncovered. Arrived at the *Orontes*, the coffin was lifted from the yard-arm and lowered on the shoulders of British sailors to the deck, where Dr Leonard, the Roman Catholic Bishop of Cape Town, with assistant priests, performed the usual service for the dead, while her Majesty's ship *Active* fired minute guns. The officers of the *Active* and the *Boadicea*, as well as of the Dutch men-of-war *Van Galen* and *Silveren Cruis*, which arrived on the previous day, took part in the solemn ceremony. Sir Bartle Frere, Lady Frere, the Hon W. Littleton, Captain Hallam Parr, Colonel Hassard, RE, Mr G. Sprigg, and members of the Cabinet, as well as many other visitors from Cape Town, were present and evinced marked respect, the deep grief of the Governor and Lady Frere being particularly noticeable. When the coffin was placed in the mortuary chapel, Lady Frere laid upon it a handsome cross of palm-leaves and immortelles; and the Misses Frere and Mrs Wright covered the steps with camellias and other beautiful flowers.'

Colonel Pemberton of the 3rd/60th Rifles accompanied the body; Deléage, Uhlmann and Lomas were allowed to travel on the warship.

At that time there was no cable between London and the Cape, so that the story of the death of the Prince Imperial took three weeks to transmit to Madeira, where it was known on 20 June. On 15 June, Eugenie wrote to Lady Sydney:

'I have just had two letters from my son. For the first time I breath at ease, for I see that he is well in health and is in good spirits. I am quite happy today!'

The message that had finally reached Madeira reached England on 20 June. Queen Victoria was at Balmoral; she wrote in her diary:

'At twenty minutes to eleven, Brown knocked and came in and said there was bad news; and when I, in alarm, asked what, he replied, "The young French Prince is killed"; and when I could not take it in, and asked several times what it meant, Beatrice, who then came in with the telegram in her hand, said, "Oh! the Prince Imperial is killed." I put my hands to my head and cried out, "No, no! it cannot, cannot be true! It can't be!" Dear Beatrice crying very much, as I did too, gave me the telegram. We sent for Janie Ely, who was in the house when he was born, and was so devoted to him; and he was so good! Oh, it is too, too awful! The more one thinks of it the worse it is. . . . Got to bed very late; it was dawning, and little sleep did I get. . . .
(Beatrice so distressed; everyone quite stunned.) . . . Had a bad, restless night, haunted by this awful event, seeing those horrid Zulus constantly before me and thinking of the poor Empress who did not yet know it. . . . My accession day, 42 years ago; but no thought of it in presence of this frightful event.'

The Empress had to be spared the horror of reading of her son's fate in the morning newspapers. Travelling by the first train, Lord Sydney, the Lord High Chamberlain, went to Camden Place to break the awful news. He was admitted by the elderly Duc de Bassano, who acknowledged at once that his position as Chamberlain gave him the dread distinction of breaking the news to his Sovereign. The Empress in her dressing-gown admitted him to her room and immediately read tragedy in the old man's agitated face.

'Is my son ill?'

The Duke was unable to answer.

'But . . . speak . . . speak! Is he wounded? I am going out . . . I shall start for Africa at once!'

Still unable to speak, the old man stared despairingly at the Empress and then broke down, burying his face in his hands and sobbing convulsively. Eugenie screamed and sank to the floor in a faint and remained semi-conscious for the next two days, one fainting fit succeeding the other.

Queen Victoria left Balmoral and came south, her thoughts full of self-blame; because she had done everything possible to facilitate the boy's desire to go to Zululand, she felt that she was responsible for this awful calamity. Her journals indicate that she anticipated reproaches from the distraught mother, but that she received none. The Prince and the Empress were guests of England, and the boy had been killed with all her army around to protect him, but they had failed to do so. She longed to make amends; as a woman who had also suffered a tragic loss, the Queen yearned to give the poor Empress the love and kindness that were her right. Without ceremony, Queen Victoria descended on Camden Place on 24 June and swept straight into the Empress's darkened rooms. The meeting comforted Eugenie and helped her to regain her strength so that she could face those duties which circumstances still demanded of her despite her grief. The Queen persuaded her to eat and insisted that the Empress should be attended by her personal physician.

23

For more than a week Lieutenant Carey continued his staff duties under Colonel Harrison.[1] It cannot have been a pleasant period for anyone in Chelmsford's force. Some of the Regular officers were inclined to throw the blame on to Carey; the Irregulars took the practical view that when a small party was surprised by a much larger party of Zulus, then flight was the only sensible course. There was a general undercurrent of thought that Harrison, in the first place, had not taken as much trouble about the patrol as he should have done.

C. L. Norris-Newman, writing of the days that immediately followed the death of the Prince Imperial, said:

'The whole circumstances of the affair . . . became the subject of a good deal of discussion and no little animadversion, even amounting to strong condemnation for pusillanimity in many quarters".[2]

It might have been fear of criticism of this sort, censure of faint-

---

[1] On 2 August 1879 *The Army and Navy Gazette* reported: 'We are in a position to state that an important fact bearing on Captain Carey's case has been brought to the knowledge of the Horse Guards. They were not hitherto aware of it, and naturally admit that it is one of grave moment. The last letter which Captain Carey's family have received from him is dated 10 pm on June 10th, and in it he says that he had been out that day on a reconnaissance, and was by Lord Chelmsford's side when Lieutenant Frith of the 17th Lancers was killed. This fact proves that up to within a few hours of his trial, which commenced on June 11, Captain Carey, remained, and was employed on, the Staff. The Prince Imperial was killed on June 1, the Court of Inquiry was held, we believe, on the 3rd, and was finished on the 4th or 5th. (Note: It was actually held on the 11th June, 1879). Thus, though Lord Chelmsford was, during five or six days, aware of all the grounds for a charge against Captain Carey, he did not even suspend him from duty as an officer of the Quartermaster-General's Department. This was clearly legal condonation, because the authority who ordered the trial was aware of all the facts of the case, and therefore impliedly pardoned him. Under these circumstances, we fail to see how the Judge-Advocate-General can do otherwise than pronounce the trial null and void.'

It is difficult to reconcile this account with that of the death of Lieutenant

heartedness, that persuaded Carey to ask for a Court of Inquiry. It is interesting to consider what the course of events might have been had he not so asked; he was not suspended from duty as an officer of the Quartermaster-General's Department until the actual day of the Court of Inquiry. A letter written on 10 June by Carey to his wife indicates that he had confidence in his cause and in his ability to defend himself against whatever charges were made.

'I now find that there were thirty men against us or thereabouts —some say, sixty. It was a complete surprise. Zulus are certainly treacherous. I am afraid I shall get into a row about it, but my conscience is clear. No effort of mine could have saved the Prince, though perhaps I ought to have attempted it, but my horse was nearly done and could scarcely carry me. The Zulus were turning our flanks and the horses of two men appeared fagged, and a river full of quicksands was in our rear, therefore under the circumstances I considered it necessary to find the drift over it to secure our retreat.

'Everyone is very kind about it, so I must bear up, but I can never forget the 1st June, 3.50 afternoon.

'I have asked for a Court of Inquiry, and it sits to-morrow, General Marshall as president. I shall get wigged for the positions I took up, but trust nothing more. I may be tried by Court Martial, but I trust in my cause as it is good. I certainly told the Prince I considered the kraal safe, and I did too. . . . This is a fearful business, but I do not fret, though at times I get very miserable. I do so long for the whole thing to be over. I get so done up with hard work that I can only throw myself on the ground and sleep sometimes. And now my own one, my true little wife, my own darling, kiss our Mama and our darling children.

'Yours own miserable husband.

'When I first received the Zulu fire, I felt Edie's prayers would save me! If I had been hit I must have been assegaied, or if any more horses had been shot. That was the reason why I desisted from attacking them or losing time.'

Frederick John Cokayne Frith, 17th Lancers, on 5 June 1879, given by Donald R. Morris on pages 551–2 of *The Washing of the Spears* (1966). Not only is there a difference in dates, but neither is there any mention of Lord Chelmsford or Lieutenant Carey being present.

[2] C. L. Norris-Newman *In Zululand With the British Throughout the War of 1879* (1880).

The Court of Inquiry sat on the following day; it consisted of Major-General Marshall as President; with Colonel Malthus of the 94th Regiment and Major L. Grice, RA, as members. Statements were taken from the survivors of the patrol and from Colonel Harrison. It became obvious that there was a direct conflict of opinion between Lieutenant Carey and Colonel Harrison. The junior officer contended that he had not been in command of the patrol, that, at his own request, he was permitted to accompany the Prince but had been specially ordered not to interfere with him in any way. Colonel Harrison, for his part, stated that although he gave Lieutenant Carey no orders to command the escort he was the senior combatant officer present, and therefore by the Queen's Regulations the command of the whole party would rest on him. He said that he was glad that Lieutenant Carey had volunteered to go out to look after the Prince; had Lieutenant Carey not volunteered, he would have sent another staff officer for this purpose. If the Prince had been the senior officer of the party, he would naturally have commanded it; but the position the Prince held on the staff was as Colonel Harrison's assistant. Lieutenant Carey and the Prince were performing similar duties in this department. Lieutenant Carey, having charge of the Prince, would not have been justified in leaving him entirely during the course of the reconnaissance. Colonel Harrison's written instructions, given to the Prince, were lost with him. Had Lieutenant Carey gone out alone, a similar escort would have been detailed for him.

Harrison was adamant in claiming that when the Prince was put under his orders, he had received no instructions to regard him as a Royal personage in the matter of escorts, but to treat him as any other officer, taking all due precautions.

Harrison related how he had met the Prince and Lieutenant Carey riding out with six troopers and a native guide, not waiting for the six mounted Basutos who should have joined them to complete the escort. He claimed that he was preoccupied by other matters, and that although he did notice that the Basutos were not escorting, their absence did not seem important. He agreed to the party going on, telling them that the cavalry was coming up and could act as support.[3]

[3] True, the cavalry were on the march and scouting in front and flanks of the division. They would probably prospect several miles in advance of the new camp, on the ridge where Colonel Harrison and the Prince were conversing, but it is difficult to see how they could have covered a patrol penetrating eight or ten miles beyond the site of that camp.

The Court of Inquiry into the circumstances of the Prince Imperial's death, assembled at Lieutenant Carey's request, made the following report:

'The Court is of opinion that Lieutenant Carey did not understand the position in which he stood towards the Prince, and as a consequence failed to estimate aright the responsibility which fell to his lot.

'Colonel Harrison states that the senior combatant officer, Lieutenant Carey, Deputy Assistant Quartermaster General, was, as a matter of course, in charge of the party; whilst on the other hand Carey says, when alluding to the escort, "I did not consider I had any authority over it, after the precise and careful instructions of Lord Chelmsford as to the position the Prince held."

'As to his being invariably accompanied by an escort in charge of an officer, the Court considers that the possibility of such a difference of opinion should not have existed between two officers of the same department.

'The Court is of opinion that Carey is much to blame for having proceeded on the duty in question with a portion only of the escort detailed by Colonel Harrison. The Court cannot admit the irresponsibility for this on the part of Carey, inasmuch as he took steps to obtain the escort and failed in so doing; moreover, the fact that Harrison was present upon the Itelezi range gave to him the opportunity of consulting him on the matter, of which he failed to avail himself.

'The Court, having examined the ground, is of opinion that the selection of the kraal where the halt was made and the horses off-saddled, surrounded as it was by cover for an enemy, and adjacent to difficult ground, showed a lamentable want of military prudence.

'The Court deeply regrets that no effort was made, after the attack, to rally the escort, and to show a front to the enemy, whereby the possibility of aiding those who had failed to make good their retreat might have been ascertained.'

Signed by General Marshall,
Colonel Malthus,
Major Le Grice.

Inevitably, a trial by Field General Court Martial was recommended, and a court was convened to meet on the following day, 12 June 1879, in the camp at Upoko River. The indictment read:

'For having misbehaved before the enemy on June 1st, when in command of an escort in attendance on the Prince Imperial, who was making a reconnaissance in Zululand; in having, when the said Prince and escort were attacked by the enemy, galloped away, and in not having attempted to rally the said escort or in other ways defend the said Prince.'

24

T HE officer, Lieutenant J. B. Carey, 98th Regiment, was tried on a charge of misbehaviour before the enemy, for having on June 1, 1879, when in command of an escort on the Prince Imperial, who was engaged in a reconnaissance, galloped away when surprised by the Zulus, without attempting to defend the Prince or to rally the escort. The Court was composed of Colonel Glynn, CB, President, Lieutenant-Colonel Whitehead, 58th Regiment, Colonel Harness, RA, Captain Courtney, RE, and Captain Bouverie, 17th Lancers. Major Anstruther, 94th Regiment, was officiating Judge Advocate, and Captain Brander, of the 2/24th, the prosecutor. Captain Brander said he proposed to bring evidence in support of the charge against the prisoner which would fully explain the whole occurrence connected with the death of the Prince, from the moment of the arrival at the kraal on the banks of the Ityotyozi River on the 1st June. He would first submit a plan of the kraal and the adjacent dongas, adducing evidence of their correctness, and showing also the position of the bodies when discovered the next morning. He would next call the survivors of the escort, who would give a full account of the nature of the ground, and the precautions taken before, and subsequently, by the prisoner. He would then call the Assistant Quartermaster-General, to prove that Carey was in command of the party, and lastly produce evidence of the cause of death.

'Captain A. W. Morris, of the 58th Regiment, was then called, and produced a sketch about a foot square, showing the relative positions of the kraal and dongas, or rather donga with several branches. He spoke as to its correctness, as he had been ordered, with Lieutenant Nuttall, of the 58th, to make the sketch, except as regarded the position of the bodies, which had been removed, but the places from which they had been taken had been shown to him by Captain Molyneux, Aide-de-Camp. In cross-examination, the prisoner elicited that the sketch, which was a copy of an original taken for the Court of Inquiry, which had at once assembled by command of Lord Chelmsford, had the north and south points improperly marked, that marked "N" being south, and *vice versa*. Lieutenant Nuttall, 58th, gave confirmatory evidence.

'Captain Molyneux, Aide-de-Camp to Lord Chelmsford, said he was directed by his Lordship to accompany General Marshall and the party who went in search of the body of the Prince Imperial. He could identify the spot "A" on the plan as being that where the body of the Prince was found, but not the other points, as he had only casually noticed the bodies of the two troopers, and then had gone to where the body of the Prince lay, and his duty being to take care of that, he had remained by it; and had, on the 4th, pointed out to Captain Morris what, to the best of his belief, was the position of the other two. Cross-examined by the prisoner, he said the Prince was attached to the personal Staff of Lord Chelmsford without having any particular grade assigned him. He was not aide-de-camp. He did anything he was told, and at times performed duties under the Assistant Quartermaster-General, but he was not considered as an officer handed over entirely to that department. Beyond what he had stated, he had no idea what position the Prince held. He had never been gazetted to any particular position.

'Corporal Grubb, of Bettington's Natal Horse, was next called. He said—I was one of the escort on the 1st of June. When we arrived at the kraal the Prince gave the word to off-saddle and let our horses out. The native guide, I, and Le Tocq cooked some coffee. I then went away for a few minutes to the back of one of the huts, and when I came back I heard the Prince say, "At four o'clock we will go." The native guide then came in and reported that he had seen a Zulu come over the hill. We got the order then directly to stand to our horses. I caught mine and saddled. The Prince then gave the commands, "Prepare to mount," and "Mount." He mounted along with us, and I took the time from him. I had not time to get my right foot into the stirrup before a volley was fired into us. I had my head over on the right side trying to get my stirrup. I turned my eyes, and saw Lieutenant Carey put spurs to his horse. I think all did the same. I know I did. As we were galloping between the kraal and the donga, I heard a bullet come "whiz" up, and it struck something,

I cannot say what; but I saw Trooper Abel throw up his arms and fall back. He was riding not more than half a horse's length ahead of me. Trooper Rogers, when I last saw him, was running round the kraal, with his head stooped down, and presenting his carbine at one of the Zulus, who was about fifteen yards off. After Trooper Abel fell, I galloped a few horses' lengths, when Trooper Le Tocq passed me. He said, "Stick firm to your horse, boy, and put in the spurs; the Prince is down." I glanced round, and saw the Prince hanging to something, but below his horse, the stirrup-leather, or the wallet; and the horse seemed to trample on him. I steadied my horse and unslung my carbine to have a shot at them, when my horse jumped into the donga, and threw me on to his neck. I was obliged to let my carbine drop to cling to the horse. With some difficulty I got back to the saddle, and when I had gone on about six horses' lengths, I saw the Prince's horse alongside of me. I tried to catch him, but I could not, so I drove it before me, and as I cantered along, it followed. I was away rather down to the right, and on turning my head round saw Lieutenant Carey, Le Tocq, and Cochrane a hundred yards away on my left front. I beckoned them to stop, and after a short time I drew up with them. It was then said that someone would have to ride the Prince's horse, and I told Lieutenant Carey that my horse was fagged and I would ride him. Then we all rode on together till we met General Wood and Colonel Buller. Lieutenant Carey reported to them the death of the Prince, and they went to the brow of the hill, and I heard Colonel Buller say that he saw six Zulus leading away four horses. After staying there a little while we all rode together towards General Wood's camp for three or four miles, when we turned off to the left and got to our own camp about seven or half-past seven. Lieutenant Carey reported the circumstances to Lord Chelmsford. We all went together, and I gave up the Prince's horse to his groom. I saw fresh marks of Kaffirs at the kraal, for there were heaps of the peel of infi (Kaffir sugar-cane) which they had been eating. I do not think the precautions taken for safety were sufficient. Lieutenant Carey led the party at the moment of flight. I saw Rogers try to get away or to have a shot at the enemy, but I am not sure which, for I passed him in a moment. He was not mounted, for he had been looking for a spare horse which was missing. I did not see the Prince after he had been apparently trampled on by his horse. No orders were given as to rallying or firing on the enemy.

131

'In cross-examination by the prisoner, the witness said there had been differences of opinion between the Prince and Lieutenant Carey as to off-saddling, long before going to the kraal. While still on the hill leading from the camp overlooking the kraal, the Prince gave the word to off-saddle, and then altered his mind and ordered the girths to be slackened for fifteen minutes. The Prince said, "It is hardly worth while to off-saddle for a quarter of an hour; we will go down to the huts by the river, where the men can get wood and water and cook something." There were six troopers, the native guide, Lieutenant Carey, and the Prince in the party but I do not know who was in command. There were not many words of command given during the day, but the Prince gave the word of command, "Stand to your horses." I was told by my sergeant-major I was going to escort the Prince, not the Prince and Lieutenant Carey. I cannot describe the relative positions of myself, the Prince and Lieutenant Carey, except that they were all over the place. The Prince was three or four yards from me. I was not facing the line of retreat, and the grass was so long that I do not know what I was facing. After the volley I glanced round and saw the Zulus were within ten or twelve yards, and were advancing. I should think they were from forty to fifty in number at a rough guess. I was not quite in command of my horse, for I could not turn him when I wanted, having no curb. I did not notice the prisoner's horse was fagged, but he was sweating. I saw the Prince was riding a very good horse—much better than anyone else. I do not recollect reporting seeing the infi peels. Rogers had lost his own horse, and was endeavouring to catch a spare one when I saw him last. When I got out of the kraal a little way I saw Zulus on our left, trying to surround us. I was six to eight yards from the Prince when I saw him clinging to his horse; it was not far from the donga. It was more than five minutes after that before I mentioned to any one that the Prince was down. The native guide did not seem to show any alarm when he reported a Zulu coming over the hill; he took it very quietly. I cannot answer for the others, but certainly I was taken by surprise at the attack. Every one seemed to gallop away from the kraal at the same time. I did not notice anything remarkable in your behaviour during the affair, except that you hardly seemed to believe the Prince's death when it was reported. I had not to pass the Prince in my flight. I was a little ahead of him. He was on my right. I galloped away because we all did. Lieutenant Carey, myself, and Le Tocq left the kraal by the left side; the other two men by the right, but I do not know who went first. The Prince's horse was saddled, and there was no reason to prevent his mounting. I do not think we could do anything else than gallop away from the kraal. If we had remained and fired there, in my opinion, we should all have been killed. I am an old soldier of the Royal Artillery, and have seen sixteen years' service and served in Beltini's Land and against Langalabalele. At the moment of the volley we had not time to look after each other. There was quick firing when we left the kraal, and I think if we had lost any time we should all have been killed. The Zulus were about forty to fifty in number, and were firing as we left. I did not see Le Tocq dismount from his horse. I did not see him till we got up the hill. If a man fell from his horse between the kraal and the donga he would have had no chance of escaping. No help could have been rendered by us to the Prince. I cannot say we all had an equal chance of escape as we left the kraal, for I do not know the position of the men left behind me. When I saw the Prince followed by Zulus they were ten or twelve yards behind; I was on the far side of the donga, about fifty or sixty yards off. Lieutenant Carey was then close alongside me. Nothing could have been done then to save the Prince's life; they were too close on him. I reported seeing this, but not till some time afterwards. I do not remember Lieutenant Carey asking me if there was any chance of saving his life by returning; I noticed nothing unusual in his conduct. I think I mentioned to him when I saw Zulus on our left, but there would have been no object then in getting us all together and firing on them. I do not know who was in command; no one gave any commands except the Prince to saddle-up and mount. I saw nothing of the native guide after the volley. We usually followed the Prince without word of command.

'Sergeant Robert Willis : I was present on the 1st June at the attack on the Prince Imperial. I did not see him on foot after it began. We got no orders as to rallying or firing on the enemy. No attempt was made to help the Prince by any one. I was not surprised, for I do not think any rescue could have been made. If I had been in command of the party I should have got my men together to confront the enemy when clear of the donga. I think we could have rallied about 200 yards from the side of the donga and yet made good our escape. The escort was six troopers and a native, and there were two officers. I do not know who was in command, but I think it was the Prince. I am not certain.

'Cross-examined by the prisoner : The Prince and Lieutenant

133

Carey were both engaged in sketching. I cannot say how we were standing, as I had two horses to look after; but we had got the word to mount, and were mounting, when the volley was poured in and the Zulus rushed out with a yell. I had got into the saddle, and to the best of my knowledge every one was mounted. I and a trooper left the kraal last, except the native, who was behind all. The Prince had left the kraal then. I saw two men fall from their horses before I got to the donga. The Prince's horse followed and passed me, but I only got a glance, as my foot was not in the stirrup, and I had enough to do to keep on. On crossing the donga I got firm in the saddle. On leaving I saw Trooper Rogers lying motionless against a hut, with his horse by him. I do not know whether he was shot or assegaied. It was not Rogers and the native that I saw fall from their horses. I thought that Rogers was shot. I did not see the place where Rogers' body was found. It must have been moved by the Zulus, who do not like dead bodies about a kraal. I believe he was dead when I left him. The two men I saw fall from their horses; whether they were properly mounted or not I cannot say. This was between the kraal and the donga; but I cannot fix the position. I know now the two men were the Prince and Trooper Abel. Neither of the men who fell had any chance of getting away, and nothing could have been done to save them, for the numbers of the Zulus were too great, and they were too close behind us. A man who lost his balance was done. We could do nothing but gallop from the kraal, for when they fired they were only three yards off. I had no command over my horse for 300 yards on the other side of the donga. We could not be rallied between the kraal and the donga. We were in two parties when over the donga, three in front, and Grubb and I behind. He mounted on the Prince's horse, and that delayed us. Corporal Grubb was not riding his own horse when he rejoined Lieutenant Carey. Grubb's horse was knocked up, and mine was very tired, when we got to the top of the hills. I noticed numbers of Zulus on our left in the mealies after crossing the donga. Though we could have rallied the men two hundred yards beyond the donga, we could have done no good then. I know no attempt was made to rescue the Prince, for all the men got out in front of me. From the number of shots fired at the attack, I think the Zulus with firearms must have been from forty to fifty. The firing was very rapid. The escort, by being rallied, could not, in my opinion, have defended the Prince. I was in charge of the escort till they joined Lieutenant

Carey and the Prince, as I was the senior non-commissioned officer. I thought we were sent for the protection of the Prince and Lieutenant Carey. I was not told that any one in particular was to command the escort.

'Cross-examined by the prosecutor: I reported to Lieutenant Carey on joining. I was ordered to report to the Cavalry Staff Officer, and Lieutenant Long, of my regiment, gave me a paper, which I gave to Lieutenant Carey; he returned it to me, and I gave it back to Captain Bettington.

'Colonel Harrison, AQMG, said: I gave prisoner no orders as to the command of the escort. The senior combatant officer would be in command of the whole party by the Queen's Regulations. Gave him no special orders as senior combatant officer, for I did not know who was the senior officer—Captain Bettington might have gone—not having seen the escort; but when Lieutenant Carey volunteered to go I said, to the best of my belief, "I am glad you are a volunteer, for you can now look after the Prince." If he had not gone, I should have directed some other officer of the Staff to go for that purpose.

'Cross-examined by the prisoner: I believe you volunteered to accompany the Prince to verify some work done previously. I might have said at first, "No, I want you to stay behind and finish the map"; and you may have pressed the point. If the Prince had been senior to you he would naturally have been in command, unless there had been some officer senior to him in the escort. I cannot remember, without referring to my journal, whether you have ever been alone with the Prince before on any duty. (On referring, Colonel Harrison said, To the best of my belief, No.) The Prince had only been a few days on my Staff. The prisoner and the Prince were performing similar duties. It would depend upon the distance whether the prisoner would be justified in leaving the escort to verify any part of the road. He would not have been justified in leaving the escort altogether, because I had entrusted him with the charge of the Prince. I have already stated the words in which I gave the prisoner charge of the Prince. The prisoner and the Prince were doing different work on the same road, prisoner verifying work already done, and the Prince making a more detailed report of the road for the march of the troops. The Prince had orders to choose a camp on the Ityotyozi River, which was on the road. If the prisoner had been alone the same escort would, under similar circumstances, have been detailed for him. When the Prince was put under my orders, I

135

was instructed in the matter of escort to treat him, not as a Royal personage, but the same as any other officer, taking all due precautions. My written instructions to the Prince were lost with him.

'Surgeon-Major Scott was next called. He said : At the request of Lord Chelmsford, in company with Captain Molyneux, ADC, I went with the cavalry brigade to search for the body of the Prince Imperial. When approaching near to the kraal where I was told he and his party had off-saddled, I, in company with Captain Molyneux, went ahead of the line of scouts, and, guided by one of the troopers of the escort of the previous day, I went down into a field and saw the body of one of the troopers with two or three men looking on. Finding it was not that of the Prince, I went in a backward direction, my attention being called there by another crowd, and I found there another body, but not that of the Prince. After that my attention was drawn by a shout, which turned out to be from Captain Cochrane, of the Natal Native Cavalry. I went to where he was standing by the body of his Imperial Highness. To the best of my belief his body had not been moved before I got there—that is, the body had not been dragged after death. He died, in my opinion, where I found him. He was lying on his back with the left arm across, in a position of self-defence. I counted eighteen assegai wounds, all in front. It is true there were two wounds found on his back, but from their nature I am satisfied that they were the terminations of wounds inflicted in front. Any one of five of the wounds would have proved mortal. There were no bullet wounds. I believe the body was not moved for two reasons—first, because the body of the second trooper lay on the slope of a branch of the donga a little higher up, and I saw that he had been killed at some distance, and dragged into the donga. The other reason is that there were no abrasions on the body of the Prince indicating that he had been dragged. There was a patch of blood underneath the head and neck, caused, apparently, by a wound he received on the side of the neck, and also by a wound through the right eyeball. The body was stripped, except a fine gold chain round the neck, with a medallion and locket of his mother, which he wore next the skin. In the struggle they had got behind, and seem to have escaped the notice of the Zulus.

'Cross-examined by the prisoner : Captain Molyneux, who was with me, directed my attention to the signs of a struggle about the spot, and the Prince's spurs were twisted. He might have been carried after death before being undressed, but he could not have been dragged.

'This closed the case for the prosecution. The prisoner announced that he intended to call a few witnesses, and pleaded that he had been punished already by suspension from Staff employment for the offence with which he was charged. This, however, the Court held to be no bar to subsequent trial by court-martial, the Queen's Regulations being precise on this point.

'Colonel Harrison, RE, AQMG, being called by the prisoner, said he had no fault to find with the prisoner, who had always done his duty while in the department to his entire satisfaction. He had seen, in orders on the 11th instant, that the prisoner had been removed from Staff employ. That was not done at his request or by his knowledge. He regarded the Prince as a civilian attached to the Staff. He was not aware that he had any status in the British army.

'Captain Bettington, in command of Bettington's Horse, being asked his opinion of the character of the four survivors of the escort, said, as far as character went, two of them, Cochrane and Grubb, had only once been in the orderly room during six months' service, and then for a trivial offence. The other two had not been up at all. He had no reason for discrediting any of their statements; they were four of the most trustworthy men he had got.

'Colonel Bellairs being called, said, the order removing Lieutenant Carey, dated 11th of June, was in consequence of the events of the 1st of June.

'The Court then adjourned to give the prisoner time to prepare his defence.

'Colonel W. Bellairs, DAG, was recalled, and said the events of the 1st of June, to which he had referred, were the circumstances of which the Court of Inquiry had taken cognisance, *viz*, the death of Prince Napoleon; and, in consequence of the opinion given by the Court, prisoner had been summarily removed from Staff employ, having previously been ordered to be tried by court-martial.

'The prisoner said he hoped that statement would remove any bias the present Court might receive from such removal, supposing it to be from some other cause.

'Prisoner asked that Colonel Bellairs might produce his report and rough sketch made on the night of June 1st, to which the Court assented.

'Witness said he could not specify any special circumstances of the 1st of June, for which the prisoner had been removed. He could only speak generally that the prisoner was removed by the Lieutenant-General on account of the report of the Court of Inquiry, he having power of selecting and removing at pleasure.

'Captain Herbert Stewart, 5th DG, Brigade Major Survey Brigade, was next called by the prisoner, and said that as senior officer of the prisoner's batch at the Staff College he had formed a very good opinion of him as a most conscientious, hard working officer. Witness knew of three kraals in the neighbourhood of the spot where the Prince's body was found within a radius of three-quarters of a mile, and a number of others towards the Emshlanwan Hill within a radius of two or three miles. From the kraals on the west, if inhabited, the Zulus could have assembled around the party in a few minutes, and from one on the east side. From the other kraals in from half an hour to an hour.

'Cross-examined by the Court: The kraals were burnt after the Prince's death, with the exception of one to the west, which he believed was not burnt yet.

'Trooper Cochrane was recalled, to bring before the Court that the escort were armed with carbines only, swords not being a part of the regular cavalry equipment.

'At the next sitting of the Court the prisoner said he had then to address them in his defence against as serious a charge as any which could be brought against an officer, for the interpretation of misbehaviour before an enemy could only be cowardice. Before proceeding to the evidence he must ask the Court to dismiss from their minds any bias which they might have received from his having been dismissed from employment on the Staff. However deplorable might be the death of the Prince, and no one regretted it more than himself, for he would willingly have changed places with the Prince, yet he should assume if he was guilty he should have been equally guilty if, by his conduct, he had caused the death of the humblest soldier of the force. The escort was said to be under his charge, but such charge had never been put upon him, and he believed he was accompanying the Prince Imperial as a brother officer of junior rank, performing similar duties. At the same time he recognised that, whether senior or junior, it was his duty to do all in his power to rescue the Prince from his perilous position, and he hoped to show that he had done so. Proceeding then to review the evidence, he showed that the witnesses concurred in saying that after crossing the donga the survivors had pulled up to a walk; and that disposed of the charge

138

of galloping away. It was true that they had galloped away from the immediate vicinity of the kraal, but that he contended was the only reasonable course open to them, and as to deserting the Prince he had seen him last with his left foot in the stirrup and his hands on the saddle, and the fair inference was that he had mounted with the rest on giving the word of command. At that instant the volley was fired, and the Zulus with a shout rushed out on them, frightening the horses. A hut was between him and the Prince Imperial, and they passed it on different sides, and that prevented him from seeing the Prince leave the kraal. The evidence showed that from forty to fifty Zulus attacked them, and that they came up in numbers on the left, and that fourteen were seen following the Prince in the donga, and the evidence of Captain Stewart proved that they were thick in the neighbourhood. With such proof of superior force about, and with the belief that the Prince was mounted, it was his duty, he conceived, for the sake of the rest of the party, seeing that they were under a heavy fire, with the enemy shouting and rushing upon them, to consider their safety; but the fact was that a rush took place, and in that rush he was carried away. That the Prince rode away with the rest he thought there could be little doubt, and once mounted, he was justified in considering the Prince had as good a chance of safety as any of them, considering the superior character of his horse. It was only the witness Grubb who said that he led the flight; every other witness said that all left together. His own impression was that two men rushed past him, and all left together. It might be said, why not rally at the kraal and charge the enemy? But was such a course possible when there were but six men with unloaded carbines, no swords, and the horses bolting along across an unknown country? He contended it was not, and that there was no course open to them except to bolt from the kraal. He was next charged with not rallying the escort between the donga and the kraal. He had not done this because he had judged it at the time to be impossible; he had shouted at the time to every one to keep to the left, because he wished to direct them, knowing the country better than the men, to the best place for collecting. The charge was of so general a nature that the whole *onus probandi* was thrown upon him as regards the possibility and utility of doing so at all. He would, however, address himself to both points. With regard to the possibility of rallying between the kraal and the donga, they might reflect for a moment on the evidence of Le Tocq, who passing Grubb urged him to spur faster, as the Prince was ┄┄┄ nd Zulus upon them, while he himself was riding on his ┄┄┄ in the saddle, and could only recover his seat when ove ┄┄┄ . Sergean Willis's horse had bolted with him, and he ┄┄┄ ve rallie on the kraal side of the donga. Grubb said ┄┄┄ othing but gallop till far beyond the donga, and all ┄┄┄ concurred in saying that they considered any attempt ┄┄┄ the kraal side of the donga as utterly useless, and he at ┄┄┄ e had to deal with the facts of long grass, an advancing e. ┄┄┄ frightened horses, and scattered men, and with the Prince no ┄┄┄ sight, nor was he told of his fate until long after, so that he was under the impression he had got away, while all the while the Zulus were pursuing hotly on the left. They, however, soon walked their horses, and then he, as surviving officer, came to the conclusion of the rest of the party as to the impossibility of doing anything for the rescue of the Prince. With regard to the futility of rallying, all the witnesses agreed that nothing could have been done to save the Prince's life, and it then became his duty to take the steps necessary to save the rest of the escort. He had, therefore, shouted to the rest of the men to join him, and he asked the Court to consider the position he was in, with four men scattered and disorganised, out of reach of fire on the donga, Zulus seen everywhere and still rushing forward, and with nothing seen on the right but a riderless grey horse. Judging from the rapidity of fire, which all the witnesses confirmed, he saw no reason to doubt then that the Prince must have been shot off his horse. Considering, then, his duty with regard to the rest of the escort, he had called them to join him. When he had learnt the truth with regard to the Prince, the Zulus had already passed the spot where he had been last seen by the only witness who had seen him in the donga, and he thought any one who was present could have come to no other conclusion than he and the witnesses had come to, *viz*, that nothing could be done then to save the Prince. He thought the Court would be of opinion that the evidence proved he had been calm and collected, and he hoped they would believe that he had acted under very difficult and perilous circumstances in the best way for the safety of the party. No one more deeply regretted than himself the loss of the Prince, but he honestly believed that no effort of his would have saved his Highness's life.

'At the prisoner's wish the report he made on the night of the 1st June was put in and read. Its main points were that the escort ought to have had, in addition to the six white troopers of

140

Bettington's Horse, six Basutos, who, however, had never joined; that the prisoner had differed with the Prince as to the place for off-saddling, he desiring to remain on the ridge, while the Prince insisted on going nearer the river; that he had suggested saddling-up at thirty-five minutes past three pm, but the Prince said wait ten minutes longer, though in five minutes more he had given the order to stand to their horses. The report said that the prisoner heard the order given to mount, and at the same time saw the Prince's foot in the stirrup, and a number of black faces come rushing up behind the troopers, within twenty yards of them; and at the time of the volley he did not think any one was wounded, on account of previous experience of the bad shooting of the Zulus. It concluded by announcing the loss of the Prince, two white troopers, a native, and five horses missing.

'For the prosecution, Captain Brander, in summing up, first dealt with the question of the command of the escort, asserting that there was no ground for the prisoner trying to evade that responsibility, seeing that Captain Molyneux's evidence showed the Prince to have no status in the British Army, and therefore no authority over any of Her Majesty's officers or men. Colonel Harrison, RE, also showed that he had specially charged the prisoner with the duty of looking after the Prince, showing that the Prince had been committed to his special care, and that the charge was well founded. The prisoner himself had admitted that it was his duty to rescue the Prince, and he had gone on to say that he hoped to convince the Court he had done what he could; but he had utterly failed to do so, and for the very good reason that nothing had been done whatever. All had galloped away, and the evidence of Grubb went to show that the prisoner had put spurs to his horse and was the first man to start after the volley. No orders had been given to rally or fire, though Le Tocq said that after getting seven hundred yards away they might have done so, and yet got away. Cochrane's evidence showed that no attempt had been made to help the Prince, and he expressed surprise that it was not done. The prisoner had no right to take credit for saving any of the escort, for it had been a clear case of each man for himself. It was shown by the evidence that the Prince had been seen in the donga, so that he had been able to run two hundred and fifty yards after the vanishing horsemen; and yet nothing had been done, and he had been left to his death by a party of men armed with breechloading rifles, who had not fired a shot in defence. Only Le Tocq, who had dismounted to get his rifle,

141

and Rogers, who was seen taking aim at the kraal, had come well out of the affair. As to the possibility of rallying, the evidence of Sergeant Willis and of Le Tocq showed that it was quite possible to rally on the further side of donga, while it was there that Grubb had caught the Prince's horse. It was the prisoner's duty after passing the hut to see that the Prince was mounted or not, and that he was safe. He had not done so, and it was for the Court to decide whether the evidence did not establish the words of the charge—that the prisoner had been guilty of misbehaviour before the enemy.

'The Officiating Judge Advocate also summed up against the prisoner, enforcing the points referred to by the prosecutor, and the Court was then cleared to consider their sentence.'[1]

The Court sat for two days and then closed to consider its findings. It was later reopened to take formal evidence as to the prisoner's service—this was the usual sign that a verdict of guilty had been returned.

Lieutenant Carey was reported as facing the Court with coolness —partisan biographers of the Prince Imperial claim that he disgusted everyone by appearing quite unconcerned! In his book *The Prince Imperial* (London, 1959), E. E. P. Tisdall gives a highly coloured version of the scene :

'The prisoner, perceiving that the members of the Court were puzzled and uneasy on account of the conflicting evidence of the survivors, each man striving to clear himself, had the boldness to assert, "I did everything possible under the circumstances to save the Prince."

'But Carey's bland declaration was a mistake. At once the Court, divided on several points, turned against him. All believed he had been panic-stricken, even if they were unsure of the

---

[1] To this point, the proceedings have been taken, in their entirety, from Appendix 'H', p 301 *et seq* of the book by C. L. Norris-Newman, *In Zululand with the British throughout the War of 1879* (1880).

The particular copy of this book was seen in the War Office Library, London; written in longhand across the top of p 301 is the following:

'The original proceedings of the Court-martial destroyed (26-Records A-2441 refers). The Judge-Advocate-General's Summary and Recommendations are preserved at the Public Record Office, London, in WA 91/48 and are not open to the public until the year 1979.'

Previous enquiries at the Public Record Office had elicited the non-availability until 1979 of these documents and a subsequent request to the Ministry of Defence for their release was refused (D/DPR/233/2/95 (DRO(AD)) of 27 February 1967 refers).

measure of his military guilt. He was a brazen liar, and the prosecutor immediately arose.

' ". . . You did absolutely nothing !" he snapped, and heads almost perceptibly nodded in agreement. The air was full of anger round the President's table." '[2]

Handling his own defence competently, Carey obviously felt that he had a good case with a better-than-average chance of acquittal. However, the Court closed without being able to publish its findings and sentence until they had been reviewed by the authorities; and Carey was sent under arrest to England. Except by the fact that he was being returned home, Carey had no way of telling what his judges had decided. Knowing that the war was nearing its end, Carey asked to be allowed to remain and fight until it was over. His request was refused. Before he left the force, Carey wrote the following letter to Major Grenfell:

'My Dear Major,

'I return you the residue of the foolscap with very many thanks. Kindly let me know what I am indebted to you for my share of messing. I cannot close without thanking you from the bottom of my heart for all your sympathy in my trial. My military career is now closed but I can never forget your sympathy, even on the night of the 1st June. Five superior officers have found me guilty,

---

[2] *The Army and Navy Gazette*, 26 July 1879, criticises Captain Brander, the prosecutor:

'. . . seems to have been under the mistaken idea that it was his duty to do his utmost to procure the conviction of the prisoner. This may be the idea of a barrister, but it certainly has not hitherto been the impression of the British officers.'

On 2 August, in the same journal, the following letter appeared: 'To the Editor of *The Army and Navy Gazette*.

'Sir—May I be permitted to notice a remark in the leader in *The Army and Navy Gazette* on Capt Carey, to the effect that "a barrister might have deemed it his duty to endeavour to bring about the conviction of the prisoner?" Now I have always endeavoured to explain to officers that this is the great military error, and I have laid down the following rule in my little book on *Military Law*, "when a prisoner is undefended, it is the duty of the prosecutor to ask questions of witnesses favourable to the prisoner, for his duty is to lay all material evidence before the court," and it is to be wished that this were more constantly attended to by military prosecutors. The drawing-up of the charges by the temporary deputy judge-advocate and the conduct of the prosecutor is, to say the least, most characteristic of unfairness and ignorance. I am, etc,

'H. B. Franklyn, LLD, Barrister-at-Law.
'Middle Temple, July 29.'

but to the end of my Life, though I bow to their decision, I cannot think that I could have done anything else.

'Kindly say goodbye to Colonel Buller and Colonel Harrison for me and tender my sincere apologies for having so bothered them at my trial—I could do nothing else and wanted Colonel Harrison's evidence to clear myself.

'Forgive my bothering you and believe me,

'Yours very sincerely,

'J. Brenton Carey.'

Two interesting points arise from this short letter—first, it seems clear that Grenfell, at least, felt sympathy for Carey. Second, although he is not mentioned in the only-available proceedings of the Court-Martial, it would appear that Colonel Redvers Buller was called as a witness. Apparently, we must wait until 1979 for Buller's true version of the meeting between himself and General Evelyn Wood and the fugitives.

Lieutenant Carey was shipped home on HMS *Euphrates*, tran-shipping to the Indian troopship, *Jumna*. Although the findings and the sentence arrived in England four weeks before Carey did they were not made public, thus causing the wildest conjecture. One much-repeated rumour had it that he had been found guilty on all charges and sentenced to death! Reporting these rumours, *The Times* of 23 August said:

'. . . though this story did not meet with credence among well-informed and intelligent persons, it is possible that it may have been believed abroad. The finding and the sentence of such a court-martial had no validity till they have been reviewed and confirmed by the superior authorities at home . . . who have power not only to alter or remit the punishment, but to determine whether the conclusions of the court, both in respect of facts and of law, were justified.'

25

THE news of the Prince's death horrified the people of Britain far more than did the news of Isandhlwana, where 900 Europeans and 500 Natal kaffirs were killed. Filling the newspapers day after day, its facets were considered and re-considered, and it became the most discussed event of the year.

Shouting newspaper boys sold special editions in the streets of Paris. Hearing them, old Filon, the Prince's tutor, lying ill and almost blind, grew worried, but he was calmed by the lie that it was the Prince of Orange who had been killed. For two months neighbours stopped the newsboys at either end of the street; then Filon regained his sight; he saw his wife dressed in black and knew the truth.

As further details of the tragedy reached France, national feeling mounted, and it was not long before Anglophobia, which was never very deep under the surface, burst forth. Rumour and counter rumour flew about, fanned by the popular press:

'Oh! to see it printed in their journals and to think the Nation is not wiped out, and that it is impossible to sink their accursed Island *et ce peuple froid, barbare, perfide, enfame*!'

It was popularly believed that the Prince's death was not an accident; the wildest stories gained substance and were believed. Gambetta had conspired with the Prince of Wales to send the victim to Zululand, and they had employed Carey to do the rest. Colonel Harrison was in it; Chelmsford, an accomplice after the fact, had been awarded a CB. That it was a plot arranged by the Freemasons; this theory was nurtured for a long time, even appearing as a book in 1891. The French playwright, Rostand (who was only eleven years old in 1879), wrote a play called *Napoleon IV* in which the Prince Imperial was led into an ambush plotted by Queen Victoria!

The Empress was both hurt and indignant when she heard of these rumours from her mother. She wrote:

'One can understand the people being taken in, but you, an intelligent woman, who should have more judgement, how can you say my dear child was assassinated? He died like a hero among the enemy, there was no betrayal, leave that word to the ignorant who can talk of nothing else: we heard enough of it in 1870 without rhyme or reason, applied to all and sundry! . . . There may be cowardice without adding treason as well; it's terrible enough, dramatic enough, without adding what has no existence. It's for those who were with my child to ask themselves that question. Did they act like brave men or did they run away? They can answer, and have been obliged to answer. It's frightful enough like that. I beg of you, never say again that my boy was murdered; you can't conceive how you hurt me. He fell fighting like a hero.'

In England, the affair had been taken up avidly by the two leading military journals of the day, each pursuing a line different to that of their rival. The opening shot was fired by *The Army and Navy Gazette* on 21 June 1879:

'We are without any detailed accounts but it certainly does appear that there is a *prima facie* case against the officer in command of the party. That officer must have been Captain Carey and we consider he was guilty of two faults. In the first place, he selected for his halt a spot which seemed expressly to favour surprise, in the second place, he kept no look out.'

In its next issue, on Saturday 28 June, this magazine devoted its entire leader page and more, to the death of the Prince Imperial:

'The grief of the British nation . . . and its sympathy with the heart-broken mother, seem to increase rather than diminish. It is almost as if we had lost one of our own Princes and were sharing the sorrow of our own Queen. Everything known . . . was to his advantage. He possessed . . . every quality which constitutes the true hero. Amiable, unselfish, upright, single-minded, clever, clear-headed, of noble sentiments, pure in morals, high-spirited, and endowed with rare personal courage, he was a noble example to his age.

'We must not, however, allow our feelings of sorrow for the

lamentable event to hurry us into injustice. We have the reputation of being a phlegmatic race, yet there is no nation which, on occasion, can be roused to greater enthusiasm, and we are easily led by our best feelings into unmerited harshness towards those of whom, in our excitement, we fasten the responsibility of a public misfortune. In the present instance, in the heat of our grief, our admiration for a dead hero, our compassion for a bereaved lady, we are displaying an impulsiveness and lack of ordinary justice which we venture to pronounce highly discreditable and cruel. We have in our anger, for it is nothing else, at the death of the Prince Imperial while serving in our ranks, assumed that some person or persons were to blame for the catastrophe, and having but slight data to go on, we have sought to justify our hasty verdict by arguments which, to say the least, are rashly put forward.'

Mentioning that blame had been cast on Lord Chelmsford, Sir Evelyn Wood and Lieutenant Carey, the article sternly rebuked those who would blame before knowing all the facts :

'It would ill-become us as the recognised organ of the Army, and the champion of its interests and reputation to be silent . . . our only object is justice and we shall be among the first to condemn those who are now visited by popular censure should their conduct, after due investigation, prove deserving of blame . . . we deny that, with our present information, we are entitled to soothe our wounded national vanity and excited sentimentality offering up as sacrifices to popular clamour the officers already named. At the same time, we are bound to admit that there is an almost universal consensus of opinion that much blame attaches to the three officers whose names we have given above . . . we deplore the flunkeyish spirit which appears to animate certain critics who are positively beside themselves with indignation that a Prince should be no more exempt from the hazards of war than ordinary individuals.'

After explaining the reasons for the Prince's ardent desire to serve in South Africa, the writer justified the conduct of Lord Chelmsford :

'The cares of the Commander of an Army in the field are too absorbing to admit the functions of Governor of a Royal visitor being added. The Prince was simply a private individual . . . acting as a simple volunteer, and had to take his chance with

147

other private individuals present, such as newspaper correspondents. The Prince was, for the time, sunk in the rôle of a volunteer.

'We now come to the conduct of Lieutenant Carey, which has, with shameful haste, been most cruelly condemned.'

Saying that an officer of Carey's experience should not have allowed himself to be so careless, the writer claimed that, by allowing himself to be surprised, there were grounds for trial by court-martial. However, the most serious accusation against him was that he deserted the Prince Imperial, and the writer indignantly rejected this : 'It may be that he did abandon the Prince in a discreditable manner, but the presumption is that, as Lieutenant Carey is a British officer, he did nothing of the sort.' It was the opinion of the writer that it was the duty of the patrol to endeavour to avoid a fight and to escape capture, so he felt that they were justified in their decision not to stay and fight.

The writer ends with a remarkable demonstration of *volte-face* :

'What, then, ought Lieutenant Carey and his party to have attempted? According to some, they ought to have thought of nothing but the safety of the Prince, and every man should have perished, rather than that harm should have happened to him. If the Prince had been seen to have been in more danger than his companions, the latter ought certainly to have tried to bring him off, equally with any other comrade. But it was not known but that he had escaped. As to the idea that any special devotion was due to him, we repudiate it energetically. The Prince was a self-invited guest of the Army, if not also self-invited companion of the expedition, and no more care of his person was called for than if he had been an officer of the English Army. Indeed, we should think little of any one who, perceiving a brother-officer and a volunteer foreign Prince in equal danger, did not aid the former, in preference to the latter. To say otherwise, is to talk like a lackey.'

Throughout, *The United Service Gazette* took a much sterner attitude towards Carey, the tone being set by their leader-article of 28 June 1879 which was entitled '*Sauve Qui Peut!*'

'In the grave disasters which have befallen our arms, with their terrible tales of butchery and death, we had at least the proud consciousness that our fellow-countrymen did their duty stoutly and bravely to the last. They died as British soldiers have been wont to die, back to back, with their faces to the encircling foe. But the dread news of the Prince's death, and the details, meagre though they be, of the manner in which he came by it, have filled every true English breast with misgiving. The story as it stands reads like a national disgrace. Shame is the overpowering emotion which takes precedence of all others when we hear that a gallant youth—not only an Imperial prince, the hope of a great party, the sole comfort and support of a widowed mother much buffeted by adverse fortune, but a comrade in arms—had been abandoned to his fate, while companions fortunate and more swift galloped off for their lives. So far as we can rely upon the information which has come to hand, the shameful fact remains that a British officer so far forgot what was due to himself, and to the uniform he wore, as to put his own personal safety above all other considerations, and, without waiting to see what had befallen his companions, ignobly take to his heels.

'To say that dissatisfaction amounting to disgust is the prevailing sentiment towards the unhappy subaltern whose conduct is at present darkened by such sombre colours is to understate the case. No doubt a revulsion of feeling will secure him at least a hearing, and the verdict of condemnation will be stayed until he has spoken in his own defence. But it is difficult to imagine how he can justify himself. He may say, with some show of reason, that the panic was sudden and uncontrollable; that the alarm given, the cry of *sauve qui peut!* was raised, and acted on almost without a second thought, that in such a momentous emergency every man naturally looked to himself. These are the obvious excuses of a man arraigned on such a charge. He may add to them the known fact that nerves vary, that all men will not act alike with the same fortitude when brought face to face with extreme peril. And, humiliating as their acknowledgment may be to us, who have looked always for finer traits in British officers, we cannot but in part admit the force of the explanation. But what can explain away the subsequent desertion of the Prince? What can excuse the pusillanimous eagerness to escape which led Lieutenant Carey to gallop five hundred yards before he turned his head? Can this be explained away? There is no one amongst us who does not devoutly and sincerely trust that it may be; who does not eagerly desire that the unhappy survivor of this most unfortunate episode may not rehabilitate himself and his good name as a brave soldier and true. But unless he can do that to the full satisfaction of the whole world, we may fairly say that not all the invective of our bitterest foreign critics, nor all the sneers of continental brethren-in-arms will at all deepen the shame and condemnation we shall suffer ourselves.'

The Army and Navy Gazette, 5 July 1879 :

'Hitherto, the public have confined themselves to blaming Captain Carey for his apparent indifference as to what became of the Prince; but we would point out that he had equally duties to perform in connection with the trooper Rogers, who, unable to mount his horse, stood at bay behind one of the tents, and the friendly native, who sold his life so desperately. What do we find, however? As soon as the Zulus fired their unexpected volley, every one spontaneously gallops away, without taking the least heed of comrades; and, at first at all events, Captain Carey led the fugitives. No attempt was made even to save their honour by a single discharge of firearms when the donga was crossed, and the only order given by Captain Carey was, "Let us make haste and go quickly." The flight was, indeed, continued at a gallop, and when it was represented to Captain Carey, after going some distance, that two of the troopers could not catch him up, and he was asked to wait for them, he replied, "We will cross the spruit, and wait for them on the rise on the other side." In short, throughout Captain Carey set an example of excitement and selfishness. It may be that evidence was given before the formal court of inquiry assembled by Lord Chelmsford, the proceedings and opinion of which have not yet been divulged, which may place Captain Carey's conduct in a somewhat better light. It may be that he lost control of his horse during the first 50 yards' mad gallop, and could not pull him in so as to bring up the rear, which was his proper post. If such should prove to have been the case, we shall greatly rejoice, but we fear that it is impossible to explain away the fact that when the kraal had been left some distance behind, his only thought was to escape; and that he rejected the proposal that the party should wait till the two troopers on tired horses should have caught him up. Indeed, as far as we can see at present, the best that can be said of him is that he lost his head, in the excitement of the moment. As to actual personal cowardice, we cannot believe that, considering his previously gallant conduct, he could have incurred such a stain on his manhood.'

The Army and Navy Gazette, in its next issue on 12 July,

devoted its leader-article to discussing the opinions of the Court of Inquiry and to prophesying the verdict of the court-martial which they knew to have ended by that time. The writer found the opinions of the Court of Inquiry '. . . somewhat singular. Its chief characteristics are want of outspokenness, want of logic, symptoms of a desire to exculpate Colonel Harrison for making a scapegoat of Captain Carey, and the absence of any mention of Trooper Rogers, who was quite as much left to his fate as was the Prince Imperial.' An entire coloumn was devoted to a discussion of whether or not Carey was in command of the patrol; the writer summed up by saying, '. . . we consider that Colonel

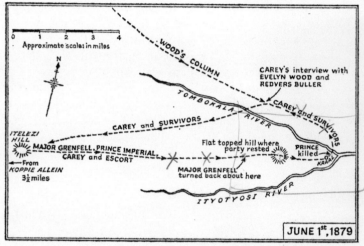

Plan of the route to the kraal and the path of the fugitives.

Harrison was more to blame, in this respect, than Captain Carey.'

The writer agrees with the fourth clause of the Court's opinion, in which they commented on the fact that no effort was made to rally the escort, saying that whether he was in command or not, Captain Carey, as the only commissioned British officer present, ought certainly to have shown more coolness and, bringing up the rear, to have done his best to assist those who were in difficulties—Trooper Rogers and the native guide equally with the Prince Imperial.

Discussing the wording of the charge made against Carey at his court-martial, the writer said that he had read it only in *The Times*, but that it was given fully '. . . the charge reflects little credit on the Judge-Advocate, who drew it out, and the persons who approved it. Anything more vague, loose, and wanting in clear specification, can scarcely be conceived. We shall not be surprised if the very wording of the charge causes the whole of the proceedings to be quashed.' Later, he writes:

'The fact is that the whole party was startled by the sudden volley, and lost their presence of mind. When they regained it, half a minute later, the Prince's fate had been sealed.'

Towards the end of the article, he displays a nationalistic bias typical of the majority of these articles:

'It would appear to be thought both by the authorities on the spot and the public at home, that the first duty of everyone was to look after the Prince Imperial; and an insolent priest has even . . . had the audacity to speak of "English cowardice". The party was sent out to reconnoitre, and it was only incidentally their duty to defend the Prince who had no more claims on their devotion than Trooper Rogers and the friendly native guide. We trust that all these facts and arguments will be duly taken into consideration by the authorities . . . and that they will not allow their natural grief at the unfortunate death of the gallant young Prince to induce them to yield to sheepish public clamours, and commit a judicial injustice.'

The United Service Gazette, 19 July:

'It may not be consistent with that spirit of fair play, which is the proverbial love of Englishmen, to comment further on Captain Carey's conduct until the proceedings of his court-martial have been published; but it is equally objectionable on the part of his friends to be puffing him and his family in the columns of such newspapers as they have access to. Who cares to be told that the maternal grandfather of Captain Carey was "that able and courageous sailor of Nelson's time, Sir Jaheel Brenton, who received a baronetcy for his blameless career"? What, too, does it signify, that Captain Carey himself received the thanks of his commanding officer on board the *Clyde*, for "having spent the whole night at Cape Town, urging on the coaling of the ship, so that the reinforcements which she carried might arrive without delay at Durban"? What the public of England is concerned about is, whether an English officer did or did not "misbehave" before the enemy. That is the question which a court-martial has had to try, and the answer to which is impatiently waited for.'

The Army and Navy Gazette, in spite of the known facts, persistently confused its readers by likening the ambushed group to a regular cavalry patrol on a serious scouting mission :

'The duty of a patrol is to . . . scatter in all directions and make their way as speedily as possible to camp, carrying the news to the General in command. This is what Captain Carey did and for doing what was right an ignorant public would condemn him to death.'

Everyone, the foreign Press, serving soldiers and the man in the street, had opinions about the affair and about Carey's share of the blame. There was a universal feeling that something was being kept back, that those who had allowed the Prince to serve and those who should have looked after him were in need of someone to take the blame, and that they meant the defenceless Carey to pay for all. Hence, in *The United Service Gazette* for 19 July :

'It is to be hoped that the Government will give full publicity to all the explanations, however "private and confidential" they may be officially worded, regarding this most wretched business. The truth, and the whole truth, should be made known, irrespective of consequences to individual rank or reputations.'

The Echo, in an article which strengthened the general conviction that the death of the Prince was due more to his own carelessness than to that of anyone else, concluded :

'The more the circumstances of Carey's case are looked into, the more reason is there to believe that the court-martial was got up to find

                                               uch of it fell upon

                                                          m, that
he   on this
reconnaissance. Be it so, but   confession most
damnable? Ought he not to have kr   and would he not have
known had it been one of our Gracious Majesty's sons? Think
you the Duke of Connaught or the Duke of Edinburgh would have
been allowed to risk his life in this way? And if he had, what think
you the Queen would have said, when the news reached her that
her son's body had been found hacked and mutilated with eighteen
wounds?'

The Italian newspaper, *Italie*, in a leader-article, pointed out that competent military critics in England, Germany and Austria were unanimous in justifying Carey's conduct. The article went on to say:

'If the officer who fell had been an ordinary mortal, instead of being Prince Louis Napoleon, no one would have dreamed of blaming Carey. Rather it would have been said that in not uselessly exposing his own life and the lives of those who were with him, he had acted as a sensible officer. The good people who sit at home by their fenders and send others out to fight their battles, will surely admit that when one risks one's life it should be to good purpose.'

The Times, 1 July 1879.

'Lord Chelmsford . . . had given general verbal orders that the Prince Imperial should not be allowed to go on any expedition without a fitting escort. And that in any case, he should not be committed to incur undue danger. Suppose Lord Chelmsford had issued orders in writing to this effect, and that these had been published, as they assuredly would have been, in France and elsewhere, what would have been the consequences to the Prince? He might have escaped risks; but an injury would have been inflicted on his reputation from which he would have found it very hard to recover. A Napoleon without a military reputation is not half himself. . . . It became the natural—perhaps the commendable—desire of the late Prince Imperial to afford the world, at all hazards, incontestable evidence of his gallantry and military capacity. This was the very purpose for which he went out, and it commanded sympathy both here and in his own country. But if an order could have been produced by the enemies or critics of the Bonapartists showing that the Prince had throughout the campaign been shielded by the vigilance of the British General and his Staff, the whole scheme would have collapsed, and the Prince's expedition would almost have become a subject of ridicule.

'The conclusion, we apprehend, which the public will be apt to draw from . . . these facts will be by no means that which the chief military authority in this country seem to suggest when the sad news first arrived. That which is of importance to observe at the moment is that the disaster arose essentially out of the fact of the Prince being present in South Africa in a false position, which exposed both himself and all around him to constant difficulties and temptations. It would have been wonderful if no error had been committed in dealing with such exceptional circumstances, and any error might be fatal.'

A spate of letters from serving soldiers of all nationalities were published and commented upon in *The Army and Navy Gazette*. An officer who had served with some distinction during the Franco-Prussian War of 1870 wrote one headed 'Justice To All':

'I am pained to see that everybody seems to be more or less prejudiced against that unfortunate officer, and that people seem to be determined not to give him a fair chance. I have seen a large amount of service myself in the Franco-German campaign, and although I must confess that Captain Carey lost a most brilliant chance of distinguishing himself, I cannot see why he should be held entirely responsible for an occurrence which, after all, is bound to happen in every campaign, for the simple reason that the victim was in this case a person of rank. We all, when going into action, must take our chance, and every soldier knows this. To condemn a man, as the civilian Press seems disposed to do, because he got away, and a brother-officer had the bad luck to be killed in a surprise, appears to be most monstrous, and adds a new danger to the profession of a soldier. It is all very well to read a newspaper report in cold-blood after a thing has occurred, and to say I should have done this or that. Although I have not the honour to belong to the British Army, I cannot help feeling for a brother soldier who is placed in so unfortunate a position, and I beg you will allow me to express my sympathy with him in his misfortune.

> 'I am, &c,
> 'A Soldier.'

ng the attention of his readers to this letter, the editor
y and Navy Gazette wrote in his leader-article:
officers will, we feel certain, be grateful to him for
defence of a comrade in his misfortune.'

rote to the same journal on 2 August:

r in the hail of prejudice and one-sided criticism
as been hurled at the unfortunate Captain
Lieutenant Carey was responsible for the sad
dity, only entertained by prejudiced persons, who

persistently ignore every part of a subject but the one they wish to see. If the Prince had got away safe, it would have been considered a fortunate affair even if all the remainder (Lieutenant Carey included) had perished. As however it was as it happened, the horrible clamour has been raised, and it is deemed necessary to hang someone for it, and the scapegoat fixed upon is Lieutenant Carey. If I thought the officer in question had been guilty of conduct at all savouring of cowardice or anything of that kind, I would be the first to "throw a stone at him" but as I firmly believe it to be otherwise, I sincerely hope that the gallant young officer may be honourably acquitted and I am sure the hope is echoed by the majority of the Army.'

'E.C.H.' of the Bengal SC wrote on the same date :

'Sir, I cannot tell you with what pleasure I read your articles in defence of Captain Carey. Had the Prince effected his escape should we have been as hard on him for leaving a British soldier, and one of his own escort, as we have been on Lieutenant Carey, who, by all accounts, simply accompanied the party as a volunteer?'

A German officer of 'high rank', pointed out in *The Army and Navy Gazette* of 9 August :

'. . . that by the ignorance of the British public the Military Authorities are being advised to commit . . . one of the greatest errors which it would be possible for them to be guilty of. By even reprimanding Captain Carey, they would lay it down as a rule in the British Army that an officer of the Intelligence Department should show fight, when any General who has seen service in a European war must at once see how dangerous it would be to establish any such
to mak
He w
— an it i
w nould c
g n charg
seem forgo
distress, he mig
General in comm
not be justified in c
constituted intelligenc
ment of Europe is in

be promulgated, for the question which has to be considered is one which deeply affects every military power.'

Not all voices spoke in Carey's favour. But those who dissented were taken to task roundly in the pages of *The Army and Navy Gazette*, as this example from the issue of 16 August indicates:

'A Cavalry officer has addressed us a letter, in which he endeavours to make out that Captain Carey was guilty of conduct so cowardly as to have ruined the character of the British Officer in the eyes of the whole Continent of Europe. It is fully time that the country came to its senses, and certainly we had hoped that the Army had long since done so. We have from the first maintained that there is absolutely no case against Captain Carey, and in taking this view, it is gratifying to find that we have with us every Continental journal of any note. The German army, we are told, "sympathises with Captain Carey to a man, and it would rather astonish some of your English writers to hear the warm language that is used in every German garrison when this cause is debated, not a single person being found to support the arguments of your mad-brained and most ungenerous critics." Another foreign officer says it is the prevailing opinion that "the authorities at the Cape must have gone out of their minds for the time". Captain Carey's case, it is satisfactory to know, is in good hands, and we may rest assured that full justice will be done him. He must have suffered enough in mind and body already, and we only hope that reparation may be made for the cruel injustice he has suffered.'

In addition to taking to task those who did not agree with its editorial policy, *The Army and Navy Gazette* even had a go at the prosecutor who had served at Carey's court-martial. In its leader-article for 26 July, he was dealt with sternly.

'Captain Brander is almost amusing in his argument, and we would recommend him to study the English language a little before he again acts as prosecutor on a court-martial. He said that as it had been proved that the Prince held no status in the Army, and therefore no authority, he could not have been in command. Of course he had no status, of course he could legally exercise no command, yet that did not prevent him, under a mistaken impression of Colonel Harrison's hazy intentions, from acting as commanding officer. It has happened before now that a colonel has inflicted a punishment which was illegal, yet the punishment has not been the less inflicted. But it is idle to confute such a manifest absurdity as Captain Brander's argument. Captain Carey, displaying far more manliness than many of his accusers, and an absence of that flunkeyism which has been painfully prevalent in connection with this lamentable affair, said that he would have been equally guilty had any misconduct on his part caused the death of the humblest soldier in the force. It would seem that with many, horror at the death of a prince had made them forget that a private trooper and a friendly Zulu equally owed their deaths to the retreat of the party.

'This is the pith of Captain Carey's defence, and it bears the marks of truth and sincerity upon the face of it. What influence it had on the Court we shall soon know. As to public opinion, both in South Africa and at home, it is noteworthy that it is beginning to veer round. This is important, for the severest punishment he has to dread is, after all, not the award of the court-martial, but the condemnation of his countrymen.'

26

O<small>N</small> 9 July, HM troopship *Orontes* was signalled off Plymouth. After communicating with the authorities on shore, the vessel proceeded up channel to meet the Admiralty yacht *Enchantress* at its Spithead anchorage at 7 am on 10 July. On board the *Enchantress* were Lieutenant-General the Hon A. E. Hardinge, CB; Prince Edward of Saxe-Weimar; Prince Joachim Murat; Comte Davilliers; Vicomte Aguado; Baron de Bourgoing; Marquis de Bassano; Comte de Turenne; M Rouher; M Pietri; Dr Corvisart; Louis Conneau; Bizot and Espinasse. The Admiralty yacht came alongside, and the coffin was transferred and laid in a saloon on the after-deck of the *Enchantress* which had been transformed into a mortuary chapel. The coffin was accompanied by Arthur Bigge, Uhlmann, Deléage and the two soldier servants.

It had been intended that a simple religious ceremony would take place during this transhipment of the remains. The Rev Father Ballard, the Naval Roman Catholic Chaplain at Portsmouth, and the Rev W. Legrave, one of the military chaplains, were to be on board the *Enchantress*, and these clergymen, with Father Rooney who was already on board the *Orontes*, were to give a short service for the dead. The act of transhipment was to be announced by the firing of twenty-three minute guns from the flagship *Duke of Wellington* and the lowering of ensigns throughout the squadron. These proposed arrangements were altered on account of the rough weather.

Arriving at Woolwich at four o'clock on 11 July, the *Enchantress* was received by the General Officer commanding the Woolwich District; the Company of Gentlemen Cadets formed a Guard of Honour on the quay. The band of the Royal Artillery was drawn up at 'T' pier and saluted the body as it was landed. Nearly every soldier and civilian of the garrison had come to the riverside to watch the Imperial coffin carried ashore.

The body was to rest in an isolated octagonal building at the western end of the wharf, formerly the Watergate Guardroom, which was now being used as an armoury by the 26th Kent (Royal Arsenal) Rifle Volunteers. It was only about twenty-four feet in diameter and consisted of a single room '. . . in shape and size and with its dome-like appearance external and internal, singularly forming an appropriate resting place for the deceased Prince. . . .' The interior of the building was draped with black. Here the Prince of Wales and the Dukes of Connaught, Edinburgh and Cambridge came to pay their respects; all exhibited signs of profound emotion. Then the English departed and the French heads of the Imperialist Party and Louis' friends surrounded the coffin to undertake the necessary legal ceremony of formal identification of the remains.

The casket was prised open and the observers leaned forward. They turned away, recoiling in horror; Uhlmann collapsed in a dead faint. The hasty embalming had failed, and the horribly grotesque face bore no resemblance to that of the young man they had known. The medical men now inspected the remains and confirmed that the body was indeed that of Louis—Doctor Conneau recognised the scar of a childhood abscess on the hip which he had lanced, and Doctor Evans, an American dentist who had treated Louis, identified the teeth.

The remains were placed within a leaden shell, and the whole was enclosed within an outer coffin of mahogany covered with dark violet velvet and decorated with gilt handles and enrichments. Upon the gilt nameplate was engraved :

'Napoléon Eugène Louis Jean Joseph,
Prince Impérial.
'Né à Paris, le 16 Mars, 1856.
'Tué par l'ennemi, en Zululand (Afrique Australe),
le 1 Juin, 1879.
'Deposé dans l'Eglise Catholique de Sainte Mary de
Chislehurst, le 12 Juillet, 1879.
R.I.P.'

The coffin was placed on a Royal Artillery gun-carriage and escorted to Chislehurst by three squadrons of the Royal Horse Artillery and by the 5th Lancers. Minute guns were fired on the Common from the time the party left the Royal Arsenal until it passed the Herbert Hospital.

The coffin was carried into the hall at Camden Place by the

officers of the Royal Artillery. The picture gallery, in which the late Emperor had lain in state previous to entombment at St Mary's, had been converted into a chapel. The walls were draped in white festooned with black crape, relieved with silver lace; the roof was covered with the Imperial flags. The bier occupied the centre of the room, and the coffin rested on a couch of violets. The English withdrew; Marie de Larminat cried:

'Ah! Let them disappear! We gave them our Prince in all the splendour of his beauty and youth, and they return us a coffin!'

Eugenie spent the night beside the bier. At five o'clock in the morning, she retired to her room; she did not attend the funeral.

Queen Victoria had given considerable thought to the funeral; she had made up her mind to send the young hero to his grave with every honour she could devise. Her Ministers, on the other hand, wanted everything to be done as quietly as possible; the Prince's death was no fault of theirs, and they felt that a royal funeral would be an insult to the French Republic. They were particularly worried by the Queen's desire to lay the Order of the Bath on Louis' coffin with her own hands. On 30 June, in the House of Lords, Lord Beaconsfield announced that it was not intended to propose a public funeral of the Prince's remains, as there were obvious reasons why such a proposal would be out of place. Indignantly, the Queen argued the point with her Ministers; she got her way about the public funeral but was obliged to give up the idea of bestowing the Order of the Bath. All the members of the Cabinet declined to be at the funeral, but this decision aroused such anger in the Queen that they thought better of it. In the end the Ministers of War and of the Colonies decided to go, in full dress.

The funeral took place at eleven o'clock in the morning; Queen Victoria was present with her daughter Beatrice and four Royal Dukes. Officers of the Royal Artillery carried the coffin from the house and placed it on the gun-carriage. With arms reversed, the Gentlemen Cadets of the Royal Military Academy of Woolwich led the way followed by the mounted band of the Royal Artillery, and finally the gun-carriage.

From Camden Place to the little church of St Mary's, on the opposite side of the Common, was barely half a mile, and part of the route lay along a narrow lane. But, in spite of rain, 40,000 mourners and onlookers swamped the little village. The 5th Lancers and other regiments lined the route, and three batteries of the Royal Artillery fired minute-guns on the Common from

F
161

the moment the procession started from Camden Place until the body entered the church. At that moment, the Gentlemen Cadets, who had formed a lane for the coffin to pass through, fired three volleys from their rifles. The officers who carried it into the church filed out by the side door, leaving the rest of the duties to friends of the deceased Prince. A short Mass followed, and the Prince Imperial was laid to rest beside his father in the private memorial chapel which Eugenie had had erected in 1873.

Archibald Forbes wrote a florid Victorian epitaph :

'I will call him happy in the opportunity of his death. Had he lived, what of artificiality, what of hollow unreality might there not have been in store for him? As it was, he had moved in the world a live ghost; better than this, surely, to be a dead hero : to end a Napoleonic serio-comedy with his young face gallantly to his assailants and his life-blood drawn by the cold steel !

'Poor Prince Louis' life was fragrant with naturalness from the time that the fall of the Empire emancipated it; but before then it was among the most artificial of the Imperial phenomena.'[1]

In a later book, he wrote :

'To be slain by savages in an obscure corner of a remote continent was a miserable end, truly, for him who was once the Sun of France.'[2]

At a dinner of the Trinity House Corporation, the Duke of Cambridge stated that the Prince Imperial had been bent upon going to South Africa in order to show his gratitude to the Queen and the country for the manner in which he had been treated while living here.

'As to his conduct, I think that there can be no doubt, he was a thoroughly good, high-minded, high-principled young man. As to his courage, singly enough I had observed on several occasions the intense dash in his character, and in a letter I have from him he thanks me for having given him a hint on that very subject. I had said to him that he should not run unnecessary risks or expose himself unnecessarily; I gave him that hint; but so strong was his desire to see service, and to show the noble spirit which dwelt within him, that he could not restrain his feelings in any way, and if the opportunity occurred he would only be anxious to go to the front. The result is deplorable; but there can be no

[1] Archibald Forbes, *Souvenirs of some Continents.*
[2] Archibald Forbes, *Memories of War and Peace* (1895).

question the feelings were noble and generous, and I am only grieved that a life so valuable should have been so unhappily cut off.'

The Prince of Wales, in a speech at the West London Hospital, similarly spoke of Louis as 'a brave young man who was a guest of this country'. The Duke of Cambridge, as Commander-in-Chief of the Army, gave his sanction to a proposal for raising a general Army Subscription for the purpose of erecting a memorial to the Prince Imperial. A committee was formed consisting of the Duke of Cambridge as President, the Prince of Wales and the Duke of Connaught, Field Marshals Lord Strathnairn and Sir Charles Yorke, Lord Napier of Magdala and other officers of high rank. The subscription was not to exceed one pound from any individual contributing. *The Times* commented :

'. . . there cannot be a doubt that the Army will eagerly seize this opportunity of testifying to the intense feeling of sorrow and pain which pervades its ranks. It will be seen from . . . correspondence . . . how profoundly the Prince's death has moved the Army in South Africa, and at home the feeling grows deeper every day. Few events in our time have aroused among all classes such overpowering sympathy, and it is well that this sentiment should be expressed by some memorial which will be a permanent and public record of it. The Royal Artillery have expressed their desire to attend the funeral of one whom they regard as a brother-in-arms. But, though the Corps to which the Prince once belonged will alone take part in this sad office, the rest of the Army will testify in another way the honour in which the Prince's name is held among them, and their regret at his lamentable fate.'

Thus Louis was given a monument in St George's Chapel; and Eugenie stayed in England for life.

In *The Echo* of 21 August there appeared a letter signed by Harriet, Carey's mother, dated 11 August, from Brixham Vicarage, Torbay, Devon. In it she stated that she had noticed the question asked in the House of Commons as to whether the bodies of the two troopers of Bettington's Horse were recovered and buried. She could answer in the affirmative. Her son, Lieutenant Carey of the 98th Regiment, had stated in a letter home relating to the Prince's death, that he personally had remained behind to see to the burial of the two poor troopers.

Lieutenant Carey had always been the soldier's friend, and the relatives of the dead troopers might rest assured that no tender office or consideration was wanting on her son's part for the mortal remains of those who had been his comrades, even if for only an hour or two.

27

WHILE Carey was at sea, the Zulu War was brought to an end at Ulundi on 4 July 1879. The Zulus were mowed down by massed artillery and rifle fire from Chelmsford's force which was formed in a huge square and were then harried by the 17th Lancers. With this operation the Zulus ceased to be an army.

The *Jumna*'s voyage home was uneventful and marked by exceptionally fine weather. All ranks greatly enjoyed singing on deck each evening accompanied by a pianist and a fiddler. They reached Madeira on 4 August, and arrived at Plymouth Sound on the 20th. Carey had been refused permission to go ashore to meet his wife and parents, but newspapermen were allowed on board. It was reported that Carey appeared to be in '. . . splendid robust health and apparently in excellent spirits. . . .' *The Daily Telegraph* of 21 August reported, 'It was the first occasion on which Carey had been addressed as Captain, the promotion having been announced in *The London Gazette* on June 6th.' He asked the Press to thank everybody '. . . for the consideration and sympathy manifested towards him on board the *Jumna* in the passage home.'

The Morning Post reported :

'Captain Carey seemed in excellent health and spirits. That he feels the loss of the Prince—and this quite apart from any personal considerations affecting himself—was very evident; but that which seemed to affect him most for the moment was the information given him that an address had been numerously signed in Plymouth for presentation to him expressive of sympathy for him in his unfortunate and trying position, and of confidence in him as a brave officer and a true Englishman.'

Carey was amazed and heartened to hear of the deputation who had come from Plymouth, complete with a brass band, to present him with an address signed by nearly three thousand Devonians. He was disappointed, however, to be told that the rules of the Service precluded the presentation to a serving officer of the address. It was sent by post, with a letter from a former mayor of Plymouth and Carey received it in Southsea a few days later :

'Sir—When it became known that her Majesty's ship *Jumna* would probably call at this port to disembark Royal Marines who have been serving in South Africa, many of the inhabitants of this borough deemed it right that occasion should be taken of your presence on board that vessel to convey to you the sympathy of a large number of your countrymen at the moment of your arrival under circumstances of peculiar hardship and anxiety. The gentlemen who have been prominent in initiating the address which I now place before you did me the honour to invite me to present it to you in person. The rules of the service having prevented the desired interview, it becomes my duty to transmit the address for your acceptance. I do so with the greater boldness because the expressions in it of sympathy and confidence proceed from no particular section of the inhabitants, political or social. It has been felt that your life, short in some degree as it is, has testified of certain characteristics which go far to make up the reputation of a British officer and gentleman.

'At an early period your career at Sandhurst secured the free commission by which, in 1865, you found employment in Her Majesty's service. Returning from your first appointment, the desire to become thoroughly efficient as an officer appears to have led you to Hythe, where I apprehend, you gained a first-class certificate. I find that in 1870 you were a volunteer in France, taking part during the Franco-German war in deeds of mercy not unattended by personal danger. Your services with the English ambulances were signalised by the presentation of the cross and ribbon, honourable distinctions of which any man may well be proud. Still advancing successfully in your studies at the Staff College, on the break out of the Zulu war your appointment to the 98th Regiment placed you in a routine of arduous duties until the unhappy moment which has become historic by the sad fate of Prince Napoleon.'

When the address was refused, Mr H. Lewis, representing the Plymouth deputation, sent Carey a telegram. Carey answered at once :

'HMS *Jumna*, Plymouth, August 21, 1879.

166

'Gentlemen—Will you allow me to offer you my most sincere and grateful thanks for your unexpected kindness—a kindness more especially gratifying as coming from inhabitants of my own county. You can well imagine that I have gone through a period of great trial, and that I look forward with great longing to the moment when I shall be out of suspense. It would not do in my present position for me to comment on the events of June 1, but I may be allowed to assure you that what I desire is justice —not mercy. Had not the justice of my cause, and trust in God and my fellow-countrymen upheld me, I could never have supported the time of suspense. When your promised letter reaches me I shall not fail to reply to it; but, in the meantime, will you kindly allow me to express to all the gentlemen who have signed the address my deep sense of gratitude. Believe me, gentlemen, your grateful fellow-Devonian,

'J. Brenton Carey, Captain 98th (Prince of Wales) Regiment.'

At the same time he received a similar address from Dartmouth, containing the names of the mayor, magistrates and members of public bodies as well as the principal tradesmen:

'To Captain J. B. Carey, We, the undersigned men of Dartmouth, in welcoming you back to your native country, desire to express our entire confidence in your valour as a British officer, and our sincere sympathy with you in the unfortunate circumstances in which you have been placed.'

On board the *Jumna*, Carey gave a statement to the Press. As reported in *The Morning Post* on 22 August, it read as follows:

'Captain Carey has made the following statement as to the circumstances connected with the death of the Prince Imperial. He says: "Lord Chelmsford sent me out to choose the line of advance for the army, and, after several hits, I chose one road, which, in my opinion, was best for the purpose. When I reported the result of my survey of the country, he said, 'I want you to make a map of it, so that I may send it home to the Horse Guards.' Everything that was decided upon went home. The day before that I had ridden out within two miles of the kraal, which lay in front of us, accompanied by Captain Buller, and when I told him of the road I had selected, he laughed at my choice, and told me there was a donga thirty feet wide lying right across it, and asked me how I intended to cross it. I told him I did not think

167

he was right, but his lordship's assertion worried me. When I got back to camp, Colonel Harrison, the quartermaster-general, said to me, 'The Prince is going out to-morrow over your ground to make a more detailed report and to choose a camping-ground, and you had better stop at home and finish your map.' I replied, 'Well, to-morrow we shall be advancing. I shall not be able to touch the map. Do you mind my going out with the Prince, because I want to go over the ground again to verify a certain point I am not quite sure about?' The Quartermaster-General, in reply, said at first, 'You had better stop at home and do your map'; but afterwards he said, 'Very well, you may go.' Now, since then, and particularly at the court, Colonel Harrison has asserted to the best of his belief that what he said was this—'I am glad you are going, because you can look after the Prince'; but to the best of my belief Colonel Harrison never said anything of the kind. But still, even if he had, I maintain that that was not in any sense giving me the command of the party, nor was there any reason to suppose that I was undertaking any such duty. He was simply directing me as the elder officer to keep my eye upon him, in order that he did not do anything rash; at any rate, that was how I should have interpreted any remark of the kind, supposing it to have been made; but as I have said, so far as my recollection goes, and to the best of my belief, nothing of the kind ever passed. Next morning I went to the Prince and asked him when he was going to start. He replied, "About half-past eight,' but I did not see anything of the escort, and I then went to Colonel Harrison, and found that the escort had not been warned. It was simply for the purpose of saving the Prince the trouble of doing this that I undertook to go and ferret out an escort, and I soon got one together. But the Prince gave every word of command. I never once interfered with him, and I do not consider that I should have been justified in doing so. The Prince Imperial was engaged in doing a particular duty, and I was merely accompanying him for my special object for the sake of obtaining for myself the protection of his escort. I could not have been on duty because I had received no instructions, and I had never once gone out on duty without having from Colonel Harrison full written instructions. The fact of my not having the slightest written instruction on this occasion is, in my opinion then, even by itself, pretty conclusive proof that I was not in charge of the escort, and that I was not on duty, I was simply and solely acting for my own convenience, and in order to gain the necessary information for completing the map to which I have referred. There were heaps of staff officers from whom to have selected someone to accompany the Prince if it had been required, and for me to have gone with him other than as I did would have been a simple waste of time."

'In respect to the court-martial, when questioned in relation to its proceedings, it appeared that Captain Carey did not himself know the real finding and sentence of the court. He laughed at the idea, however, that the sentence was death. He complained bitterly of the course adopted, that the proceedings at the court-martial, although the evidence has been in England for such a length of time, have not been published. "I feel confident," he said, "if it were published it would completely justify me in the eyes of my fellow-countrymen. I feel that, at the very worst, the court could only have reprimanded me for not going back to assist the Prince when the attack was made, but in the stampede that ensued it was utterly impossible to rally, owing to the horses being so terrified. Even if they had not been, and we had rallied, the result could only have been the slaughter of the entire party." Upon this point Captain Carey said there could not be the smallest doubt. As to the details of the surprise and death of the Prince he had nothing to add.'

In another statement to the Press, Carey gave five reasons why he felt that the court-martial proceedings should be quashed on the grounds of illegality:

Reason No 1: The general vague nature of the charge. It was true that he had pleaded to it, but only in order that his conduct might be inquired into fully. He was charged with 'galloping away, etc.', and he asked how that act could be considered criminal if no other course were open to him? If it was impossible to rally the escort, no blame could attach to him for having failed to accomplish an impossibility. He maintained again that if the evidence proved that no effort of his could have saved the Prince, he cannot properly be charged with not having attempted it. If the witnesses considered it impossible he claimed to be entitled to the advantage of their opinion. Was he to be blamed because he formed a similar opinion, and acted on it? The charge was so general that no court-martial could have acquitted him.

Reason No 2: He was removed from the Staff by General Order of June 11: he was thus punished for an alleged offence, for which he was only afterwards tried.

Reason No 3 : His case was never inquired into in his presence by his immediate commanding officer, Lord Chelmsford; the charge was based solely on the opinion of the Court of Inquiry, which opinion did not bear on the charge. The Court blamed him for not having obtained the Basutos of the escort, without inquiring why Captain Shepstone, who received a written order to supply them, did not do so.

Reason No 4 : His case was gravely prejudiced by his dismissal from the Staff.

Reason No 5 : The command of the escort was the essence of the charge. This, the evidence failed to prove.

Soon after ten o'clock on the morning of 22 August, the *Jumna* steamed into Spithead. A large crowd had assembled at the railway jetty in the dockyard, and at neighbouring piers and landing places, to greet the returning Portsmouth and Chatham Divisions of the Royal Marines; however, baggage was unshipped as soon as the vessel tied up, but the troops did not disembark until later in the day. Carey's wife and his parents had been in Southsea for the past week, awaiting his arrival. They came on board as soon as the ship was alongside, and were followed by a crowd of newspapermen. *The Morning Post* reported that the reunion was '. . . very affecting. . . .' A representative of the people of Portsmouth came aboard and told Carey that '. . . a written expression of their confidence in his gallantry and soldierly qualities would have been prepared but for the news of the refusal of the Plymouth address.' However, he assured Carey that '. . . at all events, he would receive a hearty welcome on his stepping ashore as public opinion in Portsmouth was pre-eminently in his favour. . . .' *The Western Daily Mercury* said :

'In the course of an interview with the Captain, in the course of the day, I was informed that the gallant officer himself was to that hour totally ignorant of the finding of the court-martial.[1] He said that he believed the General in command at Portsmouth was no better informed; in fact, so much in the dark has everybody been kept that on the Rev Mr Carey seeing an announcement that quarters had been prepared for his son at the Anglesea Barracks, he applied during the present week to the colonel commanding the 12th Regiment for information, and was courteously

[1] *The Times* of 22 August, the day on which the *Jumna* docked, forecast that Carey would be released and the findings quashed. Carey's parents and the newspapermen were almost certainly aware of this and probably told him at the first opportunity.

informed that room had been provided, and that the arrest would be rendered as little irksome as possible, though indeed Captain Carey makes no complaint, believing that the rule of the service has been strictly complied with. It is generally felt that due consideration has not been manifested towards the relatives who, up to the moment of his discharge, were left in the most painful suspense as to his fate.'

When the *Jumna* had been berthed for about an hour, Colonel C. A. B. Gordon, the Assistant Adjutant-General at Portsmouth, came aboard. A few minutes later, he left the ship with Captain Carey; and the two officers drove off in a cab to Gordon's office in the High Street. Here Carey had an interview with Prince Edward of Saxe-Weimar, General Commanding the Southern District, who, on instructions from the Duke of Cambridge, acquainted him with a document which had been sent from the Horse Guards. *The Western Daily Mercury* reported that Prince Edward addressed Carey in '. . . a kindly and sympathetic tone. . . .' Neither Carey nor the Press was given a copy of this document, and it was reported that at this stage Carey was still not told of the finding and sentence of the court-martial. Indeed, it was claimed that Prince Edward himself was equally ignorant in this respect.

However, the Press appears to have been aware of the contents of the document—*The Western Daily Mercury* quotes from it the following passage:

'Her Majesty has been advised that the charge brought against Captain Carey has not been sustained by the evidence, and the decision of the court-martial has, therefore, not been confirmed. Captain Carey is to be released from arrest and from all consequences of the trial, and is to rejoin his regiment. Captain Carey was released accordingly, and left the office to rejoin his friends at Southsea.'

The Morning Post reported it also, in a different wording:

'The General's instructions were from the Duke of Cambridge, and he was directed to explain to Captain Carey that the Queen manifested considerable interest in the case, and had graciously expressed her entire concurrence with the decision which exculpated him from the grave charge which has been alleged against him. Captain Carey might, therefore, consider himself released.'

At the conclusion of the interview, Carey was officially released from custody, and he left the office to join his family in Southsea, where they stayed with General Cox.

A week later, on Wednesday, 27 August,[2] Carey was again called to the office in the High Street, to be informed by Prince Edward that the Court had found him guilty and had sentenced him to be cashiered. However, they had recommended mercy on five extenuating circumstances.

Carey was permitted to read the findings of the Court-Martial, which were as follows :

'The Court held the opinion that Lieutenant Carey did not understand the position in which he stood to the Prince, and in consequence failed to estimate aright the responsibility which fell to his lot.

'Quartermaster-General Harrison stated in evidence that Lieutenant Carey was in charge of the escort; while Carey, alluding to the escort, says, "I do not consider that I had any authority over it."

'After the precise and careful instructions of Lord Chelmsford, stating, as he did, the position the Prince held, and that he was invariably to be accompanied by an escort in charge of an officer, the Court considers that such difference of opinion should not have existed between officers of the same department.

'Secondly : the Court is of opinion that Lieutenant Carey is much to blame in having proceeded on duty with part of the escort detailed by the Quartermaster-General. The court cannot admit the plea of irresponsibility on Lieutenant Carey's part, inasmuch as he himself took steps to obtain the escort, and failed; moreover, the fact that the Quartermaster-General was present on Itelezi ridge gave Carey the opportunity of consulting him on the matter, of which he failed to avail himself.

[2] Concerning the delay in informing Carey of the findings and verdict of the court-martial, *The Army and Navy Gazette* wrote : 'There is no actual law or even regulation that the finding and sentence should be communicated to the prisoner; but it is the invariable custom of the Service that he should be made acquainted with the facts before he is released or punished. Why should an exception have been made in Captain Carey's case? The comment of the Authorities is the more unaccountable, as a prisoner has the right, by the Articles of War, to obtain a copy of the proceedings within a reasonable time. It is most improbable that Captain Carey would dream of bringing an action against the President and Members who wrongly convicted him; but an action would lie, and he would obtain damages against each individual member of the court. No doubt there may be found by the Dryasdusts of the Judge Advocate-General's Department a precedent for this extraordinary proceeding, though we are not aware of one.'

172

'Thirdly : the Court is of opinion that the selection of the kraal where the halt was made, surrounded as it was by cover for the enemy, and the adjacent difficult ground, showed lamentable want of military prudence.

'Fourthly : the Court deeply regrets that no effort was made to rally the escort and show a front to the enemy, whereby the possibility of aiding those who had failed to make good their retreat might have been ascertained.'

The sentence for dismissal was accompanied by recommendation to mercy on the following grounds :

1. The smallness of the escort.
2. The insufficient armament of the escort.
3. That the men with him were not soldiers accustomed to military discipline.
4. That he, Carey, had other duties to perform besides taking command of the escort.
5. His long and honourable service.[3]

These recommendations were supported by a memorandum from Lord Chelmsford which requested that they might be favourably considered. He added that he considered that Lieutenant Carey was not deficient in personal bravery, but that he might have lost his head in the crisis by which he was confronted.

Finally, Carey was given a copy of the Official Despatch from the Horse Guards.

OFFICIAL DESPATCH FROM THE HORSE GUARDS ON THE
COURT-MARTIAL

'Horse Guards War Office,
'August 16, 1879.

'Sir—The proceedings of the general court-martial assembled at Camp, Upoko River, Zululand, on the 12th June, 1879, for the trial of Lieut J. B. Carey, 98th Regiment, on a charge of mis-

[3] In considering the recommendations to mercy, *The Times* stated: 'The extenuating circumstances justifying the recommendation to mercy were, no doubt, discovered in the situation in which Carey had to act when, as was alleged, he failed in his duty, and which may be held to excuse errors in judgement and deficient presence of mind. It is difficult to see how the admission of these excuses for Carey's conduct in a moment of confusion and urgent peril is consistent with a verdict of guilty.'
The Army and Navy Gazette of 30 August 1879 claimed that the first four extenuating circumstances were rather arguments for an acquittal than a recommendation to mercy.

behaviour before the enemy, having been submitted to the Queen, Her Majesty has been advised that the charge is not sustained by the evidence, and has accordingly been graciously pleased not to confirm the proceedings, and to direct that the prisoner be relieved from all consequences of his trial. Captain Carey is released from arrest and will rejoin his regiment for duty.

'The trial having been set aside, the Field Marshal Commanding-in-Chief offers no remark on the proceedings, but His Royal Highness has received Her Majesty's commands to make known his observations on the occurrences of the 1st June last, as they have come under his notice in official reports.

'His Imperial Highness Prince Napoleon was, at his own request, permitted to proceed to South Africa, in order to witness the operations in Zululand. He was provided with private letters to Lord Chelmsford, describing his position, and stating that it had not been thought right, even if it had been possible, to comply with his earnest desire to be commissioned as an officer of the British Army. The Commander of the forces in South Africa made such arrangements as seemed to him desirable under the condition of the Prince's non-official position, and attached him at first to his own personal Staff, and afterwards, with a view to provide him with occupation, to the department of the Quartermaster-General.

'The Prince was treated in all respects as if he had been a junior officer of the General Staff, with this exception, that Lord Chelmsford gave the most stringent instructions that His Imperial Highness was not to be permitted to proceed on any distant reconnaissance without his special permission, and that, when employed in surveying operations in close proximity to the camp, his party was always to be provided with a sufficient escort and to be accompanied by an officer.

'His Royal Highness desires it to be known that he entirely approves of Lord Chelmsford's arrangements for the reception and occupation of the Prince; and that he considers the orders issued for his protection were marked with judgment and adapted to the occasion.

'The reconnaissance which the Prince was allowed by Lieut-Colonel Harrison, the Assistant Quartermaster-General, to make on the 1st June extended to a considerable distance from the camp. Lord Chelmsford's permission had not been sought or obtained; all the arrangements were made under Lieutenant-Colonel Harrison's orders; and the Lieutenant-General commanding had reason to believe that throughout the day the Prince was in the company of Lieutenant-Colonel Harrison, who was occupied in guiding a column in its change of camp.

'Lieutenant-Colonel Harrison doubtless believed that in his arrangements for the expedition he had sufficiently complied with Lord Chelmsford's instructions to himself. In the opinion of the Field Marshal Commanding-in-Chief he was mistaken. His orders to Lieutenant Carey were not sufficiently explicit, and he failed to impress upon the Prince the duty of deferring to the military orders of the officer who accompanied him, and the necessity of guiding himself by his advice and experience.

'If Lieutenant-Colonel Harrison had displayed more firmness and forethought in his instructions to Lieutenant Carey and to the Prince, His Royal Highness cannot but think that that train of events would have been averted, which resulted in bringing a handful of men, in the middle of the enemy's country, into a position so well calculated to invite surprise and to court disaster.

'Lieutenant Carey from the first formed a wrong conception of his position. He was sent, not only to perform the duties of his staff office, but to provide that military experience which his younger companion had not yet acquired. If his instructions were defective his professional knowledge might have prompted him as to his duty.

'He imagined, but without the slightest foundation for the mistake, that the Prince held a military rank superior to his own, and acting throughout on this strange misconception, he omitted to take for the safety of the party those measures of precaution which his experience had taught him to be essential.

'At the moment of attack defence was impossible, and retreat imperative. What might have been done, and what ought to have been done when the moment of surprise had passed, can only be judged by an eye-witness; but His Royal Highness will say, and he feels that he speaks with the voice of the army, it will ever remain to him a source of regret that, whether or not an attempt at rescue was possible, the survivors of this fatal expedition withdrew from the scene of disaster without the full assurance that all efforts on their part were not abandoned until the fate of their comrades had been sealed.

'I have the honour to be, Sir, your obedient servant,

C. H. Ellice, Adjutant-General.

'To the General Officer Commanding in
    South Africa, Natal.'

175

In the days immediately following his release, Carey found that the great British Public had come out on his side. Aristocracy, generals and even royalty (of any nationality) were not popular at the time, and rumour had it that the humble Carey was to pay for the mistakes of his superiors. Overnight, he became a hero.[4] Carey began assiduously to court the public through the Press.

In an interview given to *The Western Daily Mercury* on 23 August, Carey persisted in the denial that he was in command of the reconnoitring party. He said that his only guilt was an excess of zeal, in that he wished to be perfectly certain as to the accuracy of the report and the map on which he was engaged. For this purpose he had decided to avail himself of the protection of the escort, but he had no written instructions, as he invariably had when on ordinary duty, and as the Prince had on the fatal day. He desired it to be distinctly understood that he cast no reflection on the unfortunate young Prince for the choice of the spot for off-saddling, the selection being one for which, perhaps, all were more or less responsible.

Biographers of the Prince Imperial write that Carey, 'speaking to those who knew no better', described Louis as '. . . tenacious of rank and quite insubordinate. . . .'

He said that it was for these reasons that the patrol stopped in such a bad place, since it would have been useless to protest.

The same writers claim that Carey, when he realised that the

---

[4] At the end of September, on his return from the war, the journalist Archibald Forbes gave a lecture at Shoreditch. In telling of the finding of the Prince Imperial's body, Forbes remarked:

'I wish to speak to-night only of brave men, and therefore I will ask to be excused from making any reference to Lieutenant Carey.'

The United Service Gazette for 29 September reported the event:

'Thereupon came a demonstration of Shoreditch emotion. The radical Christians, who constituted the majority of the audience, displayed open sympathy with Captain Carey, one enthusiastic idiot actually calling for "three cheers for Captain Carey". Some other idiots responded to this call, and there was a good deal of what the lecturer happily described as the "shoddy swagger of the music hall". Why any body of Englishmen should have cheered Captain Carey must be a puzzle which common sense cannot solve. Opinions may differ as to the quantum of blame to be attached to that officer, but surely it is a new interpretation of British pluck to cheer a man for running away from danger, and leaving his comrades to their fate.'

The audience were expressing an emotional sympathy for a man whom they felt had been wronged—not for a man who had run away. It was a characteristic expression of the British love of the under-dog.

176

letter which he had written in his tent during the night of 1 June had been read by eyes other than those of his wife, changed his tone, and instead of laying all the blame on the Prince, he took refuge in a plea of divided responsibility.

On 28 August, Carey issued a statement to the Press in connection with the addresses he had received from the people of Plymouth and Dartmouth. This was published in *The Morning Post* on the following day :

'Captain Carey. Captain Carey has forwarded a reply to the address which was signed and sent to him from Plymouth. Captain Carey says in his letter that he offers his most sincere and heartfelt thanks for the cordial and sympathetic address, which was most gratifying to him, especially as coming from men of his own county, who were best capable of judging his character. During the period of his arrest, from all ranks of the army in Zululand, and also during his journey through Natal, he had, however, received the most sincere kindness and sympathy, and further, on arrival at Simon's Bay he was made aware by a visit from the leading colonial clergy that truth was beginning to prevail. He had been sure from the first, and this feeling had buoyed him up during the homeward journey, that his countrymen would ultimately see the matter in its true light; and that in their eyes he would be absolved from all blame as to the death of the young Prince, whose fate Captain Carey says, "No one could have regretted more than myself, and for whose rescue, had such been possible, I would most willingly have remained on the fatal spot at any hazard. The circumstances attending the transaction are fully explained in the proceedings of the court-martial, which have not yet been published. I hope, however, that as I have done nothing to be ashamed of, and I desire nothing more than ample publicity and inquiry into all the facts of the case, a full and complete account of these proceedings may yet be given forth. In the meanwhile, the satisfactory assurance has been made to me that although the court appear to have come to an adverse finding, her Most Gracious Majesty has been advised that, as the charge was not sustained by the evidence, the court-martial has not been confirmed, and is therefore invalid, and that I am freed from all consequences of the trial. I have been further gratified by the opinion on the subject officially conveyed to me from his Royal Highness the Field-Marshal Commanding-in-Chief that, "at the moment of the attack defence was impossible and retreat imperative", and that, "what might have been done, and what ought to have been done when the moment of surprise had passed, can only be judged by an eye-witness", so that these opinions having now been ratified by the voice of my fellow-countrymen I feel that my honour and character as a soldier, and as an English gentleman, have been vindicated. Therefore it is, gentlemen, that I am doubly grateful to you for having been the first to announce to me, and to proclaim to the world at large, that such was your verdict and opinion.'

On 29 August, Carey left Southsea and went to London, where he was interviewed by the Adjutant-General of the Forces. He applied for, and was granted, three months' leave before rejoining the 98th Regiment in Malta. After spending a few days in London, Carey and his family went home to Devon.

28

LETTERS written by Louis before his death, including the last hasty note he had written, using his saddle as a desk, continued to arrive at Camden Place, and they tore at Eugenie's heart. Then some of his personal effects were delivered to her. A will made by the Prince Imperial on 26 February 1879 included the following paragraph :

'To MM Conneau, Espinasse, Bizot, J. N. Murat, A. Fleury, P. de Bourgoing, S. Corvisart, my arms and uniforms, except those I may have last worn, which I leave to my mother.'

On these instructions, someone sent to the Empress a box containing his slashed and bloody uniform, still marked with the mud of the donga. On the day after the funeral, she wandered into her son's room only to be confronted by the shoddy saddle that had betrayed him. Eugenie crumpled to the floor in a faint.

The Empress was obsessed by a desire to know every smallest detail, reading all the papers and freely discussing what she read. She sought assurance that her son had not suffered, and Louis Conneau told her that in the heat of combat, the Prince could not possibly have felt anything. The Empress wrote to a friend :

'This evidence is terrible ! ! Indeed, every word seems to me most unfavourable in every way towards all those who deserted the poor young Prince. All seem to have been so indifferent as to his fate.'

She had been unable to speak Carey's name, until, five days after the funeral, she spoke of him to Princess Beatrice. In her journal, the Princess recorded that the Empress suddenly exclaimed 'with the greatest of fervour' :

179

"Tell me, they'll do nothing to that poor man? Oh, no, I beg of you! He may have a mother! . . ."

'I hesitated, and said of course it was not entirely in my hands, but that I would try and see what could be done, to which she exclaimed: *"Merci, merci."* I then said how unhappy in fact he was, and alluded to the grief and shame we felt, upon which she hastily answered: *"Je ne veux rien savoir. Je sais qu'on l'a tué, voilà tout."* '

The Empress communicated to Queen Victoria that both the English and the French people must understand that it was not her desire that anyone should suffer as a result of the events of June the first. She did not want revenge on the man who was with him when he was killed, although she dearly wished it to be made clear that her son was not in command of the party and therefore not responsible for the deaths of the two troopers. Greatly moved, the Queen promised to write to the reviewing authorities; at the same time she pointed out that the matter was not entirely in her hands.

It was at this time that there came into her hands the letter that Carey had written to his wife from Itelezi Hill during the night of 1 June. Annie had given it to Miss Olivia Scotchburn of Dartmouth, who had called upon Mrs Carey, claiming to be an ex-member of the Camden Place staff who was collecting details of the tragedy for the Empress. Convinced as she was that her husband was blameless for what had happened, it is possible that Annie Carey felt that the letter might arouse compassion in the Empress, should blame be cast upon Jaheel. Miss Scotchburn, in a covering note, wrote that she believed the Empress would wish to read an eye-witness account of her son's last moments.

Much has been made of this incident: asserting that 'by his own pen Carey was a craven and a liar. . . . Eugenie had in her hands a signed confession of his guilt', biographers claim that her reaction was one of deep disgust. The letter showed Carey panting with fear, blessing heaven that he had escaped the bullets, praising the horse that had 'done so well coming back'. Because in the letter he cursed his folly in having chosen the kraal in which to halt, whereas at his trial he had disclaimed all responsibility for the choice, it is claimed that he is a self-confessed liar. Marie de Larminat, the Empress' maid of honour, saw it as an appeal by a distraught wife, hoping for forgiveness by exposing her husband's wretched nakedness. Carey himself later denied this, saying that '. . . no Carey would stoop to such a thing. . . .'

Eugenie saw it as a wordless plea from Mrs Carey, who had entrusted the letter to her. In spite of the urging of her friends, she refused to publish the letter. She did not want revenge—that was beneath her great grief, she 'accused no one'. Also, she felt for the Queen and her Army and wished to spare them humiliation; she reasoned that publication of the letter would only fan the flames of anti-British feeling in France. She had it translated into French and showed it to a few friends, pledging them to silence. Then she issued a public statement :

'The one earthly consolation I have is in the idea that my beloved child fell as a soldier, obeying orders, on a duty which was commanded, and that those who gave them did so because they thought him competent and useful.

'Enough of recriminations. Let the memory of his death unite in a common sorrow all those who loved him, and let no one suffer, either in his reputation or in his interests. I who can desire nothing more on earth, ask it as a last prayer.

'Speak to all, English and French, in this way.
                                        'Eugenie.'

Reading these lines, the Duke of Cambridge, the Commander-in-Chief, could not fail to respect them. He had appointed a Commission to examine the case of Lieutenant Carey; he counselled them to show the moderation which the Queen urged upon him.

There seems little doubt, however, that Eugenie believed Carey guilty, and his statements concerning the Prince's attitude during the patrol caused her some distress :

'My poor child was worshipped by the soldiers and esteemed by the chiefs, therefore they all mourned him. M Carey is the one exception, but I prefer not to touch on a subject that wounds my heart and awakens many sufferings, for if I wished him pardoned, I was far from expecting the apotheosis of a man who has no other claim to go down to history than that of having run away as fast as his horse could carry him, leaving behind a comrade and two men. But let us not stir the bitter cup. . . .'

29

IN trying to discover a reaso⋯ ⋯ for rele⋯sing ⋯rey
and putting an end to the ⋯⋯ ⋯ ⋯ ⋯ ⋯ ⋯ike
of Cambridge had had to wri⋯ ⋯ ⋯ himself. On the one
hand he knew that both the public and the Press were convinced
that Carey was being used as a scapegoat to cover the failings of
officers of higher rank. On the other hand, he had to contend with
the demands of Queen Victoria and the pleas of the Empress
Eugenie that Carey should not suffer '. . . either in his reputation or
interest'. The end result of his deliberations appeared to please no
one. The Queen was said to have been 'raised to a fury of
sarcasm' by his report, while the Empress was horrified to find
that it more than half-justified the man she had magnanimously
wanted to forgive. It was said at the time that 'if he had contented
himself with quietly pardoning Carey, that could have been taken
by everybody as a kind of homage to the Prince's memory'.

The Duke, once he had decided on his course of action, had
allowed the affair to run away with him. His re-considerations
blamed Carey, but half-justified him by emphasising the shared
responsibility and doubtful command. Coupled with the Duke's
tacit acceptance of *'sauve qui peut'* and his acknowledgement
that offensive action by the patrol was probably not possible, these
points added up to a kind of verdict. Unfortunately, it was a
verdict which embodied the implication that British officers were
entitled to run away—that Carey had carried on in an acceptable fashion.[1] Anyway, that was how the Press read it, as *The
Morning Post* indicates,:

> *'Sauve qui peut* is admitted, upon cool reflection, to be the
> legitimate and customary word of command when a recon-
> naissance party is suddenly attacked.'

[1] See Appendix 2—The Harward case.

Sir Lintorn Simmons sent an indignant reply :

'There had been *no* word of command,' he said, 'after the word "mount".' If Carey believed the Prince to be in charge, how had he dared to go off and leave him without an order? But, in any case, 'what was military duty at such a time?' No written law was needed, any more than it was needed by a climbing party in Switzerland; men held together, and helped each other out, 'by the laws of comradeship'. There were no cases in which the party had deserted a comrade, so long as there was the slightest chance of saving him. And then he cited the deeds of Buller, Beresford and others, 'who, at the imminent risk of their own lives have given glorious proof during this unfortunate war that they did not recognise the *sauve qui peut* principle when on reconnaissance'.

The newspapers received the report with mixed views. *The Daily News* said :

'There are probably few persons who will not be glad to hear that Captain Carey was yesterday released from arrest . . . in retreating before a vastly superior force of Zulus, Captain Carey was simply doing his duty as a member of a reconnoitring party. (General Nuthall explained in a letter to *The Daily News* that a reconnaissance party's duty is to discover not to fight.) Even therefore if Captain Carey had been in command of the party there would be nothing in his conduct to call for blame. Captain Carey was in no way responsible for the chance of a dangerous situation and so far as appears did nothing but his duty from first to last.

'When the reputation of a gallant officer and the honour of an English gentleman are concerned, it is not enough that an unjust judgement should be peremptorily set aside. If blame attaches to anyone in South Africa except the unhappy boy himself, for Prince Louis Napoleon's death, it must certainly be to some more influential person than Captain Carey. Captain Carey has been declared entitled to fill once more the position of a brave and innocent officer from which he should never have been temporarily extruded . . . it is not Captain Carey, but the court-martial which is now on its trial, and the opinion of their countrymen, if no more official agency, will demand to know on what grounds they convicted a brother officer on a heinous charge. For the recommendation to mercy has been substituted in reward of justice, but the acquittal of their victim is not their own.'

The *Standard*, in commenting on Carey's release, wrote:

'. . . convinced that the general opinion will be that the quashing of the sentence of the court-martial . . . is an unsatisfactory ending of an unpleasant business. The public has some rights of complaint of the official reticence which has been observed throughout in reference to the proceedings of this case, nor will they appreciate the mode in which his release from arrest has been notified, which certainly has invited a somewhat theatrical air. Captain Carey himself cannot be altogether pleased at the manner in which he has been acquitted.'

The Army and Navy Gazette—Carey's most constant supporter —delivered a strong leader-article:

'The main point, however, is that Captain Carey, after a cruel period of suspense, the pain of which was felt by his family, as well as by himself, has been released, it having been officially declared that the evidence did not prove that his conduct on the 1st of June was unworthy of a British officer. This decision will be received with almost universal satisfaction, by both the Army and the general public. The first feeling, both in military and civil circles, when the bare facts of the catastrophe were made known in England, was undoubtedly that Captain Carey had not conducted himself in a creditable manner. Those who held that no blame attached to him were few in number, but in that small minority we are proud to say we are to be counted. It is therefore with special satisfaction that we have noticed that our efforts in the cause of truth and justice were not without effect, and that by degrees the tide of defamation grew more and more slack, till at length it completely turned. The Press, the public, and the Army are now almost unanimous in asserting that Captain Carey returns to his regiment, without a stain on his honour, an imputation on his courage. Indeed, the feeling is that he is a much injured man, that nothing can compensate him for the terrible mental anguish which he has undergone, and that he ought never to have been brought to trial. Many persons do not, moreover, hesitate to say he had been made a scapegoat of, that he bore the burden of the offences of others, and that had the comrade whom he was accused of forsaking been plain Smith or Jones, instead of the Prince Imperial, Captain Carey would never have been brought to a court-martial. It must be a consolation to him that at the first place at which he touched on arrival in England, public feeling was so strongly pronounced in his favour, that without waiting to know what was the decision of the authorities, some two or three thousand respectable persons placed on record their conviction that he had in no way sullied his ancient and honourable name. Considerations of discipline prevented the Admiral at Plymouth from giving his sanction to the public presentation of an address, but the fact remains that it was drawn up, and that it has provoked an echo throughout the land. That similar manifestations of sympathy will be distasteful to the Government is certain; but for them, Captain Carey is not responsible, for he has throughout displayed a most soldierlike subordination and resignation under his sufferings. It must also be gratifying to Captain Carey and his friends that both officers and the military Press of foreign countries, especially those of Germany and Italy, have expressed a strong conviction of his entire innocence and have even derided the bringing him to trial.'

The loyal readers of *The Army and Navy Gazette* similarly rallied round; the following letter is representative of many received :

'To the Editor of *The Army and Navy Gazette*

'Sir—Public indignation in the case of Capt Carey having subsided, and a deep feeling of sympathy for that gentleman and his family ensued, extending, apparently, throughout the country, while the sentence of the court-martial—alleged to have been "cashiering"—has been set aside by the Queen, at the recommendation of the Judge-Advocate-General, not being borne out by the evidence before it, will you, Sir, allow me to inquire what amends is to be made to the victim of all this commotion, seeing he has for nearly three months been deprived of his sword, and I might say made "the song of the drunkards", for alleged "misbehaviour before the enemy", etc, than which no more humiliating stigma perhaps could have been fixed on an officer and a gentleman, while all this hubbub, or any ground for it, it now turns out, is the outcome of stupid misapprehension (or whatever else one may see fit to term it) of certain officers in South Africa, who seem to have been incapable of discriminating between what constituted command and duty, evidence and no evidence, guilt and no guilt etc? Capt Carey, further, has thus, through the cutting-short of his career by his arrest, previous to the battle of Ulundi and the winding-up of the campaign in Zululand, been deprived of the reasonable hopes of his service and Staff employ—a deprivation which cannot but be most galling to him, as, indeed, it would be to any brave soldier. If political or military expediency seemed to demand, for the moment, this severity of scrutiny on some one, to justify, or to seem to justify, the honour of the nation and the Army before the world, I submit that this, having been vindicated, justice now demands restitution for the victim of that severity, who has so well stood the ordeal, and who, it seems, had by his previous services pretty well established a claim to the brevet rank of major. A mere release from arrest can scarcely be deemed sufficient. He never should have been tried. It is but just, after the cry that has been raised in all the world, that it should be as fully known that Captain Carey's conduct stands unimpeached, and, therefore, that he needed no mercy, but justice,—no, not even the palliation from alleged "loss of presence of mind."—I am, etc. A Colonel.'

With characteristic forbearance, *The Times* gave its opinion :

'The authorities have acted in this matter with caution and impartiality. Not only the character and career of an individual officer, but, to some extent, the reputation of the British Army were at stake. At the same time there was a natural, though possibly a too anxious, desire to prove that, if the Prince Imperial lost his life through the mis-conduct of any English officer, justice would be promptly and strictly meted out. The decision which has been adopted shows at least that there is no wish to secure a scapegoat. We cannot help feeling that there has been both un-necessary mystery and unintelligible delay, and the public will rejoice that these are at an end. Captain Carey has been absolved by the reversal of the sentence passed by the court-martial. He will always bear about with him the sad remembrance of the fatal day on which he accompanied the Prince Imperial's reconnoitring party; but neither his personal honour nor his professional future need be affected by those melancholy recollections.'

On 30 August, *The Army and Navy Gazette* returned to the attack :

'The ill-judged remarks of the Duke of Cambridge, the Commander-in-Chief . . . have somewhat qualified the satisfaction which Captain Carey must feel at his virtual, though not technical acquittal.

'Read carelessly, these remarks rather commend themselves to the judgment and heart of impartial persons. When, however, they are carefully examined, it will, we think, be found that they are illogical and unfair. It almost seems as if the writer were actuated by two opposite motives, each of which ultimately got the upper hand. Evidently the Duke, in his sorrow for the Prince's death and sympathy with the Empress, is indignant with the person who has been so unjustly held responsible for the catastrophe. At the same time, he does not like to run directly counter to public opinion, which pronounces Captain Carey to have been an unlucky scapegoat. Besides, after Her Majesty's virtual acquittal of that officer, it is disrespectful for any one else to cast implied blame upon him.

'His Royal Highness completely clears Lord Chelmsford and, whilst being lenient towards Colonel Harrison—who has already been consoled for censure at home by being pitchforked into the command of a column, he is by no means tender in his criticism of Captain Carey.

'In expressing these opinions, the Duke declares his confidence that he is the mouth-piece of the Army. We believe that he is mistaken, and that the large majority of the Army share our views on the subject.[2]

'In an ingeniously worded sentence . . . (the Duke) intimates that Captain Carey was intended to act as the guardian of the Prince. It strikes us that if the Prince needed a guardian, he ought not to have been sent on the expedition . . . we are surprised that the Duke, in spite of the convincing evidence in Captain Carey's favour, will persist in implying that he was the Prince's guardian, and therefore bound to take every precaution to shield him from the danger which is the general accompaniment

---

[2] One member of the Army, who did not share these views, wrote as follows:

'To the Editor of *The Army and Navy Gazette*.

'Sir—Referring to your article on Captain Carey's court-martial in your last issue, in which you express an opinion that the Duke of Cambridge is mistaken in believing that his remarks thereupon will be re-echoed by the Army, I am constrained to remark that I am satisfied the public opinion of the Service will only differ from it in the belief that the Duke has not said half enough in reprobation of Captain Carey's conduct. This, at all events, is the belief of

A COMMANDING OFFICER.'

'We insert this letter, as our pages are open to advocates on both sides of the question. We have, however, better means of ascertaining the feeling of the Army than "A Commanding Officer", and we are convinced that he is mistaken.—Ed. A. & N.G.'

of all those, whether Princes or privates, who take part in a campaign. The Duke says that Captain Carey acted under the strange misconception that the Prince was his senior officer; but we have no evidence to bear out this statement. The misconception, if there was any, was that the Prince was in command of the party, and this misconception was shared both by the Prince himself and the troopers.

'The question whether, when the first moment of surprise had passed, anything further could have been done, he (the Duke) reasonably says, "can only be decided by an eye witness". Yet, though the Duke was not an eye witness, he says in effect that Captain Carey ought to have remained till all efforts had been made to ascertain the fate of the missing. He thus completely stultifies himself.

'After all, however, this is a comparatively minor matter, as far as Captain Carey is concerned. His alleged offence was that he misbehaved in front of the enemy, and her Majesty has declared that the evidence does not support the charge,—that is to say, that he is innocent of the misbehaviour attributed to him. Therefore, Captain Carey owes his escape, not to any technical flaw, but simply because, though the Court found him guilty, the legal and military advisers of the Crown were of opinion that there was nothing to show that he was to blame in the essential point.

'We now take leave of this painful subject, with an expression of hope that nothing will occur to reopen it, and that Captain Carey himself will observe a discreet silence concerning the wrongs he has undoubtedly suffered.'

On the other hand, *The Daily Telegraph* considered that the decision of the Duke of Cambridge and the judicious comments which accompanied it would be considered satisfactory by the public.

If *The Army and Navy Gazette* steadfastly supported Carey, its rival and counterpart, *The United Service Gazette*, consistently set itself up as the stern defender of the highest morals and principles in the Service. Its leader-article of 30 August sets a typically high note :

'The Canticles of Carey

'Captain Carey has demanded a hymn of praise from his "fellow-believers". He is of opinion that his prayers to Providence, whom he says he "reminded constantly", have caused the quashing of his sentence and his release from arrest. A section of the world not altogether irreligious may think that the stupidity of the judge-advocate who framed the charge for the court-martial had also something to do with bringing about the happy result. Whether Providence secured Captain Carey's freedom by causing the legal official to blunder is a theological problem which may be left to those "fellow-believers" in and of the Captain, who are requested by him, in his extraordinary letter to *The Christian*,[3] to offer up a thanksgiving of praise for his successful wrestling with Heaven. A more curious production from the pen of a British officer has seldom ever appeared in the public press, and that it will be read with feelings of contempt and disgust by the majority of the Army is an opinion which we think will not be singular to ourselves. It must have struck many soldiers of "the old school" with astonishment that a prisoner under arrest, waiting the issue of a court-martial, should have been permitted to hold communications with newspaper correspondents, to have been interviewed by them, and through their means to have commented on his own case in the newspapers. Nobody of course has a right to interfere with the expressions of admiration and sympathy which a certain number of people at Plymouth chose to embody in an address to Captain Carey, but it certainly shows a considerable change in the manners and customs of the service that he should have been allowed to interchange complimentary communications with the shore whilst under the ban of arrest. It may be a proof of the progress of the age that military justice should be so tempered with mercy as to allow such latitude, but as a matter of good taste it might have been better had Captain Carey declined to be interviewed, and kept discreet silence until the order of his release came. Lord

[3] Carey's letter in *The Christian*, Southsea, 25 August 1879: 'My Dear Sir—May I ask you to kindly insert a request for praise on my behalf in the next number of your journal? Since the first moment of my arrest I took the whole matter to my Heavenly Father. I left it in his hands, reminding Him constantly of His promise to help. He has borne my burden for me, He has sustained me, my wife and family, in our distress and He has finally wiped away tears from our eyes. There were certain circumstances at first that seemed, owing to the bewildered statements of the survivors, difficult to explain; but though my faith wavered, His promises endured, and He in His good time brought me to the haven where I would be. I feel that it would be wrong to keep from my fellow-believers such a wonderful example of God's goodness and power in influencing the hearts of men; and though I hate publicity, I feel compelled to add my testimony to the power of prayer. Believe me dear sir, Yours faithfully, Jaheel Brenton Carey.'

189

Chelmsford and his staff were wise in their expressive reticence, and it is a pity that Captain Carey did not show equal good sense. As to good taste, that, after the publication of the sanctimonious epistle which is going the round of the press, need not be considered as a Carey virtue. He declares that he hates publicity, but after doing his best to pose as a military victim he now strikes an attitude as a Christian martyr. It will no doubt take with those who appreciate peculiar forms of heroism and pious testimonials to Providence. Captain Carey "feels it would be wrong" to keep from the world the discovery that Providence is neither unjust nor ungenerous, and through the medium of the press he has caused this satisfactory assurance to be made wide known. Though there are some who may see in his letter not a little of vanity, and something of irreverence, it cannot be doubted that a large portion of what is called the "religious world" will accept it as a valuable testimony, and make much of the writer. Captain Carey may be exalted to higher fame than he has already achieved in the eyes of his friends and fellow believers. Nobody need grudge the saints their idol, but it is to be hoped that the strong common sense of the nation will assert itself in passing a final verdict on the case. The letter from the Horse Guards, reviewing the whole affair, is anything but satisfactory. There is in it the usual official dislike of telling the whole truth. It was clear that somebody had blundered, and so an attempt has been made to shift the burden of responsibility from one shoulder to another, until it was made at last to settle on those of Captain Carey. Public opinion has very properly been against that officer being made a scapegoat, but it can hardly go the length of saying that no responsibility of any kind should rest with him. His Royal Highness the Duke of Cambridge, Lord Chelmsford, and Colonel Harrison must each and all accept a share in the responsibility which was attempted to be fixed on one. But this fact is surely not sufficient to make Captain Carey a hero and a fitting subject for public praise. Taken in its most generous meaning, the language used to explain his conduct has had to adopt the form of apology. He has had to excuse himself, and although we would not quote the French proverb to his detriment the fact remains. In his letter to *The Christian* he owns that "there were certain circumstances that, owing to the bewildered statements of the survivors, were difficult to explain". What were these? Simply that all the survivors stated that they had galloped away, each man to save himself, and no one took thought of his neighbour.

190

We have no intention of discussing here whether Captain Carey acted in proper accordance with reconnoitring rules, nor do we intend to question his caution or his courage. The whole affair was a deplorable one, and can bring back no recollections of pride to the mind of any officer or soldier. The sooner it is buried in the merciful oblivion of forgetfulness the better. But it is because Captain Carey and his friends will not allow this to be done that we raise our voice in protest. Captain Carey is neither a hero nor a martyr, and this commonplace view of his position must sooner or later be accepted by the Army and the nation.'

Later, the same journal commented :

'Some curiosity exists as to the grounds upon which Lieutenant Carey's court-martial was quashed. It was thought at first that Lord Chelmsford had no power to order the assembling of such a court, but this was not the case. Lord Chelmsford had ample powers under the warrant which he held as commanding Her Majesty's forces in South Africa. It is said that the illegality which nullified the proceedings of the court-martial was the blunder of the president of the court in not having recorded that the witnesses had been duly sworn. As a matter of fact the witnesses were sworn, but the fact was not recorded on the proceedings. *Hinc illæ lachrymæ.*

'The military authorities have committed a greater blunder in not publishing the evidence taken and recorded at the court-martial. Captain Carey has been able to make (unintentionally no doubt) considerable capital out of this reticence. His friends will have it that there is something in the background to his credit which the Horse Guards do not choose to disclose. This is not so; His Royal Highness the Duke of Cambridge has shown more than tender mercy; but if a portion of the public insists upon making Captain Carey a hero and a martyr, it is not improbable that further light may be let in upon the whole affair, which seems to have failed to secure a charitable oblivion.'

In mid-September, when the affair was fading from the public mind, *The United Service Gazette* was still unable to resist a few jibes :

'Two privates of the 8th Foot have been sentenced by a court-martial to five years' penal servitude and dismissal with ignominy from the Army for running away from their posts in a sudden panic which took place at the Peiwar Kotal in July last. The court recommended them to mercy, but Sir Frederick Haines refused to give effect to such recommendation, His Excellency remarking :

' "Had the sentence been more severe I could have added my approval. The scare which impelled Privates George Smith and Alfred Spencer to headlong flight might, under other circumstances, have endangered an army. There was no strain upon their courage; the possession of ordinary firmness would have enabled them to act creditably in the position in which they found themselves. Their conduct, on the contrary, was disgraceful. They must take the consequences."

'If Privates Smith and Spencer have been allowed to read the newspapers lately, they must regret that they ran away in Afghanistan and not in Zululand. Had it been their happier fortunes to have taken flight in a scare there, they might have been sent under easy arrest to England, have had congratulatory addresses presented to them on arrival, been interviewed by representatives of the press, and their likenesses put into the illustrated papers, and after the announcement that their court-martial proceedings had been quashed, have been played home in triumph by a volunteer band.

'Opinions, however, *do* differ, and it is said that there is a scheme on foot to get up a subscription in order to present Captain Carey with a sword. Would not a pair of spurs be a more appropriate compliment?'

With Carey free and enjoying leave with his family, the newspapers played out the final rounds with conjectures as to his future. *The Western Daily Mercury* said :

' . . . his future procedure will depend upon the course of events at the Cape. An officer, and a gentleman of much modesty, he naturally shrinks from the empty parade of applying for further service in Zululand at the close of the war, but should it appear that more fighting is in store for the British forces, and military men who have recently returned from the Cape are of opinion that the struggle is not yet over, he will ask for permission to return to the post he vacated when placed on his trial. Although the finding of the court-martial has been set aside, the consequences to Captain Carey have been serious. As the public are aware, he was holding a staff appointment in Zululand. But for the deplorable event of the 1st of June, and in the ordinary course of affairs, he would have advanced with the Commander-in-Chief, and would have been present at the battle of Ulundi. Some recognition of service, in the shape, perhaps of a Brevet-Majorship was, therefore, not too much to have anticipated. If compelled, however, to rejoin his regiment (the 98th) which, as stated on Saturday, is now at Malta, all chance of professional promotion at the close of the war is at an end.'

The United Service Gazette endeavoured to have the last word :

'It is said that Captain Carey will not, on the expiration of his present leave of absence, rejoin his regiment. It is not true that he has asked to be transferred to the West Indian corps in which he at one time served, but it is possible that he may retire from the service altogether if he gets a fair price from the purchase commissioners, and may enter another body "militant"—the church.'

30

DURING his leave, Carey seems to have decided upon a course of action that could be construed as one of calculated expediency. At best, it can only be viewed as an attempt at self-justification by a man of weak character. Knowing that friendship with the French royal family had given a certain standing to Bigge, Slade and Wodehouse, Carey apparently reasoned that his vindication lay in his reception by the Empress Eugenie. He wrote a letter, addressed to the Duc de Bassano at Camden Place, in which he said that as long as his name was under a cloud he had thought it right and proper to be silent, that he had hesitated to approach the Empress with the possibility of guilt hanging over him. However, now that he was freed from that restraint,

'. . . now that I think I may say I stand freed from the charge of cowardice or misbehaviour . . .', he asked that his deepest sympathy be conveyed to the Empress and suggested that she might like to see him to hear about her son's last hours.[1]

Bassano answered with dignity, requesting that Carey withdraw statements he had made in the Press imputing blame to the Prince accusing him of obstinacy and self-will that had cost three lives. In the correspondence that followed, Carey became repetitive and provocative:

'I know what Captain Molyneux says about resistance, and I was there, too, but I don't see it. Each is entitled to his own view, but I don't want to impose mine on anyone more than his.'

He repeatedly denied being in command:

'The truth is I never knew I was to be considered responsible

---

[1] *The United Service Gazette* 6 September 1879: 'The Empress Eugenie has not, we believe, intimated any anxiety to see Captain Carey . . . she has seen Lord William Beresford, Redvers Buller and Lord Chelmsford.'

for his safety—or I should have acted very differently! . . . I feel sure that all people whose judgment is worth having will at least look leniently on any error of judgment we, or rather let me say I, committed that day. In the letters to my wife, to which you refer, you will see that I never implied I was in command, but merely that the responsibility of the choice of position must be mine. This responsibility I have always accepted and I felt at the time, though few would have acted differently, that this was the only thing for which I could be blamed. . . .'

To each letter came a restrained and courteous reply; carried beyond the bounds of sensible restraint, Carey continued to plead his case with increasing insensibility. Throughout, the Empress remained aloof; to her Carey was the officer '. . . who had run away as fast as his horse could carry him leaving behind a comrade and two men.' However, at last she could take no more; at her orders, Marie de Larminat closed the correspondence :

'L'Imperatrice juge inutile de poursuivre cette correspondence.'

Frantic, Carey continued to write himself into a contradictory morass. Saying that '. . . he was deeply grieved and pained at the tone of her letter . . .' he wrote that he was horrified that anyone should think his wife had asked the Empress to 'intercede'. 'Only the guilty criminal or the friends of such plead for mercy, and no Carey would ever have descended so low . . . I cannot bear to think that any of my friends have been supposed to crave for mercy.' Miss Scotchburn had offered, but '. . . Mrs Carey had said no . . . she relied on the merits of the case. . . .'

None of these letters was answered, and the Empress eventually passed them on to Queen Victoria. The Queen in turn showed one of them to Disraeli, commenting that it was disgraceful that Carey should have got off so lightly. The Prime Minister replied that under the circumstances, it was probably the best thing :

'He is a caitiff, and yet the court-martial has so mismanaged the case that it is highly probable that if their verdict had been sanctioned, this mean wretch might have been transfigured into a hero or a martyr.'

31

THERE is rarely a single cause of any tragedy; rather, the climax is the inevitable culmination of a chain of events. The Prince Imperial did not die solely because the character and temperament of a fellow-officer decreed that it was preferable to be a live coward than a dead hero. Perhaps the first link of the chain was forged in July 1870, when Bismarck manœuvred France into a disastrous war with Prussia. There were many other agents—Carey, Harrison, Bettington, Buller, Chelmsford, the Zulus Langalabalele and Zabanga, a grey named Percy, the Empress Eugenie—and the French people. Is it unfair to single out Lieutenant Carey's share of the blame as being greater than the collective contribution of the others?

Perhaps it really began when the Prince was permitted to go to Natal—*The Times* of 1 July 1879 certainly thought so:

'With respect to the cause of the calamity, our correspondence of yesterday has afforded considerable light on the circumstances, and though there is still a good deal of uncertainty respecting details, there are some important points on which there can be no little doubt. It now appears that Lord Chelmsford, as might have been expected, had given general verbal orders that the Prince Imperial should not be allowed to go on any expedition without a fitting escort, and that in any case he should not be permitted to incur undue danger. So far as the General in command was concerned, nothing more could well have been done for the Prince. Suppose Lord Chelmsford had issued orders in writing to this effect, and that these had been published, as they assuredly would have been, in France and elsewhere, what would have been the consequences to the Prince? He might have escaped risk; but an injury would have been inflicted on his reputation from which he would have found it very hard to recover.

'His difficulty is forcibly illustrated by the proceedings of the Bonapartist party in France at this moment. M Rouher, while "recognising" Prince Napoleon, has nevertheless resolved to retire into private life. In other words, he feels that he and Prince Napoleon could not act together, though at the same time the Prince cannot be formally put aside. What is the secret of this general unpopularity of Prince Napoleon? It is known to arise in great measure from the fact that the Prince has been singularly unfortunate in his attempts to display his military qualities. He returned from the Crimea too soon to have exhibited his valour, and he has similarly found himself unable to come to the front in the other great wars which France has waged during his lifetime. But a Napoleon without a military reputation is not half himself, and Prince Napoleon is now paying the penalty of his misfortunes in this respect. With this example before his eyes, it became the natural—perhaps the commendable—desire of the late Prince Imperial to afford the world, at all hazards, incontestable evidence of his gallantry and military capacity. This was the very purpose for which he went out, and it commanded sympathy both here and in his own country. But if an order could have been produced by the enemies or critics of the Bonapartists showing that the Prince had throughout the campaign been shielded by the vigilance of the British General and his Staff, the whole scheme would have collapsed, and the Prince's expedition would almost have become a subject of ridicule. It was therefore quite inevitable that the Prince should in great measure be left to himself; and the natural consequences of his anomalous position are clearly visible in the reports we have published. The Prince, being for a little while out of Lord Chelmsford's hands, persuaded the Acting Quartermaster-General to allow him to reconnoitre and to choose a suitable place in advance for a new camp. It is not surprising that such a request was at length granted. It was not easy for an officer in subordinate command to refuse an appeal urged on him with the eager gallantry which the Prince displayed. Our Correspondents describe him as anxious beyond all measure to see actual fighting. He thought it dull work being shot at, and even expressed his wish to experience a slight assegai wound. He was allowed to have his way; and perhaps it is due to the informality of the whole procedure that no adequate escort seems to have been provided for the party. So far as can at present be learned, the whole conduct of the reconnaissance was left in the Prince's hands, Lieutenant Carey being directed by Colonel

Harrison to allow the Prince to have the sole honour of selecting the new camping-ground. The same eagerness is conspicuous in all the arrangements of the reconnaissance. The Prince would hear of no danger, and the party seem to have acted as coolly as if they had been taking a ride in a friendly country.

'The conclusion, we apprehend, which the public will be apt to draw from these facts will be by no means that which the chief military authority in this country seemed to suggest when the sad news first arrived. The chief blame or error of judgment will be seen to lie in the original consent to the Prince's enterprise. It was impossible for an overworked body of officers to be always watching the Prince, and he was sure sooner or later to find some one among them more complaisant than the rest who would allow him the opportunity for which he was eagerly craving. He was not under orders, and could not be positively commanded, and his personal influence rendered it very difficult to resist him. There must, indeed, be a very careful inquiry into the details of the disaster itself, which, as narrated in our columns yesterday, seem very unsatisfactory. But the judgment on these points must be referred to the military authorities, and the public will be very reluctant to anticipate their decision. That which it is of importance to observe at the moment is that the disaster arose essentially out of the fact of the Prince being present in South Africa in a false position which exposed both himself and all around him to constant difficulties and temptations. It would have been wonderful if no error had been committed in dealing with such exceptional circumstances, and any error might be fatal.'

The reader will by now have formed his own views on whether or not the patrol were justified in *sauve qui peut*. One officer in Lord Chelmsford's army did not think they were :

'. . . everyone here believes that if Lieutenant Carey had kept his men together, and faced about too, opening a fire as they came on the Zulus, if they had been cool enough to do it, the Prince would have been saved. It was the stampede that encouraged the enemy to leave the hiding-place from which they had fired. The whole story is too dreadful, and one does not like to think about it now. What we all want is to get away from the country, and leave the Zulus and the Colonists to adjust their future relations.'

Bear in mind, however, that the Prince Imperial, equally with Carey, was leaving Trooper Rogers and the native guide to their fates. The French Press and biographers of the Prince Imperial have consistently attempted to minimise this fact by claiming that the Prince was abandoned by the rest of the party at the moment of surprise. In even stronger terms, the same writers have gone to immense pains to prove that Lieutenant Carey was in command of the party and not the Prince. They obscure the possibility that it was the Prince who led the party into a death-trap and failed to take the most elementary military precautions :

'Besides, what reason would there have been for the Prince to go down from the heights to the kraal? Nothing would have suggested it to him, whereas there was an obvious interest to Carey in the points that remained uncertain on his maps, for it was his business to find in those low-lying marshy places a way for the guns and transport.'

In the records of the British Headquarters at Utrecht in the Transvaal, the name of the Prince Imperial was shown in Orders and Field States as being without military rank but as an extra aide-de-camp to Lord Chelmsford. On 19 July 1879 *The United Service Gazette* wrote :

'The first blunder committed was perhaps in recognising the presence of the Prince Imperial as attached to the Staff of the British Army at all.'

Because he wore the undress uniform of an officer of the Royal Artillery, most people invested the Prince Imperial with the status of a British officer—it is recorded at least twice in contemporary papers that he was 'an honorary Captain'. The notoriously lax staff-work of the Zulu War may well have countenanced such a grading. The other aides on Chelmsford's staff were puzzled by the Prince's status; Molyneux, the senior of them, later testified on oath to this fact. Carey asserted consistently that he believed himself to be inferior to the Prince in military rank.

In connection with the question of command, there was an amazing sequel, claimed by a member of Empress Eugenie's entourage to be '. . . a voice from the tomb . . .' which proved Carey's responsibility. Later in the year 1879, after the war had been concluded, Louis's sword and uniform were recovered from Cetewayo and sent home to his mother. Among this kit was a light waterproof said to have been worn by the Prince when he set out on the fatal patrol. In the ticket pocket, Eugenie came across a leaf from her son's notebook, with the following note in what appeared to be the Prince's writing :

'June 1st—Started from Itelezi to find camping ground for 2nd Division. Escort under Captain Carey.'

General Sir Evelyn Wood writes about this incident in his book *From Midshipman to Field Marshal.* However, although he played a relatively prominent rôle in the events of the time, it is almost the only mention of the Prince Imperial that he makes in his book :

'The officer, arraigned before a Court-Martial for misbehaviour, alleged the Prince was in command of the party, but I have had a strange and convincing piece of evidence before me for many years, in the Prince's own hand-writing, that he was serving under the British officer, and was therefore in no sense responsible for the disaster. Light rain was falling early on the 1st June, and when the party started the Prince was wearing a Pocket Siphonia.[1] He had been unusually well taught; his plans submitted for redoubts to defend depôts showing not only great natural talent, but that he had thoroughly assimilated the sound instruction imparted at the Royal Military Academy at Woolwich. On previous patrols he had taken full notes, and on the 1st June had filled the sheet of a writing pad thus : "1st June.—Started from Itelezi to find camping-ground for 2nd Division; party under Captain ——"; and then follows an itinerary with a panoramic sketch, the last entry being dated 1.30 pm. The Prince, tearing these notes off the pad, had put the paper into the ticket pocket of the waterproof; and when, after the war, various articles belonging to His Imperial Highness were recovered, the coat, having been sent to Chislehurst, was being sponged and straightened out, for the waterproofing had caused it to stick together, a lump in the ticket pocket was noticed, which was found to be the sheet of the writing pad.'

If these facts are true, there is no question that the Prince was in command of the party; but there seems little doubt that this note is a forgery. The patrol did not start from Itelezi, but from the old camp on the left bank of the Blood River. It was to Itelezi that the fugitives returned late on 1 June. But the main

[1] A very light waterproof of the day, advertised 'to be carried in the pocket'.

reason for considering the note to be other than genuine is that Carey did not at that time hold the local, honorary, or temporary rank of Captain; in Zululand, he was always 'Lieutenant' Carey. The Prince and he were often together on previous duties, and both were in the same small section of the Headquarters Staff; and the Prince was notoriously punctilious in such things as rank. It was not until five days after the Prince's death, on 6 June, that Carey's promotion was shown in *The London Gazette*. In England and France, Carey was known as a captain because by the time he came to public attention the *Gazette* had published his new rank. Thus the press invariably described him as Captain, and very few people in England realised that Carey, when the Prince knew him, had been a Lieutenant.

Every record and account indicates that the Prince Imperial was the man who exercised command of the patrol, that he was *de facto*, if not *de jure*, in command. Even M Deléage, correspondent for *Le Figaro*, a violently anti-Carey writer, inadvertently admits this fact. Describing the surprise of the party in a report to his paper, he used these words :

'*Il résulte un point certain et réel. C'est que le Prince, mettant le pied a l'etrier, donna immédiatement quelques ordres brefs et rapides pour maintenir ses hommes et réprimer tout affolement.* (One certain real point emerges. That is that the Prince, putting his foot in the stirrup, immediately gave certain brief and rapid orders to sustain his men and quell panic.)'

In any military group, the man who gives the orders is the man who is in command; and '*ses hommes*' (his men) tells its own tale.

The United Service Gazette deals sternly with a Government spokesman on this point :

'Lord Bury's plea that the Prince Imperial could not have been in command of the party because ". . . he did not hold the Queen's commission" would be amusing were it not so utterly lame and unsatisfactory. Does every officer commanding men in the Cape hold the Queen's commission? Do the numerous leaders of Irregular troops—Commandant Lonsdale, Major Bengough, Major Dartnell and a dozen more? Does Captain Bettington, whose Irregular Horse furnished the escort? It would have been much better for Lord Bury to have confessed openly and at once that he did not know, or that if he knew he did not choose to say.'

It might have turned out differently had Major Bettington been in command of the party. In his diary, Bettington wrote:

'If I had been there, I should have saved him or I would have stayed there with him.'

Madly courageous men like Bettington or Buller probably would have stayed in the kraal—and if they had decided that discretion was the better part of valour, then their reputations would have justified their actions. Bettington never went out without his mounted Basuto scouts; a British correspondent wrote:

'In all probability had those quick-sighted and sharp-witted natives (the Basutos), thoroughly experienced in Zulu tactics, accompanied the party, the catastrophe would never have occurred.

'They would most certainly, being so near akin to the wily Zulu and his cunning tricks, never have permitted the party to have off-saddled in such a dangerous position, with dense cover on two sides, a steep hill shutting off retreat on the third side, a deep donga on the fourth, wherein, as it proved, the Zulu ambush party were hidden.'

Another relevant factor must be the size of the party; had it been stronger it might never have been attacked, or it would probably have made possible aggressive resistance after the surprise. It might be that Carey was loath to take out a larger party as a result of the recent chaffing he had suffered when he had taken out a whole squadron of Regulars. But in this connection, Colonel Harrison must shoulder some of the responsibility. After entrusting a responsible and dangerous task to the Prince, he saw how scanty was the protection afforded to him; but he had still allowed them to continue.

Harrison was a harassed and over-worked officer, and had an extra burden placed upon him when he was put in charge of the Prince Imperial. Lord Chelmsford's verbal instructions to Harrison left to the latter's discretion the particular duties to which his Royal charge was assigned, providing that they were not dangerous. Obviously, when Harrison sent the Prince and his party out to select a new camping ground, he had no anticipation of danger; he saw it as a safe day's outing. The whole tenor of the morning reflects this interpretation, from the happy-go-lucky departure of the party with only half their escort to the mesmerised indifference with which they picnicked in the enemy's country.[2]

It seems inexplicable that Colonel Harrison should have assigned to the Prince Imperial the task of selecting a new camping site. In enemy territory this can be done only by an experienced and highly-trained officer, who can adequately consider the many problems such as defence, water-supply, command of view, hygiene and approaches and exits. It is difficult to accept that Lord Chelmsford, still recovering from the disaster at Isandhlwana, could have known that his army was marching to a camp chosen by a young and impetuous man backed by only two years' training at 'The Shop'.

Colonel Harrison is said to have performed all his military duties in an excellent fashion throughout the Zulu War. When Sir Garnet Wolseley arrived in South Africa he selected Harrison

---

[2] *The Army and Navy Gazette* remarked bitterly upon this:

'That the party should have been surprised, is extremely discreditable to us. It is incontestable that the most ordinary precautions against such a catastrophe were neglected. The expedition was not more hazardous than a patrol in an enemy's country must always be, and considering that the Zulus have no cavalry and that the Prince's party was well mounted, there ought to have been no exceptional amount of risk. The party, however, had they wished to be surprised, could scarcely have taken measures better calculated to ensure the success of their object. They first of all placed themselves on a high hill, where they must have been visible from any spot within several miles. They continued there for some time sketching, so as to obviate any chance of their having escaped notice by the keen-eyed Zulus. They then off-saddled in a kraal which showed signs of having been recently occupied, and turning their horses loose, simply indulged in a picnic. Except on one side, the kraal was surrounded by high grass and maize, yet not only did they turn their horses loose to graze, but they never searched the neighbourhood, did not post a single sentry, and did not even load their rifles. It is a well-understood rule that the horses of a cavalry picquet should be kept constantly saddled, and that the bridles of only from a third to a half of the horses should be removed at a time, for the purpose of feeding or watering. If this is the rule for outposts, it is still more essential that it should be observed by cavalry reconnoitring. Again, Clery, in *Minor Tactics*, says, regarding halts by cavalry thus employed, "They should never be made in inhabited places, but either in secluded spots, where surprise is not to be apprehended, or on elevated ground, where a good view can be obtained. During a halt, vedettes should be thrown out, and every precaution taken for security." For the neglect of these elementary rules of war, the poor Prince himself was responsible, for though he had no commission, and therefore could not properly exercise any authority, he was expressly placed in command of the party. At the same time, we should like to know whether Captain Carey—a passed Staff-College officer—made any representations to his Imperial Highness on the subject. If he did not, he clearly neglected his duty.'

a comparatively junior officer, for the command of a brigade. This caused considerable comment in England, and one military journal of the time set forth its views as follows :

'It certainly seems somewhat extraordinary that a comparatively junior officer like Colonel Harrison should have been selected for the command of a brigade in Zululand, when so many experienced and senior officers are left out in the cold. Colonel Harrison has had little practice in handling troops—indeed, it is seldom that Engineer officers obtain that practice. Moreover, considering the great want of discretion displayed by him in connection with the expedition when the Prince Imperial lost his life, he was scarcely the man to obtain such exceptional advancement as that which has fallen to his lot. Here at home everyone is crying out that Captain Carey has been made Colonel Harrison's scapegoat; and it is, under these circumstances, rather a wanton defiance of military public opinion that Sir Garnet Wolseley should have gone out of his way to give Lieutenant-Colonel Harrison the command of a brigade.'

When Colonel Harrison learned of the reprimand contained in the Duke of Cambridge's statement, he issued a personal statement that appears to have satisfied those in authority at the War Office. He came out of the Zulu War as a Companion of the Bath; he eventually retired as a full General.

The United Service Gazette also criticised Lord Chelmsford :

'Lord Chelmsford was . . . anxious that the youth's impetuous gallantry should be curbed and that he should not be permitted to run needless risks; but he appears to have allowed him to go on reconnoitring parties as his fancy led him. Colonel Harrison may or may not be a courtier, but in directing Captain Carey not to interfere with the Prince, but to allow him to have the full credit of the work undertaken, he took a responsibility on himself which was hardly in the routine of his duties.'

The officers of higher rank stuck together in the support of Harrison. Redvers Buller later told the Queen that 'Colonel Harrison *could not* be blamed'—he had 'most nervous and responsible duties to perform' and it was 'a shame' to try to put this calamity on him. As he made no excuse, but left his case entirely to his superiors, they felt for him all the more. The outer world, however, thought harshly of him.

A letter written by an officer serving in Natal at the time spoke of the Prince's horse :

'It is about 15·2 hands and is very quiet and easy to mount, a grey, with a hard mouth and good action, rather fiddle-headed, which I see mounted by Clifford's aide-de-camp, Lieutenant Westmacott, every day of my life. The fact is that the Prince, who was a centaur when once in the saddle, did not get into it well unless he vaulted in clear, as he was fond of doing; and Captain Bettington says he remarked frequently that the Prince got his stirrup with difficulty. The Prince seized a near wallet with his left hand, and tried to spring into the saddle. It is nearly certain that he caught the rotten leather strap of the wallet and that when it gave way he fell, his hold on the stirrup leather by the left hand throwing him rather under the horse till he let go.'

Contemporary opinion felt that the force of circumstances was against Carey. *The United Service Gazette*—never pro-Carey—expressed this view in one of their editorials :

'. . . the Court speaks in language which is guarded yet perfectly plain . . .', and goes on to say that Carey's trial by Court-Martial was the inevitable result of adverse public opinion. The main indictment, '. . . stripped of verbiage and reduced to plain English, accuses Lieutenant Carey of cowardice and nothing less . . . the word is painful to pen . . . it is an aspersion which has never, if at all, been cast upon an English officer before, and no one will deny commiseration to the unfortunate man who finds himself arraigned upon so terrible a charge. So long as the case is *sub judice* it is but right to refrain from comment. But while all will unite in hoping that Mr Carey may clear himself from a shameful imputation, which, if proved, must alike ruin his character and his professional prospects, there is but too much reason to fear that public opinion upon the spot, as expressed by Sir Evelyn Wood's scathing censure when he encountered Lieutenant Carey returning alone, has already condemned a comrade who appeared to have been unfaithful to the traditions of his cloth.'

One writer of the time came nearest to the truth :

'The excitement is too great to reason calmly upon this subject; but the reflection is forced upon us, that here has been solved one of the most difficult problems of French history.'

32

W HEN his leave ended, Carey rejoined his regiment, the 98th, who were at Litchfield, prior to their departure for Floriana in Malta; the regiment was commanded at that time by Lieutenant-Colonel Attilio Sceberras. However, the prospect before Carey was not a happy one. Officially he had been relieved of all consequences of his trial, but the stigma of a conviction for misbehaviour in the field is not one to be lifted by a formal phrase—certainly not in the eyes of the officer-class, obsessed by traditions of honour.

It has been generally accepted by everyone who has written about the tragedy that Carey was a military pariah from the moment when he dug his spurs into his horse. Without exception, all assert that '. . . he rejoined his regiment a broken man. . . .' In *The Prince Imperial* (1959) E. E. Tisdall writes:

'The unhappy Carey departed for India, where as the most miserable and shunned of officers he died in the service several years later.'

Katherine John, in her book *The Prince Imperial* (1939), says:

'That was the end of Carey. He never got off; he never got away from that kraal. The utter ruin of his career—his promising career —became the least circumstance in the life of torture. Officers turned their backs as he approached. When he spoke, there was no reply; if he tried to join a conversation, it stopped at once. The name of Carey was felt a disaster and a stigma by those who had no connection with him. After so much volubility, a silence fell around him. . . .'

In *Service Trials and Tragedies* (1930), F. E. Whitton, probably the most sympathetic of the writers on this subject, writes:

206

'. . . a broken man. No one, of course, ever referred to the Zulu campaign in his presence; he never alluded to the subject himself. Although he had received numerous letters of congratulations from home and abroad on his release, he was a man who disliked publicity and he knew well that his career was broken for ever. He was not, however, called upon to carry his cross for long. . . .'

The latest book in which the subject is mentioned is *The Washing of the Spears* by Donald R. Morris (1966). On p. 543 he writes :

'He was finished. He rejoined his regiment, which did not want him, and he was put in Coventry for the rest of his life. Officers turned their backs on him when he approached; conversations he tried to join ceased. He had neither the sense nor the courage to resign.'

It is not to be expected that French authors would write well of Carey. Auguste Filon, the Prince's tutor, wrote in *Memoirs of the Prince Imperial* (1912) :

'When Carey, full of assurance, would have taken his place again in the Service, the greetings he received taught him what feelings were entertained towards him without any expression of those feelings in words. He knew the bitterness of that dumb ostracism which isolates its object in the middle of the most animated company, which ignores his presence and even his very existence, does not see him when he is there, does not hear him when he speaks; the eyes that turn away, the hands that shun, the conversations that stop when he enters, and begin again when he goes; all that world of signs, and above all of silences that make of him an outsider among his comrades, an inferior among his equals, a stranger in his own house, a dead man in the midst of living. Carey held on, convinced that time would work for him. He dragged his isolation and rancour from garrison to garrison until the day when disease carried him off. Were those few years of wretched life worth the price with which he had bought them?'

There is a marked similarity in the expressed sentiments which could indicate that each writer is perpetuating a legend. Closer examination indicates that these are expressions of opinion based upon what the character and temperament of the writer leads him to feel *should* rather that *would* have occurred. On Carey's subsequent Army career, the views of these writers appear to be based more upon conviction than upon evidence.

If it is to be accepted that Carey was treated in this manner by his fellow officers for the remainder of his military career, then it must also be accepted that Carey must have been a man of exceptional character in order to withstand such treatment and to continue to soldier. And an unimaginative, stolid, self-sufficient man might possibly have shrugged off such treatment or allowed it to pass over his head. However, there is every indication that Carey was none of these things—he was a highly-strung, emotional, voluble, ambitious man who gained his self-assurance from the esteem of others.

Carey would appear to have possessed a sort of courage, and resistance to adversity that is quite unlike the craven character that these same writers claim for him. It can be fairly claimed that Jaheel Brenton Carey has emerged from the pages of this book as a resourceful man, with a quick and perhaps flashy intellect; obviously good at his job, with no record of reproof or censure against him so far as his military duties are concerned. He was an excellent linguist, with Staff experience that would fit him for the handling of men in other capacities. His family were comfortably off, and the favourable opinions and expressions of confident goodwill that abounded in 1879 throughout the country and in the Press would most likely have led Carey to feel that he was capable of making a worth-while career for himself outside the Army. He did not have to tolerate humiliation and crushing indignities. It seems unlikely that he did, in fact, suffer as the authors quoted above would have us believe.

Brave men can be tolerant of those who show less courage. Both Sir Evelyn Wood and Redvers Buller had won the Victoria Cross and were known to be men of exceptional courage bordering almost on foolhardiness. They say very little in reproof of Carey in their respective biography and autobiography; and few of Chelmsford's force in Zululand recorded any denunciation of Carey. Perhaps the tradition of sticking together silenced those Regular officers who may have felt strongly about the affair; and the casual, eminently practical Irregulars probably tolerated the expedient of *sauve qui peut* as being the only sensible course of action under the circumstances.

The manner in which *The Army and Navy Gazette* championed Carey, and the sympathy expressed in numerous letters from serving soldiers, indicate that military opinion was not entirely against him.

The son of an officer who served with Carey in the 98th Regiment during the early 1880's, recalls that his father 'spoke of Carey's tragedy several times'. He goes on to say :

'He always spoke very kindly of him and sympathetically as a very smart officer who had the bad luck not to have risen to the occasion when the opportunity arose. I understood him to say that Lieutenant Carey said the order was given for a general *"sauve qui peut"* and he was under the impression the Prince Imperial had got away. . . . I understand Lieutenant Carey had trouble with his own frightened horse at the time. It sounds at least as if the officers of the 98th did not "black-ball" him.'

33

Early in 1880, the Empress Eugenie decided to make a pilgrimage to Zululand, to spend the first anniversary of her son's death in the kraal and donga where he died. The Empress wrote of her resolve to a friend, M Franceschini Pietri:

'. . . I feel myself drawn towards this pilgrimage as strongly as the disciples of Christ must have felt drawn towards the Holy Places. The thought of seeing, of retracing the stages of my beloved son's last journey, of seeing with my own eyes the scene upon which his dying gaze has rested, of passing the anniversary of the night of the 1st of June watching and praying alone with his memory, is for me a spiritual necessity and an aim in life. Since the end of the war has allowed me to regard this possibility more hopefully, it has become my dominant thought. . . . This thought sustains me and gives me fresh courage; without it I should never have sufficient strength to endure my life, and I should allow myself to be submerged in my sorrow. . . . I am under no delusions as to the painful experiences which await me in Africa, or the long and trying sea voyage and the strain of a hurried journey, but all this vanishes when I think of Itelezi. . . .'

Displaying the greatest solicitude, Queen Victoria insisted that General Sir Evelyn Wood should accompany her to act as escort, for her safety and to make her journey as easy as possible in an uncivilised country. Captain Slade and Captain Bigge also accompanied the party, together with the Marquis de Bassano, son of the Duke, and Doctor Scott, who had served as an army surgeon throughout the Zulu War. Sir Evelyn Wood's wife and another lady, the widow of an officer killed at Ulundi, who was bound on a similar pilgrimage, accompanied Her Majesty.

The Empress left England on 28 March and arrived at Cape Town on the morning of 16 April, where she stayed at Government House, as the Prince had a year before. On 18 April the Empress wrote to M Pietri :

'We have arrived at Cape Town after twenty days' journey. I can well understand the tedium which my poor boy must have endured, as the voyage is most monotonous, and the heat is intense near the Equator. I have never slept a single night! I found here on my arrival the *d'Estrées*, the French despatch vessel which was commanded by M des Varannes when he fell ill with yellow fever. . . . I would not land at Madeira, and since my arrival at Cape Town I have only been in the garden of Government House. I cannot express to you what I felt when I entered this house, the first halting place of my beloved son! . . .'

While the party was at Cape Town, the Marquis de Bassano visited the castle in which Cetewayo, the ex-King of the Zulus, was imprisoned. It is recorded that Cetewayo expressed in suitable terms, through the medium of an interpreter, his regret at the death of the Prince; he could tell nothing of the details of the tragedy, but he recalled that as soon as he realised its importance to the Europeans he sent the Prince's sword back to the authorities.

After several days' journey by steamer the party reached Durban and travelled on from there to Maritzburg, from where the Empress wrote to M Pietri on 3 May :

'My reception everywhere is of the most touching character; not a sound, not a shout, but a respectful silence similar to that which one tries to maintain in a sick room, and everyone uncovers his head. Even the blacks seem to understand that she to whom God has given so much, yet from whom He has taken, one by one, all the gifts which He had bestowed, leaving her the heart's bitterness as her only companion, is indeed past all wishes. . . . I saw some Sisters this morning who have prayed over my lost beloved one. Everybody speaks of him in terms which make my grief more intense, but which at the same time appeal to my pride as a mother. . . . Oh, why was he taken so soon, and why was I left behind? . . . I do not know exactly where this letter will find you, but give your news of me to those who are anxious to hear, if any still exist. . . .'

The journey up-country began in the first days of May. A letter from M de Bassano furnishes some details as to the conditions under which it was made. A letter is dated from Seven Oaks (South Africa), the third stage of the journey :

'My Dear Friend—I am writing a few hurried words to tell you that all goes well up to the present time. The Empress is not too fatigued with the journey, although unfortunately she is sleeping badly. . . . Our slow progress gets terribly on her nerves; although she keeps her feelings well under control, I can see plainly that her sadness increases day by day. I dare not picture her grief when we arrive at Itelezi!

'She travels with Lady Wood in a carriage driven by the general himself, and the carriage has been made as comfortable as possible. The days are very warm, and the nights are cool. The Empress's tent is wonderfully well arranged. We have with us as escort twenty of the Natal Mounted Police, and we number in all seventy-five persons and two hundred animals, horses and mules, the greater part supplied by the Government. . . .

'Please give our news to Corvisart, and tell him that Scott says he has written to him by each mail.'

On 11 May the Empress wrote to M Pietri:

'. . . One can almost imagine it possible to trace his footprints, so far is one from mankind in these immense solitudes. . . . And, as the moment approaches when we shall reach our journey's end, I am torn between impatience to arrive there, and dread. . . . I should wish to stay there for as long as I have courage to remain.'

And again on 23 May:

'. . . We shall arrive on the 25th—that is to say, on Tuesday. I shall like that better than this long waiting, which terribly unnerves me. . . .

'I am very tired. I have been suffering with fever for some days. The weather has been shocking; one night at Kambula we thought that our tents would have been swept away by the heavy rain and the strong wind. That very day was the worst day of the fever. . . .'

They crossed the Zulu border at Landman's Drift and reached their destination, the kraal at Ityotyozi, on the evening of 25 May, and it is recorded that the Empress walked straight to the spot where her son fell, guided only by her intuition. But she did not find it as she had imagined.

'Near the cairn raised by the soldiers on the morning of June 2nd, 1879, a cross had been erected by order of Queen Victoria. All vestige of the grass trodden by her son and watered with his blood in his last fight had disappeared beneath a layer of white cement, surrounded by an iron railing. The soil of the donga had been carefully raked as far as the top of the banks which bordered it. The two soldiers and the Basuto guide who were killed in the skirmish of June 1st at the same time as the Prince were buried a few paces away, with the result that the spot presented the peaceful and orderly appearance of an English cemetery instead of that of a wild ravine which had witnessed a scene of death and carnage. The Empress experienced a bitter disappointment, if one can rightly apply this commonplace word to this particular instance.'

Her feelings were understood by her companions, and the next day Captain Slade removed the layer of cement which offended the Empress. The Marquis de Bassano wrote on 29 May:

'. . . The Empress can see from her tent the road taken by the Prince from the kraal to the donga; and as it is exactly the same season, the maize and the grasses are the same height as they were this time last year. As she goes from her tent to the donga she can picture the poor Prince, running by the side of his horse, vainly trying to mount him, and prevented from so doing by the tall grass (taller than myself by 30 or 40 centimetres), crossing a first branch of the donga, climbing a bank, and then stopping to meet his foes in a small hollow before one reaches the main donga— which was crossed by Carey at a point eighty paces away from the Prince with great ease as we have all been able to verify for ourselves. The Empress is continually going over this tragic road, and passes most of her time in what we may now call the cemetery.'

1 June:

'She has planted with her own hands the willow and the ivy which we brought from Camden Place. Yesterday morning the Empress insisted upon going alone to find the spot selected by the Prince for the camp of the second division, where he made his last sketch; in order to do this she had to walk for over three hours. I accompanied her in the afternoon, and we went over the same ground together. . . . She ate nothing all day; her wonderful energy alone sustained her, and she walked with a sort of feverish strength. . . .

'I have already told you, I think, that we had arranged to have collected here as many as possible of the Zulus who took part in

213

the attack of June 1st. Eighteen men have come, about the same number are still missing. As the Empress wished that the inquiry should be conducted by General Sir Evelyn Wood, he began to question the Zulus the day after our arrival. I am the only other person present at these examinations, which have now lasted three days. Nothing is more painful than to find one's self face to face with these savages, and to listen to them explaining how they pursued and killed our poor dear Prince, accompanying their recital with what they consider appropriate gestures, and which are horribly significant! Up to now we cannot draw any very certain conclusions from their confused and often contradictory accounts; but they all agree that the Prince turned and fought like a lion, and fired three revolver shots, and that they left the medals on his corpse, as their custom is not to despoil of their neck ornaments brave men who die fighting. They all confirm the flight of Captain Carey, and they showed us the place where he crossed the donga, eighty paces above the point where the Prince stopped. We have crossed the donga on horseback, with the Empress, exactly at the same place, and we have verified that it is impossible not to have seen from it the whole of the hollow now occupied by the cairn and the cross; one of the Zulus even told us that, if the fugitives had but turned round, they would have stopped the pursuit. . . .

'Au revoir, my dear friend, I often think of you and how much you would wish to be with us near this fatal donga where passed away the last of the family which we have both served with such affection.'

The Empress described her feelings to M Pietri:

'Ityotyozi Kraal, May 30th, 1880.

'My Dear Monsieur Pietri—You are doubtless aware that I am only a few steps from the place where my beloved son rested before he was surprised by the Zulus. Here also I take my rest, but I do not sleep, my soul is full of bitterness, regrets, and sorrow; it is a curious thing, but I can only find peace near these stones which mark the spot where he fell, fighting, with his last breath, "like a lion", as the Zulus say. . . .

'If you were to see this spot, you would understand the surprise attack and the events which followed it, but what one cannot understand is how this man left a brother officer and two soldiers to their fate without giving them the least support. I have retraced for myself the road which he took, and he must have seen the

Prince and heard the revolver shots, because we have experimented with one, and the man who was sent in Carey's tracks heard the shots quite plainly. . . . It fills my heart with bitterness to think that this precious life has been so wantonly sacrificed, and that this child, left alone, fell fighting like a brave soldier with no witnesses of his courage except a handful of savages one degree removed from the brute ! . . .

'But I cannot speak of him any more; my heart overflows, and the wound bleeds anew and is powerless to heal. Even though I summon all my pride as a mother, yet I feel that my love is the stronger. . . . But what gives me courage to plunge into this abyss of sorrow is the knowledge that this may have caused him a pang of regret at the moment of death, and I owe it to his memory to let the world realise the man that he was.'

Sir Evelyn Wood continued to question the Zulu warriors who had been with the party that surprised the patrol. They told him that there had been thirty-six Zulus in the party and that seven of them had attacked the Prince. They said that the officer, realising that flight was hopeless, had walked slowly towards them, and they had watched him come. Using his left hand, he had fired twice at them, missing each time; then he was struck in the thigh by a spear, which he plucked out, and he rushed at them, fighting with his left arm. They said he would not let them get behind him and that they beat at him with their shields. Finally, he put his foot in a hole, and they assegaied him as he fell back. Wood asked them why they did not disembowel the Prince.

'Because of the gold chain hanging round his neck . . . we feared his ghost.'

'How did this young man look when he fell? Did he die like an ox knocked on the head?'

'He fought like a lion.'

'Why like a lion?'

'The lion is the bravest beast we have seen.'

The Zulus reportedly said that if there had been a stand they would have run away.

The Empress passed the night of 1–2 June in prayer by the cairn. Speaking of it later, she said :

'More than once I noticed black forms on the top of the banks, which moved silently about and watched me through the tall grasses. This scrutiny was full of curiosity, but it was not hostile.

I believe these savages wished rather to express their sympathy and their pity ! . . . And doubtless these were the very men who had killed my son on the same spot. . . .

'Towards morning a strange thing happened. Although there was not a breath of air, the flames of the candles were suddenly deflected, as if someone wished to extinguish them, and I said to him: "Is it indeed you beside me? Do you wish me to go away?" . . .'

Exhausted both physically and emotionally, the Empress fell into a state of prostration. The date on which the party left the area is not known, but on 17 June the Empress wrote to M Pietri from Mooi River:

'This letter will reach you by the mail which precedes our arrival. I am excessively tired and anxious for physical rest, as for fifty days we have slept under canvas. In two days we shall once more have a roof over our heads, and I am counting the hours, as all the interest which previously sustained me is now over.

'I wish particularly to find at Camden Place only its usual occupants, and these only if they desire it. My one longing is for rest; any visit would be unwelcome at present.

'Besides the farther I travel down the sorrowful road of life the greater is my need for rest and solitude. Nobody can fill the immense void which has opened in my existence, and to see people only wearies me without bringing comfort to my heart. . . .'

After her return, the Empress found Camden Place at Chisle-hurst to be unsuitable, more because of difficulties in housing her beloved dead than herself. She was unable to find a suitable spot in the area for a new chapel—the existing church was very small, and the chapel built on to it to receive the remains of Napoleon III was the only addition possible owing to lack of space and the impossibility of acquiring more land. The Prince's tomb rested under a narrow side arch, incompletely partitioned off; and under no circumstances could the Empress regard it as a permanent resting-place. Eventually, the Empress decided to buy a property at Farnborough Hill in Hampshire. It was said that it was a 'mansion in mourning . . . sheltering a great life, which had been sorely wounded by the terrible blows of Fate and is here slowly awaiting the end.' Four years were spent in building a small church on a pine-covered hill, and in 1887 the bodies of Napoleon III and his son, the Prince Imperial, were transported from the

Church of St Mary at Chislehurst to the crypt at Farnborough. The tombs occupied both sides of the underground chapel.

At Farnborough, Eugenie maintained a room which she called the *Cabinet du Prince*. It was a large room in which the Prince's things were arranged exactly as they had been in the one he occupied at Camden Place before leaving for Natal. As soon as her son had started for Zululand, Eugenie had had all his belongings carefully covered up, the place of each marked with chalk, and the room locked so that nothing might be touched. There were even a few still unopened letters on his desk. Nearly all around the room at Farnborough were bookcases containing the Prince's favourite books, and near one of the windows was the carved silver bassinette, swinging between two solid Imperial eagles and decorated with the Prince's Arms and those of Paris, which had been a gift from the City at the time of his birth. There were several veiled pictures representing the moment of the Prince's death, and two glass cases containing all the little personal treasures and souvenirs of his father and of his childhood. In the centre of one of these cases was a small ebony compartment containing a torn shirt stained with blood, together with the medal and gold chain that was still around his neck when his body was found. It is reported that Eugenie never had the courage to look at these sad relics, and that Uhlmann kept the key. Most of the items were obtained from Cetewayo by Queen Victoria, through Redvers Buller and Sir Bartle Frere.[1]

[1] This information appears in a book entitled *The Empress Eugenie in Exile* by Agnes Carey, which was published in 1922. Agnes Carey was engaged in 1886 as a companion for the Empress Eugenie. It is odd that seven years after her son's death, the Empress had accepted the constant companionship of a person bearing the name of Carey. Admittedly, Agnes Carey was no relation of Jaheel Brenton Carey, but such was the revulsion aroused in the Empress by this name that the occurrence is bizarre.

34

CAREY went with the 98th to India, serving under Lieutenant Colonel T. T. Simpson. The Army List for October 1882, records Carey as being senior captain in the battalion. They were stationed at Karachi, with a three-company detachment at Hyderabad, but malaria was rife at Karachi and the health of the regiment was consistently bad. In December 1881 it was decided, for health reasons, to relieve the Hyderabad detachment by marching the whole regiment there and back—a five weeks' expedition, which Captain Carey accompanied.

In February 1883 orders were received for the regiment to march to Quetta. The move was to take place in two stages, at intervals of about a month. After the first party had left, there was a great deal of work to be done by those remaining in the cantonment; two of the regiment's four captains had gone, leaving Captain Carey and one other, besides the Field Officers of Battalion HQ, to march out with the second party in mid-March.

Carey was kept constantly busy, moving back and forth through the lines supervising the dismantling and packing of all the equipment that gathered around a regiment serving in India. On 21 February he stood watching a fatigue-party, who were working industriously with an officer's eye upon them; they were loading a wagon with heavy wooden half-discs that fitted together to form the floor of a bell-tent.

Hearing the soft plod of hooves, he glanced right to see his fellow-captain mounted on a grey, coming towards him. Coming level, the rider pulled up and sat looking down at Carey :
'Never seems to end, does it?'
Carey's reply was drowned by a sudden crash, as the fatigue-party, relieved to be free of critical eyes, allowed one of the heavy wooden frames to fall noisily into the wagon. The grey's head

jerked up, its hindquarters swung around, and a near leg lashed out catching Carey full in the lower abdomen. He was lifted from the ground and thrown into a heap some feet away.

When Carey regained consciousness, he was in his bungalow; Annie, his wife, and the doctor were standing by the bed looking down at him. Through a haze of nausea and pain, he heard the doctor say :

'Hot fomentations will relieve the abdominal pain, I'll come in and see him later on.'

Annie clasped her hands together :

'My husband seems to be in great pain . . . cannot you give him something . . . laudanum perhaps?'

The doctor shook his head :

'No, ma'am, I'm afraid not . . . it would relieve the pain but it would also mask the symptoms should he have a ruptured intestine. Don't worry, tho' . . . that's looking on the black side.'

For the remainder of the day, Carey lay with his knees drawn up, in terrible pain, with bouts of vomiting that drew agonisingly on his abdomen. The doctor came in at nightfall and examined him; he noted the quick pulse, the rise in temperature and the rigid abdomen, and he told Annie :

'Captain Carey is still in shock. I hope he'll be better by morning. Carry on with the hot fomentations. Give him sips of hot water.'

But the next morning brought no improvement. Aware that his patient was seriously ill, the doctor gravely observed Carey's 'facies Hippocratica'—the sunken but bright eyes, the hollow cheeks and the drawn anxious expression. He administered a turpentine enema with little effect; the temperature was still high, but as the day wore on, it became sub-normal. Towards afternoon, Carey relapsed into unconsciousness. The doctor shook his head and told the weeping Annie that he feared her husband had suffered a ruptured intestine, which had led to peritonitis, and that he would shortly go into a coma.

'Thus closed the career of Jaheel Brenton Carey—Jaheel from the third son of Zebulon, the tribe of whom, in the rapture of triumph sang Deborah, "They were a people that jeoparded their lives unto death in the high places of the field." No such pæon sounded over the grave of this luckless staff officer. His lot was the lot, not of Zebulon, but of Sisera. The stars in their courses fought against him.'[1]

[1] F. E. Whitton, *Service Trials and Tragedies* (London, 1930).

Even at his death, *The Army and Navy Gazette* was still his champion :

'Captain J. Carey, 98th Regiment, of unfortunate history in Zululand, has, we regret to hear, died under mysterious circumstances in India, a victim of much persecution.'

APPENDIX ONE

Copy of a letter from Captain J. MacSwiney, 94th Foot, to his sister Louisa.

'10 Miles East of Koppie, Zululand.
June 1st (1879)

'Dear Louisa,

'We are all very sorry tonight to hear of the sad news that the Prince Imperial was dead. We all marched from Koppie this morning at 9 and are encamping here tonight. I myself only arrived at 6 this evening and a few natives (six) and Carey of the 98th had just come in with the news that 3 of their escort had been shot and the Prince assegaied as he had his foot in the stirrup. They had gone out together with a very few as escort as Carey was making a survey of the country and the Prince was making a sketch. About 7 miles from here, they off-saddled in some long grass when to all accounts about 60 men sprang up and before they got away, 2 were shot and the Prince killed. He was very popular with everyone and such a nice fellow and very plucky— he had had a narrow escape before as I wrote. They pursued the rest for some way, so we may be attacked in camp tonight. We are not going on tomorrow—a party of the 17th Lancers are going to see if they cannot find the body. I cannot tell you how the men feel about this disastrous affair—why such a small party should be sent to our opinion is a fearful mistake—but after all this long delay has made everyone very careless. . . .

'June 2nd.
'. . . as soon as light the 17th Lancers and the squadron of KDG went out to get the body of the Prince and took with them an ambulance with horses in under Marshal. They returned about 2 bringing back the body. They found it in a donga with very

221

steep banks lying on its right side with his arms up over his head as if protecting a blow. He had 18 assegais wounds all in front. One through his right eye and nothing on except a gold chain and locket round his neck. Of course he was ripped up. We all think he must have fought with his sword at last, as he was a beautiful fencer and this accounts for so many wounds. The doctor says only 2 . . . have been fatal, one in his pulse and the other through his throat or rather the side of it. It happened thus. Carey, Deputy Assistant Quartermaster General a Lt in the 98th, went out as in charge of 6 of Bettingens Horse as escort (raised in the colony of white men) in charge of the Prince, who went out for Harrison RE who is QMS to make a sketch, as he had other work to do. They had gone about 9 miles and off-saddled close to a large mealie garden with a Kraal in it. They had just finished eating something when their horses were brought up from feeding as the men thought something was up. They saddled up and the long and short of it (20 or 30 Zulus having sprang up and tried killing 2 of the escort) bolted. The Prince caught hold of his saddle trying to get his grey (which he had bought at the . . . for £75 to replace one that he had brought out that died) when the saddle wallets which we have over the saddle split clean up and having a foot in the stirrup and the horse wanting to get after the others, got away—very few horses will stand quite still in an ordinary way much less when other horses are galloping. The saddle was bought of Fielden and King of Leadenhall Street and to this saddle the poor Prince owes his life. I always say these are very bad saddles and if it had been one of Peats it would never have happened. The flap of the saddle is just like brown paper. Whether it was got out here I don't know as everything in this colony is rubbish and the most exorbitant prices charged. He then ran after his horse down the donga a good way about 4 hundred yards where his body was found. Carey had got over the donga when up came the Prince's horse and one of the men said it must be going badly for the Prince. Now if they had only remained together and not made a stampede of it nothing would have happened. They shouted after them "you English cowards, you always run away" but Carey is very much to blame and how he could come back with a tale, knowing that the horse came after him and the last time the Prince was seen was with his foot in the stirrup (that gave cause as I said yesterday to the story that he was assegaied whilst mounting) of course it was a stampede like the Inhlobane affair—a Zulu heard if much less seen is quite enough for the whole division to immediately rush into laager, in fact what with Isandhlwana and the way Ld C goes about the most minute details to insure everyone being able to run the shortest way into laager, quite a panic has arisen. To continue, the body was brought in and the funeral was ordered for 5. 3 companies from each Regt went and formed up 3 sides of a square. Standing with our arms reversed the body was . . . in a horse blanket and put on a board and tied on to a gun drawn by 6 horses with a tricolour flag over it. The artillery officers were pall bearers and Ld C and his staff following. A RC priest in his full stoles etc going before Ld C. They halted at the end of the square where the funeral service was read and then moved out again, we giving a royal salute by fixing bayonets and presenting arms—a most solemn affair and I hope I may never see one again. The 2 bagpipers of the 21st played a pilbroch or dirge. The body is to be embalmed as soon as possible and . . . in an ambulance for Durban. Delaches, the correspondent of the French *Figaro* came to say goodbye tonight and goes with it. Poor little fellow he was awfully cut up and he is going home. He said he dared not send a telegraph to the Empress but he takes back the chain and locket, the pall cover, ie the tricolour flag, a lock of his hair and a spur and one of his socks that he found this morning.

'Both Stanley and Forbes, correspondents to the *Standard* and *Daily News* told me that they found in the kraal an old woman who told them that they were her sons that did it. . . .

'You will read enough in the papers about who is to blame as both Forbes and Stanley are very wrath. . . . Enough now of such a sad affair and I myself think disgraceful to ourselves. . . .

'With best wishes
'Believe me
'Your affect Brother
'J. MacSwiney.'

APPENDIX TWO

The Court-Martial of Lieutenant H. H. Harward, 80th Regiment.

Luneberg was garrisoned by five companies of the 80th Regiment commanded by Major Charles Tucker. Towards the end of February 1879 a convoy of about twenty wagons laden with stores and ammunition for the garrison was sent from Lydenburg. On 7 March, a company of the 80th Regiment under Captain David B. Moriarity was sent out to meet the convoy, which had arrived at the ford at Intombe River, to escort it down the lower reaches of the road. When Moriarity reached Myer's Drift on the Intombe, he found the fifty-yard wide river swollen by recent rains so that it was impassable. Seven of the convoy wagons had reached the far bank where they lay stranded in a large open area surrounded by high broken ground. The rest of the wagons were still on the road several miles north of the river. By 9 March, Moriarity had got them all down to the Intombe, but it was only possible to get two of them across the fast-flowing river, on a raft.

On the north bank of the river, Moriarity formed his sixteen wagons into a large inverted V, with the apex on the road and the base legs twenty yards from the river bank, leaving open gaps between the wagons. Tents were erected and seventy-one men remained on that side of the river, while thirty-five men with three tents guarded the two wagons that had already been ferried across on the south bank.

On the afternoon of 11 March, Major Tucker, accompanied by Lieutenant Henry Hollingworth Harward of the 80th Regiment, came to discover what progress had been made. An Intelligence Department Report states that :

'Major Tucker, on inspecting the arrangements for defence considered the wagons too far apart, and objected to the space

224

left between the last wagon of the laager and the river bank, but he did not order any change to be made.'

The rain had stopped and the river was falling, so Moriarity hoped to get the rest of the wagons across the next day. Thus he did not feel inclined to go to the trouble of altering his arrangements, although the camp was later described as being 'pitched in a most dangerous position, with its face towards some high ground, covered here and there with dense bush, while its rear was resting upon the swollen river, across which Lieutenant Harward and 34 men were posted. No particular precautions appear

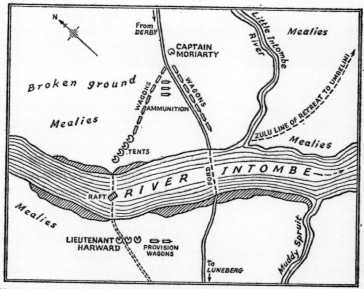

Plan of the disaster on the Intombe River, March 12th 1879, as a result of which, Lieut. H. H. Harward was court-martialled.

to have been taken, except that a sentry was posted about fifteen paces from the front of the camp, on the Derby side, according to one account; or, according to another, with the exception of a guard stationed on each bank, each furnishing two sentries, but no pickets, the force being probably too slender to provide them.' Tucker rode back to Luneberg, taking with him two lieutenants from the south bank, and leaving Harward behind. The latter, a veteran of the Ashanti campaign, did not feel inclined to entrench two wagons when they were virtually within sight of the garrison at Luneberg.

On both sides of the river the men turned in, and they were soon 'lying asleep and undressed.' It began to rain soon after dark, and a thick fog rose. At about half-past four on the morning of the 12th, the sentry on the north bank fired a shot and called, 'Guard turn out!' Harward had his men stand to and sent a messenger across the river to check with Moriarity; the Captain told the messenger that he had ordered his men to turn out; in fact it is believed that he had gone back to sleep without ensuring that the order reached his troops.

The rain ceased shortly after five o'clock and the mist began to lift, enabling the men on the south bank to distinguish dimly the wagons on the other side of the river. Suddenly, in the dim light and gauzy mist, the whole valley could be seen to be swarming with Zulus. They at once surrounded the wagons on the north bank and assegaied the soldiers, in many cases before they could leave their tents. The Zulu force, said to be 4,000 strong, was under the command of Umbelini. Lieutenant Harward had placed his thirty-four men under cover of a solitary wagon and made dispositions to fire into the enemy's flanks. This fire disclosed his presence, and several hundred Zulus broke away from the charging impi and plunged into the river.

On the north bank, Moriarity was killed as he left his tent, sword in hand; and his detachment, being completely surprised, could offer no resistance to an attack so sudden and overwhelming, and they were butchered almost to a man in a very short time.

On the south bank, the fire of Harward's party was not strong enough to keep off the attacking Zulus, and when Lieutenant Harward saw that they could not hold their position, he ordered his men to fall back on a farmhouse in their rear, and, mounting his horse, galloped off to Luneberg for aid. Colour-Sergeant Anthony Booth, with eleven men, fell back in good order to a deserted farm two miles south of the river. Booth kept them well in hand and directed volleys at every group of Zulus that approached them. He was later awarded the Victoria Cross.

Harward reached Luneberg and warned the garrison. Major Tucker started off at once with a small mounted party, followed by 150 men on foot. When they arrived at the laager they found that the Zulus had retired, carrying off with them the whole of the oxen, small-arms ammunition, rifles, blankets and every object of value. Moriarity and seventy-nine NCO's and men lay hacked to ribbons amid the wreckage.

On 20 February in the following year, Lieutenant Henry Hollingworth Harward of the 80th Regiment was tried by a general court-martial at Fort Napier, Pietermaritzburg. He was accused of abandoning his men while under attack and riding off at speed, and of having failed to take proper precautions for the safety of his camp. In his defence, Harward claimed that he had taken every possible precaution; that he had only joined the camp on the south bank the night before the attack, and that it was not possible to form a laager with only two wagons. He claimed to have been better prepared for the attack than was Moriarity, and said that he had ridden away only when his command had disintegrated, and then only because help was urgently needed to prevent complete destruction. He claimed that Colour-Sergeant Booth had done everything that he could have done himself, and as he was the only man with a horse on the south bank he was the logical person to ride for help.

The court recorded a verdict of 'not guilty' and acquitted Harward; the proceedings were sent to Sir Garnet Wolseley, now Commander-in-Chief in the area, for review. Unable to reverse the verdict, Wolseley indicated that he disapproved of the findings and refused to confirm them; in explanation, he issued the following statement:

'Had I released this officer without making any remarks upon the verdict in question, it would have been a tacit acknowledgment that I concurred in what appears to me a monstrous theory, *viz*, that a regimental officer who is the only officer present with a party of soldiers actually and seriously engaged with the enemy, can, under any pretext whatever, be justified in deserting them, and by so doing, abandoning them to their fate. The more helpless a position in which an officer finds his men, the more it is his bounden duty to stay and share their fortune, whether for good or ill. It is because the British officer has always done so that he possesses the influence he does in the ranks of our army. The soldier has learned to feel, that come what may, he can in the direst moment of danger look with implicit faith to his officer, knowing that he will never desert him under any possible circumstances.

'It is to this faith of the British soldier in his officers that we owe most of the gallant deeds recorded in our military annals; and it is because the verdict of this Court-Martial strikes at the root of this faith, that I feel it necessary to mark officially my emphatic dissent from the theory upon which the verdict has been founded.'

Back in England, the Duke of Cambridge strongly approved Wolseley's remarks and ordered the findings and the comments to be read at the head of every regiment in Her Majesty's service.

BIBLIOGRAPHY

ABRAHAMS, PETER. *Jamaica—An Island Mosiac* (London, 1957).

ASHE, MAJOR, and WYATT-EDGELL, E. V. *The Story of the Zulu Campaign* (London, 1880).

BARNES, R. MONEY. *Military Uniforms of Britain and the Empire* (London, 1960).

BINNS, C. T. *The Last Zulu King—The Life and Death of Cetshwayo* (London, 1963).

BURNS, SIR ALAN. *History of the British West Indies* (London, 1954).

BUTLER, LEWIS. *Redvers Buller* (London, 1909).

CAREY, AGNES. *The Empress Eugenie in Exile* (London, 1922).

CLEMENTS, W. H. *The Glamour and Tragedy of the Zulu War* (London, 1936).

COLENSO, FRANCES ELLEN, and DURNFORD, EDWARD C. L. *History of the Zulu War and Its Origin* (London, 1880).

FILON, AUGUSTE. *Le Prince Imperial, Souvenirs et Documents* (Paris, 1912).

— *Memoirs of the Prince Imperial* (London, 1913).

— *Recollections of the Empress Eugenie* (London, 1920).

FORBES, ARCHIBALD. *Barracks, Bivouacs and Battles* (London, 1892).

— *Memories and Studies of War and Peace* (London, 1895).

— *Souvenirs of Some Continents* (London, 1890).

FORTESCUE, SIR JOHN W. *History of the British Army* (London, 1927).

FRENCH, GERALD. *Lord Chelmsford and the Zulu War* (London, 1939).

FURNEAUX, RUPERT. *The Zulu War: Isandhlwana and Rorke's Drift* (1963).

GODWIN-AUSTEN, MAJOR A. R. *The Staff and the Staff College* (London, 1927).

GRANT, JAMES. *British Battles on Land and Sea* (London, 1886).

GRENFELL, FIELD MARSHAL SIR FRANCIS WALLACE. *Memoirs* (London, 1925).

JERROLD, WALTER. *Sir Redvers H. Buller, VC* (London, 1900).

JOHN, KATHERINE. *The Prince Imperial* (London, 1939).

MOCKLER-FERRYMAN, MAJOR A. F. *Annals of Sandhurst* (London).

MORRIS, DONALD R. *The Washing of the Spears* (London, 1966).

NORRIS-NEWMAN, CHARLES L. *In Zululand with the British Throughout the War of 1879* (London, 1880).

RITTER, E. A. *Shaka Zulu, The Rise of the Zulu Empire* (London, 1957).

ROTHWELL, JOHN SUTTON (compiler). *Narrative of Field Operations Connected with the Zulu War of 1879* (HMSO, London, 1881).

SMITH-DORRIEN, HORACE. *Memories of Forty-Eight Years' Service* (London, 1925).

SYMONS, JULIAN. *Buller's Campaigns* (London, 1963).

TALBOT-BOOTH, E. C. *The British Army* (London, 1937).

TISDALL, E. E. P. *The Prince Imperial* (London, 1959).

TOMASSON, W. H. *With the Irregulars in the Transvaal and Zululand* (London, 1881).

TURNER, E. S. *Gallant Gentlemen* (London, 1956).

TYLDEN, MAJOR G. *The Armed Forces of South Africa* (Johannesburg, 1954).

WARD, W. E. F. *A History of Ghana* (London, 1948).

WHITTON, F. E. *Service Trials and Tragedies* (London, 1930).

WILMOT, A. *History of the Zulu War* (London, 1880).

WOLSELEY, GARNET J. *The Story of a Soldier's Life* (London, 1903).

WOOD, EVELYN. *From Midshipman to Field Marshal* (London, 1906).

— *Winnowed Memories* (London, 1918).

— *British Battles on Land and Sea* (London, 1915).

WYNDHAM, HORACE. *The Queen's Service* (Boston, 1899).

NEWSPAPERS AND PERIODICALS

The Army and Navy Gazette.
The Daily News.
The Daily Telegraph.
The Evening Standard.
Le Figaro.
The Graphic.
The Illustrated London News.
The London Gazette.
The Morning Post.
The Times.

Tradition Magazine.
The United Service Gazette.
The Western Daily Mercury.

The Army List.
Report on Blue Book 1858.

INDEX

233

234

St Ann County, Jamaica: 36
St Denis: 47
St Dominique: 35
St George's Chapel: 163
St Jean de Luz: 19
St Mary's Church, Chislehurst, Kent: 160, 161, 217
St Thomas-in-the-Vale County, Jamaica: 36
Sandhurst: 21–23, 54–57, 166
San Jose, British Honduras: 28
San Pedro, British Honduras: 28, 32
Santa Cruz: 28
Sarrebrucken, battle of: 40–41
Saunders, Sir Charles: 99
Saxe-Weimar, Prince Edward of: 159, 171, 172
Sceberras, Lieutenant-Colonel Attilio: 206
School of Musketry, Hythe, Kent: 42, 54
Scotchburn, Miss Olivia: 180, 195
Scott, Surgeon-Major: 111, 112, 136–137, 210, 212
Sedan: 40
Seven Oaks, South Africa: 211
Shepstone, Captain: 90, 115, 170
Shoreditch: 176
Simmons, Major-General Sir Linton: 50, 73, 75, 76, 77, 183
Simon's Bay: 63, 121, 177
Simpson, Colonel T. T.: 218
Sirayho: 95
Sityityili: 99–100
Slade, Captain Frederick George: 52, 64, 80, 113, 194, 210, 213
Smith, Private George: 192
Smith-Dorrien, Lieutenant (later General Sir) Horace: 60, 91
Société de Secours aux Blessés: 48
Solferino: 25, 39
South Africa: 7, 57, 59, 79, 81, 104, 114, 147, 154, 158, 162, 163, 166, 174, 175, 183, 185, 191, 198, 203, 211
Southampton: 71
Southsea: 166, 170, 171, 172, 178, 189
Spanish Town, Jamaica: 33, 35, 36
Spencer, Private Alfred: 192
Spicheren, battle of: 44
Spithead: 159, 170
Sprigg, G.: 121
Stamfordham, Lord (see Bigge, Arthur)

Stewart, Captain Herbert: 90, 105, 113, 138, 139
Stewart Town, Jamaica: 36
Stony Gut, Jamaica: 33
Strathnairn, Field Marshal Lord: 163
Sweden, Prince Royal of: 19
Sydney, Lady: 121
Sydney, Lord: 122

Tashingway: 99
Tekax, Yucatan: 28
Teneriffe: 72
Times, The: 43, 109, 121, 144, 151, 154, 163, 170, 173, 186, 196
Tisdall, E. E. P.: 81, 89, 142, 206
Tombokala (Tombocto) River: 85, 101, 116
Transvaal: 199
Trelawny, Jamaica: 36
Trinity House Corporation: 162
Tucker, Major Charles: 224–226
Turenne, Comte de: 159
Turkey: 53, 65
Turner, E. S.: 22–23

Uhlmann: 50, 70, 74, 120, 121, 159, 160, 217
Ulundi, South Africa: 59, 63, 89, 165, 185, 193, 210
Umbelini: 226
United Service Gazette, The: 148, 152, 153, 176, 188, 191, 193, 194, 199, 201, 204, 205
Upoko River: 127, 173
Utrecht, South Africa: 80, 81, 85, 86, 199

Varannes, des: 211
Verriers: 40
Victoria, Queen: 53, 145, 146, 153, 171, 204
  and Prince Imperial: 67, 76, 161, 162, 212
  relationship with Eugenie: 16, 49, 82, 122–123, 195, 210, 217
  and Carey: 174, 180, 181, 182, 185, 187, 188, 195
Viet-nam: 8
Vine family: 37
Volta River: 26

239

240